RACE
and RADIO

Mohit Anand: Thank you for your support. May Success be your friend forever

Bala Baptiste 10·18·19

**RACE
RHETORIC
& MEDIA**

Davis W. Houck, General Editor

RACE and RADIO

Pioneering Black Broadcasters in New Orleans

Bala J. Baptiste

Foreword by Brian Ward

University Press of Mississippi / Jackson

The University Press of Mississippi is the scholarly publishing agency of the Mississippi Institutions of Higher Learning: Alcorn State University, Delta State University, Jackson State University, Mississippi State University, Mississippi University for Women, Mississippi Valley State University, University of Mississippi, and University of Southern Mississippi.

www.upress.state.ms.us

The University Press of Mississippi is a member of the Association of University Presses.

Copyright © 2019 by University Press of Mississippi
All rights reserved

First printing 2019
∞

Library of Congress Cataloging-in-Publication Data

Names: Baptiste, Bala J., author. | Ward, Brian, 1961– author.
Title: Race and radio : pioneering black broadcasters in New Orleans / Bala J. Baptiste, foreword by Brian Ward.
Other titles: Race, rhetoric, and media series.
Description: Jackson : University Press of Mississippi, [2019] | Series: Race, rhetoric, and media series | "First printing 2019." | Includes bibliographical references and index.
Identifiers: LCCN 2019013311 (print) | LCCN 2019022105 (ebook) | ISBN 9781496822062 (hardback : alk. paper) | ISBN 9781496822079 (pbk. : alk. paper)
Subjects: LCSH: African American radio broadcasters—Louisiana—New Orleans. | African Americans in radio broadcasting—Louisiana—New Orleans. | Radio broadcasters—Louisiana—New Orleans.
Classification: LCC PN1991.4.A2 B37 2019 (print) | LCC PN1991.4.A2 (ebook) | DDC 791.44/08996073—dc23
LC record available at https://lccn.loc.gov/2019013311
LC ebook record available at https://lccn.loc.gov/2019022105

British Library Cataloging-in-Publication Data available

CONTENTS

Foreword vii

Acknowledgments xiii

CHAPTER ONE 3
Organized Action Colorized White Radio in the Crescent City

CHAPTER TWO 21
Race and Supremacy Contaminated Media

CHAPTER THREE 37
Radio Forum Evolved from Religion to Negro

CHAPTER FOUR 57
Black Culture, Music, and "Hep Phrasing" Permeated Radio

CHAPTER FIVE 79
The Pioneer Mixed a "Batch of 'Congrats'"

CHAPTER SIX 93
Some Black Broadcasters Spoke Concerning the Civil Rights Movement

CHAPTER SEVEN 105
Entertainment Content Required on Black-Focused Radio

Conclusion 115

Epilogue 125

Notes 135

Index 153

FOREWORD

—Brian Ward—

African American deejay "Jockey" Jack Gibson once proudly declared that black-oriented radio "was the thing that caused the Civil Rights Movement to happen." Of course, no single "thing" was responsible for creating the Civil Rights Movement of the 1950s and 1960s.[1] Nevertheless, other pioneering African American radio announcers and entrepreneurs shared Gibson's belief that black broadcasters had played a vital role in helping cultivate a powerful sense of black identity, pride, and purposefulness that could be leveraged into political action. Some even saw a divine hand at work as the medium took its place alongside black schools, universities, fraternal lodges, unions, and churches at the heart of many black communities and near the vanguard of the freedom struggle. "Black radio was God-directed for the salvation of this nation and the world," explained Martha Jean "the Queen" Steinberg, a veteran of WDIA Memphis and later a station owner in Detroit.[2]

Participants in the African American freedom struggle during the so-called "classic phase" of civil rights activism in the 1950s and 1960s were equally convinced of the significance of radio and the influence on the black community of charismatic on-air personalities who drew thousands of listeners to their programs every day. Julian Bond, communications director of the Student Nonviolent Coordinating Committee (SNCC) in the early 1960s, explained that radio's speed of response and unique reach and prestige among African Americans made it an especially useful vehicle for activists: "If you wanted to get to the large mass of people, you had to go to radio. Radio was what they listened to and radio was where they got their information."[3]

During the middle decades of the twentieth century, radio station ownership and senior management remained overwhelmingly in white hands. Jesse Blayton was the first African American to own a radio station, when he purchased WERD Atlanta in 1949. Two decades later, at the end of the 1960s, there were still only sixteen black-owned facilities, ten of them located in the South, among the nation's 7,350 commercial and noncommercial radio stations.[4] Although the whites in positions of power in the industry were often indifferent and sometimes openly hostile to the black struggle for freedom, justice, and equality, their desire to maximize the economic potential of black programming created the environment within which black-oriented broadcasting emerged and flourished. Even in the segregated South, black deejays and a handful of sympathetic white announcers used the airways to showcase black musical and dramatic talent and gave unprecedented airtime to stories of black history and black political, economic, educational, scientific, artistic, and sporting accomplishments. At a time when television was geared primarily to white audiences, black-oriented radio was an invaluable source of local and national news of particular interest to black communities around the nation. Sometimes stations and their staffs were even central to local civil rights activities, as happened during the spring 1963 protests in Birmingham, Alabama—a campaign that is impossible to understand properly without taking into account the role of WENN and WJLD and announcers such as Tall Paul White, Shelley "the Playboy" Stewart, and Erskine Faush.[5]

In Atlanta in 1967, Martin Luther King Jr. spoke eloquently of the importance of black-oriented radio in black lives. He noted, with only a modicum of exaggeration, that African Americans were "almost totally dependent on radio as their means of relating to society at large. They do not read newspapers ... television speaks not to their needs but to upper-middle-class America." King had "come to appreciate the role which the radio announcer plays in the lives or our people; for better or worse it is important that you remain aware of the power which is potential in your vocation."[6]

King made these remarks at the annual convention of the National Association of Television and Radio Announcers (NATRA), one of the most dynamic and sometimes controversial of the many organizations that emerged in the later 1960s and early 1970s to try to extend black financial and editorial power within the broadcasting industry, believing black ownership was a vital factor in maximizing the potential of radio to expand black economic, political and social power. NATRA's work highlighted the fact that the broadcasting industry itself was one of many arenas in which the freedom struggle was actually being waged; it was another crucial site of conflict and negotiation between white power and black aspirations, set within the context of the regulatory power of the Federal Communications Commission (FCC).

In sum, black-oriented radio, as a business, as a news medium, as a vehicle for and expression of black culture, and as an institution with the potential for mass mobilization, was somewhere near the epicenter of African American life and politics in the middle decades of the twentieth century. Which begs the question of why, still, relatively little has been written about the topic by historians of the modern African American freedom struggle, or of black culture, community, and enterprise. It is an oversight that the richness of Bala J. Baptiste's forensically researched *Race and Radio: Pioneering Black Broadcasters in New Orleans* makes seem even more egregious. Simply put, anybody who wants to understand the black community and its struggle for respect and empowerment in New Orleans during the mid-twentieth century needs to reckon with this fascinating and revealing book.

Baptiste begins *Race and Radio* by reminding us that, though his main focus is black broadcasting in the Crescent City, this is an exercise in American, rather than exclusively African American history. While nobody can seriously question the need for ever more comprehensive and probing histories of the African American experience, there is a danger of quarantining black history, artificially and misleadingly divorcing it from the flow of the American, Atlantic, and indeed global histories with which it has intimate, complex, and reciprocal relationships. Baptiste avoids that trap by embedding the local story of black broadcasting in New Orleans within the broader history of race, racism, and the struggle for black opportunities and self-realization in the United States. And what a story it is. The book is peppered with riveting tales of powerful and alluring men and women who made a living out of promoting themselves and their wares on air. Baptiste uses the careers of black broadcasting pioneers such as Vernon L. Winslow Sr., who created the jive-talking Poppa Stoppa persona and become the city's first regular black deejay when he debuted as Dr. Daddy-O on WWEZ in 1949, to illuminate key themes in the history of the city's race relations, intra-community dynamics, as well as of its radio industry.

Understandably, Baptiste pays close attention to the economic arrangements and management structures that shaped programming content on New Orleans radio. Such factors largely, but never wholly, determined the nature and extent of black broadcasters' involvement in what we might think of as civil rights activism, broadly construed. Throughout, Baptiste explores the mix of serendipity and opportunism, as well as of careful planning and conscious commitment that defined the contributions to the freedom struggle of black broadcasters and stations such as WNOE and WMRY, which in 1950 became the first outlet in the city to switch to wholly black programming. Indeed, it is a profound strength of the book that Baptiste so deftly juggles personal, local, regional, and national factors in explaining how black broadcasting in New Orleans developed and functioned. For example, he notes how black-oriented programming in New Orleans might not have emerged in 1946 had it not been for an FCC ruling that WNOE was broadcasting too many commercials and not enough community-service programming. White station owner James Noe sought to rectify the situation by offering fifteen minutes of noncommercial black community programming once a week; thus was born the "Religious Forum of the Air." Noe had no particular desire to support the African American community or advance civil rights through progressive programming. Rather, O. C. W. Taylor, a founding member of the local chapter of the National Urban League (NUL) and subsequently an important announcer and public relations director for black programs, spotted the potential of a local radio show and used his leadership of the newly formed Negro Citizens Committee to seize the opportunity to get black access to WNOE's hitherto lily-white airwaves.

As Baptiste notes, these early forays into black broadcasting were often tentative. Thanks to Taylor, there were finally regular black voices on air, discussing matters of great moral import. However, the show did not initially engage with the social, economic, and political problems confronted by the black community in a world of segregation and widespread disenfranchisement. At first Taylor was not even allowed to record his program in WNOE's own studios and had to work in small independent facilities. Moreover, the show initially stuck doggedly to religious and philosophical questions and offered no black news, or song, or other expressions of black culture. Soon, however, Taylor had renamed the show as "Negro Forum of the Air" and transformed it into a vehicle for discussing important political, social, health, and educational issues affecting the black community. "Negro Forum" became a model for engaged black-oriented broadcasting in the area and was woven into the social and cultural fabric of the local community, which rallied to resist efforts to can the show in the late 1940s.

The story of the transformation of New Orleans radio illustrates a major theme in Baptiste's book. African Americans often found their way onto the airways in New Orleans because it made economic sense to those who owned the stations. But it was also because African Americans like Taylor were acutely aware of the potential of radio to inform, entertain, and perhaps even unite and mobilize the black community. They worked hard to make inroads into an industry that often remained resistant to black advancement, but which white owners were ultimately willing to integrate if it meant greater profits. In 1949 WWEZ put a black show on air simply because a local brewer wanted to attract black beer drinkers. Jax Beer, like many other sponsors and advertisers—including some black-owned businesses, such as the Monarch Life Insurance Company, financers of a weekly news and sports show on WNOE in the late 1940s—recognized the power of radio to reach a highly lucrative black consumer market.

Time and time again, the lure of the black dollar created cracks in the walls of prejudice that initially kept black broadcasting to a minimum. WJBW was launched in 1926 by white electrician Charles Carlson, whose wife Louise served as program director and the city's first female radio announcer. Following their divorce, in 1947 Louise became the station's owner. Struggling to compete with better resourced and, eventually, more powerful local stations, she brokered a partnership with Frank Painia, the black owner of the famous Dew Drop Inn and Café. Carlson made a concerted effort to increase the station's audience and profits by targeting black listeners with exciting live shows from the club. Within months, the cavalcade of top black musical talent was supplemented by appearances from Daniel E. Byrd, executive secretary of the New Orleans branch of the National Association for the Advancement of Colored People, who promoted the NAACP's voter registration drives. There was a similar trajectory at WMRY, which began broadcasting from the elegant white Court of Two Sisters restaurant in the French Quarter, initially and unsuccessfully targeting white listeners. In danger of bankruptcy, general manager Mort Silverman changed tack to court an underrepresented black community. Starting in March 1950 with "Tan Timers Club," a daily black music show, Silverman saw an instant spike in listeners and quickly hired another African American deejay, George "Tex" Stephens. As revenue and sponsorship soared in tandem with rising black audiences, WMRY moved to a new facility in the black-owned Louisiana Industrial Life Insurance Company building, located in a working-class African American neighborhood.

Despite a variety of economic and legal impediments, as well as the indifference and intransigence of many of the whites who controlled the industry, slowly but surely, by accident as well as by design, by stealth as well as through overt civil rights advocacy, WJBW, WNOE, WMRY (which in the late 1950s acquired new call letters WYLD), and several other New Orleans stations became important platforms for what Baptiste describes as "progressive yet controlled black political discourse." Such programming provided an important foundation for the raised black pride and consciousness that underpinned the upsurge of civil rights activity in the city during the 1950s and 1960s.

As those protests escalated, with vibrant campaigns for voting rights and against segregation in schools, on buses and in a wide range of public amenities, radio began to play a rather more conspicuous, if still somewhat cautious, role in supporting the movement. In particular, Baptiste argues for the significance of WYLD, which, under the leadership of Chicago exile Larry McKinley, become a critical source of local news about regional and national developments in the freedom struggle and sometimes offered a platform for movement leaders in New Orleans itself. As McKinley admitted, there were still constraints on full and free expression of support for the movement that tempered exactly what he and other black announcers could and could not say on air. Yet, McKinley joined other black announcers in trying to circumvent some of those constraints. One method was to interview activists and report on nonviolent direct action protests—-and the often brutal white responses to them—as part of the station's news remit. Among the interviewees was Jerome Smith, a CORE stalwart who participated in both the New Orleans sit-in movement and the famous 1961 Freedom Rides, during which he was terribly brutalized.

It also helped align broadcasters such as McKinley and Stephens with the freedom struggle that they were sometimes seen at rallies and other movement events. That said, not everyone felt that black broadcasters in New Orleans were doing enough for the cause. Baptiste gives space to some of the dissenting voices, such as Edwin Lombard, who found little support among local announcers for his efforts to organize a voter education project in the city in 1967. Lombard complained that the stations and their black deejays were simply "trying to sell records and trying to sell products." There is something to Lombard's complaint. The contributions of black-oriented radio to civil rights activities took place within the context of a highly commercialized industry, where the pursuit of corporate and personal profits played a major role. What Bala Baptiste's book demonstrates, however, is that black broadcasters were often able to transcend the base commercial imperatives of the radio business to create institutions of great cultural vitality and social significance. By their very presence on air in an overwhelmingly white-controlled medium, as well as through their championing of black history and culture, attention to news and issues of particular interest to the black community, and steady commitment to the struggle for racial justice and equal opportunity, these broadcasters made a real contribution to the long African American freedom struggle in New Orleans.

ACKNOWLEDGMENTS

If you learn something from *Race and Radio*, and perhaps enjoy reading it, I credit the individuals who assisted me. In the unfortunate circumstance that you think it is insignificant or not gratifying, it's absolutely my fault.

First let me thank Craig W. Gill, director of the University Press of Mississippi, who discovered my article published in the journal *Louisiana History*. The piece concerned the preeminent, pioneering New Orleans disk jockey Vernon "Dr. Daddy-O" Winslow. Craig asked whether I had more scholarship related to the topic. I said yes and submitted a manuscript concerning the emergence of African Americans in radio broadcasting in New Orleans. The press's board unanimously approved its publication. After reviewers provided comments, I made revisions and submitted this book.

As well, I acknowledge receiving critical assistance from Christopher Harter, director of library and reference services at the Amistad Research Center. He sent photocopies of articles from the *Louisiana Weekly* and other documents. Brenda Nelson-Strauss, head of collections at the Archives of African American Music and Culture, gave me access to audio recordings and transcripts of key informants. I am also indebted to Edwin Lombard, Don Hubbard, Warren Bell, Bill Rouselle, Paul Beaulieu, and Samson "Skip" Alexander, who unselfishly sat with me as I interviewed them. Raphael Cassimere Jr. responded to my email and provided his insightful historical memories. My gratitude is also extended to staff members at the *Times-Picayune*, the Library of Congress, the Louisiana Division of the New Orleans Public Library, and the Hogan Jazz Archive at Tulane University. I am sure I am omitting some individuals who contributed, but it is not intentional. To all of you, even those I did not name, I express gratitude.

My wife, Renee, put up with me frequently retiring to bed early and arising at 3 a.m. or 4 a.m. to drive to work at Miles College, one hour away from home in Pell City, Alabama. I prefer getting an early start, but Renee is a light sleeper and, on many occasions, I unintentionally woke her when I showered, ground coffee, or otherwise knocked things around. Several times she was unable to return to the world of dreams. She simply accepted me as a workaholic and accommodated my work schedule. I also must acknowledge my daughter, Mykia Smith, who listened closely to my tales about the book and provided useful feedback.

I extend special recognition to Miles College in Fairfield, Alabama, where I am an associate professor of mass communications and chair of the Division of Communications. The publication was not possible without the aid of the institution's leadership, under the direction of George T. French Jr.

Finally, I dedicate *Race and Radio* to my mother, Tener Cecelia Baptiste Hall, who transitioned on Sunday, March 4, 2012. From my earliest memories, she put up with this precocious little boy who could not stop asking questions. She subscribed on my behalf to the kid's newspaper the *Weekly Reader*, let me join a penpal network, bought my first reel-to-reel audio recorder, and complied with my constant requests for postage stamps and envelopes to mail cereal box tops and receive various trinkets. Such gestures and experiences steered me toward the practice of print journalism and eventually to my research interest, the study of the intersection of blacks, mass media, and history.

RACE
and RADIO

CHAPTER ONE

Organized Action Colorized
White Radio in the Crescent City

The emergence of black on-air personalities at radio stations in New Orleans changed the medium after executives diverged from white-only staffs and programming targeting Caucasians. This book, which discusses pioneering black broadcasters, is significant because African Americans need more than inclusion in broadcast historiography. In fact, broadcast historiography is inadequate without sufficient discussion of relevant black experiences.

David Nord, a former editor at the *Journal of American History*, said in order to understand American history you must have an appreciation for African American history. In other words, black history is mainstream American history. It is not merely adding history of black experiences to the American experience. Black history is American history.[1]

Similarly, the history of American radio must include the history of African Americans. Nevertheless, broadcast historiography, and radio history in particular, either interprets the experiences of white people exclusively or lacks sufficient discussion of when and why whites finally permitted blacks to broadcast Afrocentric ideas or cultural productions. Much of the role racism played in the industry is omitted. General studies of broadcasting underrepresent how the medium affected African Americans, the roles blacks played in radio, and how they altered programming.[2]

To improve the historiography of blacks in radio, a considerable amount of primary data was analyzed, including archived manuscripts, correspondences, articles and display advertisements in newspapers from the period, interview transcriptions, oral narratives and historical memories of eyewitnesses, government documents including Federal Communications Commission reports, and other data concerning black radio in New Orleans between 1945 and 1965. The historical narrative includes stories of O. C. W. Taylor, a black man whom WNOE in New Orleans allowed in 1946 to produce and host the city's first African American radio program; Vernon L. Winslow Sr., the personification of Dr. Daddy-O on WWEZ in 1949, who became the city's first black broadcast disc jockey; and Larry McKinley, a disc jockey, announcer, and station manager, who began his career in 1953 at WMRY. Further discussion explores reasons whites discontinued prohibiting blacks from entering broadcast studios and speaking on air. The book reveals the introduction of a diversity of ideas and perspectives on air and how they contributed to feelings of pride among African Americans in the New Orleans metropolitan area.

The emergence of blacks, whether in talk or music format, transformed the character of radio and reshaped the discourse transmitted via the medium.[3] Racial integration of radio broadcasting began a process of changing the medium into a more representative transmitter of black cultural structures of meaning. The rise of black announcers at radio stations provided opportunities for African Americans to have a voice to interpret their affairs and issues and use broadcast communication as a cultural resource having the potential to connect and sustain linkages among community members. Black announcers, new to the white world of radio, offered listeners a broader context within which to build community and make sense of the American experience.[4]

To build community, individuals need to create, maintain, and expand collective identities. To establish a network of camaraderie and sympathy among group members, mass communication tools must be available.[5] Community building is a function related to an alternative public sphere or discursive space within which blacks access opportunities to crystallize their collective opinions on small and large issues. In the public sphere, people discuss important issues of the day. Since white people imagined blacks outside of systems of representative democracy, African Americans constructed a version of the public sphere to build communities and gain and maintain white approval.[6]

Black Americans had very little opportunity compared to whites to reason together via the electronic media of the era. Nevertheless, radio aimed at blacks enabled them to move in mass at a stepped-up pace in a direction toward community solidarity. The inclusion of black announcers and on-air personalities therefore changed the utility of radio. The black personality's voice, articulation, black-centeredness, language, music choices, discussion topics, and cultural references were among characteristics embodied in their emergence.

Early black announcers provided status and publicity opportunities to African Americans who owned a business or worked in a profession. Black announcers, particularly in the talk-show format, provided occasions during which black decision makers in social and religious organizations could solicit donations, new members, and the attention of a widely dispersed community. The announcers provided black parents, and their family members and friends, opportunities to experience pride when their children played a musical instrument, sang, read their essays, or otherwise displayed their talents on the air.

Black pioneers in music radio disseminated a variety of incarnations of the blues, jazz, boogie woogie, gospel, and rhythm and blues. The trailblazers shared knowledge of black music traditions with their audiences and were conduits through which musicians talked to the public about their art.

The new presence of blacks on the air ushered in the process of change in the nature of programming, marketing, advertising, Euro-centeredness, and broadcast media's perpetuation of an ideology of black inferiority and white superiority. Blacks introduced a divergence in talk-show topics, music programming, strategy to attract consumer markets, and ideologies of Afro-centeredness and racial equality.

To construct a thick narrative of broadcast history, a micro-level approach is warranted. The information must meticulously address blacks and their experiences in radio as well as whites who exhibit a propensity toward racism. New Orleans is the setting for several reasons. The city possesses a significant black music legacy. Blacks laid the foundation for the late 1800s development of jazz music that defined a major stream of American culture. African Americans fused together the musical, dance, and rhythmic traditions of the eighteenth- and nineteenth-century slave celebrations in Congo Square. They developed the jazz funeral and Mardi Gras Indians and added major components to the rise of gospel, funk, and rhythm and blues. As well, during the Civil Rights Movement, New Orleans was one of the racial battlegrounds of the South wherein the descendants of African slaves marched past ramparts of white supremacy and pushed toward equal, legal protection. During the movement, leaders in the city refined what would become the Southern Christian Leadership Conference and elected the Rev. Dr. Martin Luther King Jr. as its president. Finally, the city in the bend of the Mississippi River had a sizable population of African Americans.

Blacks in New Orleans employed music to sustain themselves as they struggled with slavery and the slave trade, unjust state and local laws, separatist social structures, obstacles to educational opportunities and gainful employment, and opposition to interaction between blacks and whites. When black announcers arrived, they began a reconfiguration of radio into a utilitarian resource gradually enlarging opportunities for African Americans to pursue the American dream.[7] The racial integration of radio presented opportunities for blacks to speak more clearly, in their own voices, and with a cultural tool that laid the foundation for a broader plateau on which to build community.[8]

Broadcast historians have also focused insufficient attention on black Americans and their interest in community building. White power brokers opened the public sphere to whites but closed it to blacks. The public sphere is the space between the state and the individual where ideas and issues are debated. The implications rendered blacks virtually powerless in the South before 1965. Whites held political and economic power in the North and the South and succeeded in stopping or at least drastically slowing processes in which blacks attempted to build community. Public institutions, such as newspapers, were among principal community building tools before the rise of racial integration in radio. As staunch, overt white supremacy subsided and black empowerment surfaced, African American dissent, conflict, ideological passion, and "intermitted agitation" morphed into a strategy of nonviolent resistance.[9]

To fully understand the history of blacks in broadcasting, one has to consider factors associated with segregation and integration in mass media in the United States. Why did whites decide to hire blacks to play records or musical instruments, to sing, or talk on the air? The reasons included multilayered factors that converged in a gradual movement over time, including black cultural production,[10] the assertiveness of individual blacks,[11] the profit motive, saturated white markets, and competition.[12]

Radio stations integrated racially as social, economic, and political events unfolded, each affecting the other and influencing broadcast decision makers. Whites in some northern cities racially integrated public accommodations before their counterparts in the South. States such as Indiana, Michigan, and New York passed legislation outlawing racial discrimination in public places. For example, New York enacted a Human Rights Law in 1945. In radio an impetus for integration was the acceptance of black cultural production, such as the music genres of gospel, jazz, blues, boogie, and rhythm and blues. Whites developed a fascination for African American music and dance. Advertising and broadcast executives hired blacks to play instruments, sing, and later talk via radio in part because young adult and teenage whites in northern cities, beginning in the Jazz Age of the 1920s and 1930s, were listening. Radio audiences in Chicago heard the music of the dance band Clarence Jones and his Wonder Orchestra as early as 1922 on the city's Westinghouse station, KYW.[13]

Nevertheless, broadcasters programmed a limited amount of black music in the early days of commercial radio in the 1920s. The rise of network broadcasting did not necessarily increase black employment opportunities, but it began the surfacing of wide distribution of the African American presence on radio. National dissemination of content emerged in 1933 and advanced a slow, steady climb toward racial inclusiveness and multiculturalism in the medium. Networks began to dominate American broadcasting beginning in the mid-1930s as advertising agencies took over the production and distribution of radio programs.

The proliferation of black music continued to move station managers and advertising agencies to hire blacks at the local level, in stepped-up fashion beginning in 1948, when disc jockeys began to multiply and white teenagers hugged tighter onto risqué music.[14] Disc jockeys began in the 1930s the transition in radio from focusing on recorded music to highlighting the person who introduced the recording artists.[15] Northern broadcasters in the 1940s and early 1950s hired blacks earlier and at greater frequency than their southern counterparts. But as late as 1947, *Ebony* magazine reported radio stations employed only sixteen blacks, less than 1 percent of the three thousand disc jockeys nationally.[16]

Independent stations in big cities did not have access to programming distributed by the networks: NBC, ABC, CBS, and MBN. Non-affiliates had to produce their own content. The lack of access to network programming contributed to station managers being less resistant to hiring black talent. Independent broadcasters with stations in cities aired the music, talk, and comedy of black entertainers more than network affiliates or radio serving small markets. Approximately eight hundred local radio programs included at least one black singer, instrumentalist, comedian, or actor between 1920 and 1933.[17]

White broadcasters in the North hired blacks in part because moderate and liberal attitudes broadened their views of opportunity sooner and wider than the frame through which southern conservatives gazed. Ethnic-oriented whites established in northern cities radio stations targeting immigrants and were among the first to hire blacks. Southern whites enforced racial segregation longer than their northern counterparts and created a sociopolitical environment that discouraged the establishment of ethnic-oriented radio in the South.[18]

The continued reliance on directing the advertisement of products and services to white people interfered with decisions to hire black actors and writers. The rise of commercials as a major source of revenue in the mid-1930s contributed to the continuation of white exclusiveness. Corporate executives refused to hire advertising agents to produce programs that featured blacks in serious or leading roles. Dramas, game shows, comedies, and variety shows were among prominent radio content during the period. Broadcast managers did not want commercials or programming that overtly attracted black consumers. White consumers, they rationalized, would avoid purchasing products or services associated with blacks. White supremacy saturated the American mindset. An advertising agent rationalized: "Pillsbury flour is one of our biggest accounts. If it gets out that we were pushing Negro talent on a Pillsbury program, the next thing you know, it would be branded a 'nigger flour' and it would never move."[19]

The first radio station to air a black announcer in New Orleans in 1946 did so in part because blacks organized their efforts to obtain airtime on WNOE, an affiliate of the Mutual Broadcasting Network. It was not for an immediate profit motive, in the sense of selling black listeners to advertisers for the highest price. The owner of WNOE, James A. Noe, was a politician who envisioned running for political office. He also had his eye on petitioning the Federal Communications Commission to increase the power at which his station transmitted. Having black programming would help his causes.

Nationally, in 1941 officials at the Urban League organized blacks and convinced executives at the Columbia Broadcasting System to allow the League to produce and broadcast an African American radio program. The Urban League, founded by blacks and liberal whites in 1911, is a black-rights organization interested in urging blacks to learn skills qualifying them for high-paying jobs and in motivating public and private-sector employers to open up employment opportunities. CBS agreed to let the Urban League use its production studio and equipment to produce a black show, but limited its content to music. On March 30, 1941, CBS broadcast "The Negro and National Defense," which featured entertainers including Louis Armstrong's band and a segment from Detroit where Ethel Waters sang "Georgia on My Mind."

Urban League officials also organized at the local level in the 1940s. They urged their affiliates to approach owners of radio stations and ask them to give the group free airtime to produce public affairs shows. The national organization granted a charter to organizers in Louisiana, and they established the Urban League of Greater New Orleans in 1938. O. C. W. Taylor, who integrated radio in New Orleans, was one of the founders of the local Urban League and its first director. An article in the *Pittsburgh Courier* indicated blacks in New Orleans, led by Taylor, accepted the challenge. The group organized as the Negro Citizens Committee and later approached WNOE management and convinced station officials to provide free airtime.[20] A solid link existed between the New Orleans Urban League and the first black program, the "Religious Forum of the Air"; however, neither Taylor or the black press publicized details of negotiations between WNOE and the committee. Middle-class blacks in New Orleans in the 1940s were subdued about publicizing their efforts or victories at obtaining racial concessions.

Albert Dent, another founder of the local Urban League, epitomized the cautious approach. Dent, the president of Dillard University, engaged in quiet diplomacy typical of old-guard black leaders: "My role in New Orleans, in getting things done, is to work quietly with the power structure." Dent silenced publicity about integration of the public library in New Orleans in 1955. He called the presidents of the area's black institutions of higher learning

(Southern University at New Orleans and Xavier University) as well as the principals of the African American high schools and said a small branch of the library was opened to blacks. Direct your students there discreetly, he said. Nothing concerning the integration of the library system was published in the newspapers or broadcast on radio or television.[21]

Before World War II, radio stations, and network affiliates in particular, transmitted programs to attract the attention and imagination of whites: Women during mornings and afternoons and both genders and all age groups during evenings.[22] In 1933 CBS introduced block programming, an approach to scheduling that targeted housewives. CBS began scheduling daytime serials, or soap operas, contiguously in fifteen-minute time slots. WWL was the CBS affiliate in New Orleans. Before CBS's innovation, soap operas were scattered throughout the program day. Block-scheduled daytime serials encouraged women who worked as housewives to listen and continue listening to a network or independent station's offerings. Officials at other networks and program directors at stations throughout the country also adopted some form of block programming over the years. By 1941 networks broadcast at least one soap opera every half hour between 10 a.m. and 6 p.m. Blacks were not considered as desired listeners.[23]

Program directors, corporate publicity staffs, and advertising agents developed shows and commercial messages to appeal to whites, who represented a profitable market. A 1943 survey of radio programming and the preferences of listeners throughout Louisiana found no secular programming targeting black audiences. Instead, programmers scheduled, on occasion, black religious music. WWL's 1938 show "Deep South" comprised a "colored unit of ten negroes in spiritual and jubilee songs, also an old negro deacon as the narrator."[24]

Decision makers in New Orleans radio also avoided producing advertisements to attract black consumers. They kept away from the production of drama or public affairs programs intended to pique the interest of blacks. An occasional programmer scheduled safe shows also serving whites' perceptions of blacks' otherworldly interests, such as "Spirituals and Hymns," which WWL broadcast between December 29, 1945, and June 2, 1946.[25]

WNOE owner James A. Noe was an exception. While he did not allow advertisements or commercial programs targeting blacks, he nevertheless set aside fifteen minutes at 10 a.m. on Sundays for an African American public affairs program. That move racially integrated radio in New Orleans. He did so in part because he wanted FCC approval to change the station's position on the dial and increase broadcast power. In 1936 Noe purchased WNOE, before which was known as WBNO. Since 1922 he had lived in Monroe, a small city in north-central Louisiana, 300 miles from New Orleans. He planned to move to New Orleans if the commission approved his application.

FCC policy required broadcasters to serve the public interest by offering a balanced schedule of programming. The policy enjoined licensees to survey public opinion, determine the issues affecting them, and produce programming addressing the outcomes. Stations had to consider the desires of civic, labor, religious, educational, arts, cultural, and nonwhite groups. When a station sought a license renewal, a major change in broadcasting capabilities, or a permit to build a station, the commission held public hearings at which individuals or competitors could support or oppose requests. If it was shown that a station did not perform in the public interest, the license renewal or change in operations would be denied. The policy provided community organizations opportunities to influence programming and other station operations.

The FCC examined WNOE program logs from May 1, 1946, to July 19, 1946, and determined the station aired an average of more than a thousand commercials weekly. The May-to-July period included approximately the first eight broadcasts of the weekly "Religious Forum of the Air," the show that integrated radio in New Orleans. In response, WNOE submitted to the FCC a proposed schedule for one week of programming, including 60.4 percent of the time devoted to commercials. The FCC considered the percentage high. "We recognize that the number of commercial spot announcements broadcast by WNOE in the past has been in excess of the number which we consider should be broadcast in a well-balanced program schedule." WNOE proposed the station would reduce the number of commercials, station break identifications, and other program interruptions to five or less during fifteen-minute periods. WNOE also proposed additional programs of special interest to Negroes.[26]

The FCC held hearings between July 22–24, 1946, in Washington D.C. Noe applied for permission to change WNOE's operating assignment from 1450 kilocycles with 250 watts of power 24 hours per day to 1060 kilocycles with 50,000 watts during days and 10,000 watts at night. A competitor also wanted the 1060 frequency. The New Orleans–based Deep South Broadcasting Corporation applied for a construction permit to launch a new radio station on the same frequency and with identical wattage. The FCC considered the two applications simultaneously.[27]

Deep South Broadcasting's FCC proposal said its new station would devote a maximum of 60 percent of broadcast time to commercials, further specifying a maximum of three thirty-second spots during a fifteen-minute program. Deep South reported its programming would include a Negro news show among other public service programming. The proposal said the local unit of the National Association for the Advancement of Colored People was among black organizations with which the petitioners had a tentative agreement.[28] On January 26, 1949, the agency denied Deep South and approved WNOE's application.

General manager James E. Gordon had been in charge of day-to-day operations at WNOE since 1941. WNOE employed twenty-nine staffers. The station planned to hire thirty-five additional employees to aid in the production of new programs, commercials, and provide better service to the station's clients and listeners.

In New Orleans, racism partly explains why in the World War II era broadcasters by and large excluded blacks from among their target audiences. Low socioeconomic status of blacks also provided an explanation. Blacks in New Orleans in 1940 were seventy-five years out of slavery, lived within a white supremacist power structure, and were denied quality access to training and education. Blacks remained poor and could hardly afford to purchase radio sets or advertised products.[29]

Nationally, 14.4 percent of urban black households and less than 1 percent of rural blacks owned a radio receiver, according to the 1930 US census. In New Orleans, 50 percent of blacks owned at least one radio receiver compared to 90 percent of whites, according to the 1940 census.[30] Blacks represented 149,034 or 30 percent of the total New Orleans population of 494,537 in 1940, and 199,527 or 35 percent in 1950.[31]

In the World War II era, the dominant radio content in New Orleans portrayed Eurocentric culture and Caucasian-oriented information, sometimes conveying the interests of the privileged class. Five radio stations broadcast comedy, drama, news, music, variety, game, and other shows. Four New Orleans stations were affiliated with a broadcast network in 1945 and transmitted much of the programming the networks distributed nationwide. The network stations were WWL, Columbia Broadcasting System (CBS); WSMB, National Broadcasting Company (NBC); WDSU, American Broadcasting Companies (ABC); and WNOE, Mutual Broadcasting System (MBS).[32] The independent station held the call letters WJBW.[33]

The four network affiliates commenced daily broadcasts at 6 a.m. Mondays through Saturdays, except WSMB, which transmitted its initial programming beginning at 7 a.m. All four network stations began Sunday-morning broadcasts at 8 o'clock. All of them began broadcasts of their last daily show at 11:45 p.m.[34] Weekdays until 8 a.m., all of the networks broadcast shows primarily produced by their staffs or contractors. Stations sometimes aired consecutive runs of a fifteen-minute show for thirty to sixty minutes. The program schedules varied slightly from day to day.

Nationally, network stations did not play a substantial amount of recorded music until the rise of television in the mid- to late 1940s, when popular radio programs moved to television. In the meantime, stations in New Orleans broadcast considerably more network programs during weekday afternoons than mornings. WNOE, the MBS affiliate, was the exception. WNOE staff produced and aired more local shows than WWL, WSMB, and WDSU. In the afternoon on weekdays, those stations broadcast for at least thirty minutes: "Cinderella, Inc.," a quiz show in which four housewives competed; "Glamour Manor," a variety show with an orchestra; and "Queen for a Day," an audience participation show in which women answered questions and the studio audience chose who was correct. The stations also scheduled the programs to air in the same timeslots each weekday. The stations scheduled different programs on Saturdays. For example, the country-western musical variety "Opry House Matinee" aired at 1:30 p.m. and 1:45 p.m. on Saturdays on WNOE instead of "Queen for a Day," which aired during the timeslots on weekdays.[35]

Stations WWL and WSMB presented evening listeners more variety than during weekday mornings and afternoons. Instead of repeating shows throughout weekday mornings and afternoons, WSMB scheduled at 8 p.m. and 8:15 p.m. Monday through Sunday respectively: "Telephone Hour," "Amos 'n' Andy," "Eddie Cantor," "Music Hall," "People Are Funny," "National Barn Dance," and "Merry-Go-Round." WDSU, on the other hand, scheduled a more steady evening offering such as the comedy "Lum and Abner" at 8 p.m., Monday through Thursday.[36]

Whites wrote, produced, announced, engineered, and otherwise decided which programs were disseminated in New Orleans beginning March 31, 1922, when WWL launched the first broadcast in Louisiana. A small crack formed in the exclusivity on May 26, 1946, when WNOE integrated.[37] At the time, broadcasters imagined blacks as dull-witted caricatures of human beings. White supremacy engulfed Anglos' media presentations of African Americans as Uncle Toms, Aunt Jemimas, childlike, or other characters who need not be taken seriously. "Radio is not contributing a damn thing to better race relations," according to a panelist at a conference on radio and blacks at Ohio State University in May 1946. "With few exceptions, radio still handles the Negro in the same old Uncle Tom, crap-shooting minstrel tradition. Jack Benny's Rochester is a good example."[38]

The long-running comedy show, "Amos 'n' Andy," which demeaned blacks, represented a product of the Eurocentric imagination. The show featured Freeman Gosden and Charles Correll, two white men who pretended to be black and presented their black characters as mentally and morally challenged. WGN in Chicago introduced Gosden and Correll's blackface characters to radio in a 1926 series called "Sam and Henry." WMAQ acquired the actors' services in 1928 and changed the show's title to "Amos 'n' Andy." NBC acquired the show and began network distribution in 1929. CBS picked up the series in 1950, changed the format in 1954, and ended it in 1960. The "Amos 'n' Andy" characters thereafter became the basis of a television series bearing the same name.[39] WWL followed in the same vein in 1929, producing "Smoky Joe and Tee Tain," a long-running nightly comedy modeled after "Amos 'n' Andy." "Smoky Joe" featured white actors speaking in dialect conjuring inarticulate blacks in far-fetched dilemmas.[40]

The black inferiority/white superiority ideology is among long-standing traditions and customs in the United States. A brief history of the relationship between blacks and whites in New Orleans provides context for understanding the social and political conditions blacks experienced in the city in the post–World War II era. New Orleans gained affiliation with the United States in 1803 when the federal government purchased the Louisiana Territory from France. The 1810 census count of 17,242 residents positioned New Orleans as the fifth largest city in the nation. The city's location near the mouth of the Mississippi River attracted investment capital, commercial and employment opportunities, and contributed to the city's growth. The Mississippi River provided the principal route for the international transportation of bulk items, such as southern cotton and midwestern food products. As more investment capital arrived, migrants swelled the population. The city's growth slowed, however, as railroads emerged and offered an alternative and competitive mode of transportation throughout the Mississippi Valley, particularly after 1860.

New Orleans was a major US market at which whites bought and sold enslaved Africans and held them as personal property. Louisiana laws prohibited enslaved blacks from entering contractual relationships, owning property, or marrying. The laws prohibited anyone from teaching the enslaved to read or write. In 1830 lawmakers prohibited anyone from writing, publishing, or distributing books, pamphlets, or newspaper advocating anti-slavery.[41]

White men who conceived children via sexual intercourse with black women sometimes provided financial and legal support to emancipate their offspring, sexual partners, or both. The progeny became known as Creoles, light-skin straight hair individuals who sometimes closely resemble white people. They were privileged with more opportunities than darker blacks. Over the years, the city's population of non-enslaved blacks increased. Whites, however, denied freed blacks, sometimes called free people of color, equal legal protection and enacted legislation to codify the inferiority of the black offspring of white men. According to state law, free people of color must never insult or strike white people nor consider themselves equal to whites.

Furthermore, blacks were required to yield to whites on every occasion and only speak to them respectfully. Violators would be imprisoned and sentenced commensurate with the severity of the offense.[42]

After the Civil War, Congress enacted the Thirteenth Amendment to the US Constitution and abolished slavery in 1865. White southerners lost their black-property rights but maintained control by enacting state and local laws restricting residency, mobility, speech, voting, education, employment, and other rights and privileges.[43] Political leaders in the state organized a constitutional convention and met in New Orleans on February 8, 1898. The white elite intended to reverse the federal government's Reconstruction initiatives between 1863 and 1877, which legislated equal rights for freed slaves. The initiatives extended voting privileges to blacks and led to the appointment and election of black lawmakers. The Compromise of 1877 ended the dream. The compromise permitted white southern Democrats to invalidate equal-rights doctrine the federal government had forced upon southern whites. The Compromise codified white supremacy and manifested racial separation.

In a talk to state delegates on the first day of the constitutional convention in Louisiana in 1898, the group's president, E. B. Kruttschnitt, framed the launch of the state's post–Civil War codification of white supremacy as a corrective to political corruption of blacks and Reconstruction supporters: "We know that this convention has been called together by the people of the State to eliminate from the electorate the mass of corrupt and illiterate voters who have degraded our politics."[44]

The convention provided the Louisiana legislature the tools to deny blacks legal protection. The legislature enacted a law prohibiting blacks from occupying the same railroad cars as whites. It later broadened the law to prohibit blacks from occupying the interior of railroad stations. Louisiana restructured its constitution in 1898 and included legislation prohibiting blacks and whites from attending the same public schools. The legislature passed ordinances forbidding marriage between blacks and whites. It required circus operators to install two ticket windows, one for blacks and the other for whites.[45]

New Orleans lawmakers also enacted laws denying blacks legal protection and attempting to physically separate them from whites. New Orleans enacted restrictions in areas where state law was silent, and it acted years earlier than the legislature in some matters. City lawmakers enacted an ordinance in 1816 requiring theater operators to seat blacks and whites in different sections. The city council passed a law in 1835 requiring administrators to partition cemeteries into three zones: one half for white people, one quarter for free blacks, and one quarter for the enslaved. In 1902 lawmakers began requiring officials of streetcar companies to provide separate trolleys for blacks or otherwise install moveable partitions to distinguish sections reserved for whites.[46]

Blacks resisted white supremacy. The Creoles of mixed European descent lobbied the legislature to defeat discriminatory bills and requested federal courts to outlaw railroad segregation. Black newspapers articulated opposition to activities of racists. Teachers at black colleges in the city inculcated students to be responsible citizens and to pursue goals despite racial roadblocks.[47]

In post–World War II New Orleans, African American leaders accelerated efforts to empower blacks, gain support from liberal whites, and reform policies and practices that advantaged whites. The principals in the local branch of the NAACP were among the leaders. Blacks struggled to prepare themselves and their children to rise in the social sphere, absent substantial economic and political opportunities. Founders of the NAACP acknowledged the problems and sought solutions. They launched the NAACP in New York City in 1910 and gradually attracted men and women who developed reform strategy, organized blacks, solicited donations, and pursued in court remedies against unjust laws. Five years after the NAACP was founded, an affiliate branch was established in New Orleans in 1915.

In the thirty years between its establishment in New Orleans and 1945, the local NAACP struggled. The group agitated, submitted proposals and petitions to status quo leaders, and otherwise directed attention to problems including truancy, residential overcrowding, dilapidated housing, police brutality, discrimination in voter registration, and other issues interfering with black progress. The group encouraged blacks to pay poll taxes, join the NAACP, sign petitions, and contribute to fund-raising efforts. The NAACP leadership envisioned solutions in part via ballot access.[48]

Whites maintained the near elimination of blacks from the New Orleans electorate throughout the Reconstruction Era. In 1940 blacks numbered 149,034 or 30 percent of the city's total 494,537 residents.[49] Orleans Parish officials registered 659 blacks and 159,310 whites to vote in public elections as of October 5, 1940 (see Table 1). The officials allowed 0.4 percent of the city's black citizens to qualify to vote but let 46 percent of whites register. Black voters also represented less than 1 percent of all registered voters while whites represented 99 percent.[50]

Orleans Parish registrars continued to retard blacks from access to voter registration but, in 1946, they permitted 4,822 or 3.2 percent of the African American population in the city to register and tally 2.6 percent of the electorate. As of October 5, 1946, registrars let 178,524 whites or 52 percent of the city's Anglo population register.

Table 1
Registered Voters
Orleans Parish, 1940–1950

Year	Total	Whites	%	Blacks	%
1940	159,969	159,310	99	659	0.4
1946	183,346	178,524	97	4,822	2.6
1948	200,786	189,050	94	11,736	5.8
1950	212,895	186,866	88	26,029	12

Source: *State of Louisiana Report of Secretary of State to His Excellency*, 1940, 1942, 1946, 1948, 1950, Special Collections, Joseph Merrick Jones Hall, Tulane University Library, New Orleans.

Liberalization of thought associated with World War II and America's participation in the conflict accounted for part of the reduction in official resistance to blacks registering to vote between 1940 and 1946. A US Supreme Court decision also provided an explanation. The court ruled in *Smith v. Allwright* in 1944 that Texas Democrats violated the Fifteenth Amendment when they excluded blacks from voting in party primaries. The effect of the ruling was applicable nationwide.[51] The number of black voters in New Orleans increased between 1940 and 1950 from less than 1 percent to 12 percent.[52] The small rise in the number of African American voters also contributed to blacks' entrance in New Orleans radio beginning in 1946.

Abraham Maslow's theory of self-actualization is another factor. It seeks to explain aspects of human behavior. The theory is sometimes called the hierarchy of needs. Maslow argued that individuals encounter a psychological hierarchy of needs that must be quenched before moving to a higher realm, such as in ascending order: the necessity to eat and drink, urge to engage in sex, need to be involved in loving relationship(s), and the desire for esteem in order to reach self-actualization. For example, a hungry man cannot very well experience love until he satisfied his need for food and sex. He can only achieve esteem after he experiences love. Thereafter, reaching esteem is possible. The individual subsequently has the wherewithal to seek endeavors that satisfy his quest for self-actualization, the highest phase of the hierarchy.[53] This is relevant because black people experienced a different reality. Blacks had to satisfy at least one additional component in order to reach self-actualization.

Black people experienced sets of unimagined spaces that contrasted with white reality. Therefore Maslow's hierarchy of needs requires refinement to be applicable. Black people too had to satisfy the basic, human needs, such as hunger and sex before they could pursue esteem and self-actualization. However, black men encountered unique experiences in their travels through America. White men initially succeeded in denying black men a sense of manhood, which was reserved for Caucasian males. Manhood here means qualities associated with being a man, such as having within his grasp self-determination, authority over the nuclear family, socioeconomic status, and access to the means of production. During the periods of slavery and racial segregation, blacks could not achieve success based on the amount of energy and effort they expended. Before black men could pursue esteem, they had to find manhood.

A case in point: One month after WDIA in Memphis hired a black man, Nat D. Williams, in October 1948 and integrated its on-air staff, the *Memphis World* interviewed him. Williams articulated a version of the concept manhood. He said WDIA hired him because its decision makers recognized the existence of "... 'a new Negro' in the United States today. He's a Negro who believes he is a man..."[54]

The first African American men whom broadcasters permitted through the gates of New Orleans radio satisfied their black-exclusive basic need for manhood. Thereafter they were equipped to pursue esteem and to strive toward self-actualization. Black men whom broadcasters added to their stable of announcers had to negotiate such an additional element in the hierarchy. Their white counterparts inherited the notion of growing into manhood. White men who applied for jobs as radio announcers, program hosts, or disc jockeys individually satisfied each element of Maslow's needs hierarchy and respectively sought higher-level accomplishments and satisfaction. The founding fathers codified manhood in the Constitution and applied it to the experiences of white men. All men are created equally, as long as they were of European descent. The US Constitution, state laws, and mainstream social conventions treated black men horrendously differently than white adult males. Black men were denied equal legal protection and therefore encountered different realities and interpreted reality differently than whites.

Black people understood their limited access to opportunity, food, shelter, and other basic requirements of Maslow's needs hierarchy. They had to work without monetary gain, accept the circumstances without outward protests, and envelop themselves in Protestant Christianity or other religiosity promising deliverance, often in an afterlife of abundant milk and honey. Without manhood, blacks failed to seek experiences or access opportunities that brought about a sense of esteem and self-actualization. The pioneer black broadcasters found ways to become men and to be respected as men. They were crafty, confident, and determined to enter local radio.

Movement began, in large part, because individual black men, with a hunger for new challenges, knocked on doors at radio stations and sold their ideas. Jack L. Cooper was among blacks whom whites hired to write and perform comedy skits early in the evolution of commercial broadcasting. Cooper was a representative of the *Chicago Defender*, a prominent black newspaper distributed nationally. The newspaper's leadership dispatched him to Washington, D.C., to open an office early in 1925.

Cooper packed his radio set among his belongings and moved to the nation's capital. There he listened to shows on stations his receiver captured, such as WCAP, which had a German bandleader hosting a musical variety show. He heard what he thought was the music of a black vocal group, but he never heard a black person speak on radio. Cooper realized he never heard a black voice on the air anywhere, ". . . so I made up my mind to do something about it."[55]

Cooper went to the hotel housing the station with the intention of talking with the German. A staffer tried to turn Cooper away because the hotel prohibited blacks except if they were custodians or kitchen help. Cooper used subterfuge and said he was a deliveryman who had to place a message in the white man's hand. It worked. He talked with the German and sold him on the idea to hire Cooper to write and voice comedy. The bandleader hired Cooper but required him to use black dialect on the air. He complied. Four years later, in 1929, he returned to Chicago and debuted the radio program "The Negro Hour" on WSBC. Cooper also was among the country's first black disc jockeys.[56]

Hal Jackson was another black man with a powerful psychological drive who influenced a white man to integrate his station. Jackson also exhibited a sense of manhood and self-esteem that propelled him to seek a job in radio. Circa 1939 in Washington, D.C., Jackson had been a play-by-play announcer at sports events at Howard University. Jackson wanted the manager at WINX to hire him to announce the university's games on the air. Jackson's mentor tried to discourage him from pursuing the goal, reminding him of D.C.'s racial segregation. Shortly thereafter, Jackson went to WINX, a station owned by the *Washington Post*, at Eighth and I Streets NW. He believed the station manager was an intolerant redneck so he did not make an appointment. Jackson walked into the station and told the receptionist he wanted to see the guy who ran the station. She asked what Jackson wanted. He said he announced sporting events at the local Griffith Stadium and wanted to talk about producing sports programming.[57]

Jackson was allowed to visit with the station manager and told him he would buy airtime and sell commercial time to local businesses. He also proposed to voice the play-by-play commentary on air. The general manager laughed and said he would only hire a white announcer because "no nigger will ever go on this radio station." He called his staff into his office: "I brought you all in here because, can you imagine, this nigger is talking about going on this radio station."⁵⁸ Jackson, to the contrary, was not embarrassed or discouraged. He was angry and determined to get his show on the air.

Jackson wrote a prospectus for a nightly show he named "The Bronze Review," a code that hinted to blacks the show would target African Americans. It would feature live entertainment, interviews, and news. He got a local black weekly newspaper, the *Afro American*, to agree to publicize the show; C. C. Coley, who owned five barbeque restaurants, agreed to buy advertising time; and he hired a white advertising agency, Cal Heimlich and Merck, to enter into a contract with WINX on his behalf. WINX's sales department signed on because it assumed the broadcaster was white. Subsequently, "The Bronze Review," the first black radio show in D.C., aired for fifteen minutes at 11 p.m. Monday through Saturday, beginning November 1939.⁵⁹

Cooper's experience at WCAP was not unusual. When whites hired blacks to speak on early radio, they often required them to use a dialect to sound ignorant. Of course, exceptions are a part of every rule. William Barlow organized data of the emergence of blacks in radio and conceptualized the experiences into five periods: blackface radio, 1920–1939; the middle passage, 1939–1949; black oriented radio, 1950–1965; black controlled radio, 1965–1990; and black public radio, 1967–1990.⁶⁰

Broadcasters during the blackface period, 1920–1939, presented African Americans as inconsequential entertainers in the minstrel tradition. Gradually whites backed away from the blackface requirement and moved into the middle passage period, between 1939 and 1949. Sometimes, however, whites permitted blacks to speak standard English on radio before 1939 or required blackface vocalizations during and after the middle passage period. Some broadcasters during the period of black oriented radio, 1950–1965, devoted their entire format to programming that targeted African Americans. New Orleans radio illustrated characteristics of the middle passage between 1945 and 1950 as well as black oriented radio, 1950–1965.⁶¹

At any rate, stations diverged from white-only policies and hired blacks when management envisioned few or no other ways to produce profit from radio content. Subsequently the profit motive was among factors leading to integration. American blacks were by and large poor at least until the burgeoning economy during the World War II era influenced employers to hire blacks and paying them living wages. African Americans thereafter bought radio sets and lusted for the goods and services advertised thereon, especially after black programming surfaced.⁶²

CHAPTER TWO

Race and Supremacy Contaminated Media

African Americans' involvement in radio is under-theorized and lacks sufficient generalizations. Scholarship concerning blacks in broadcasting needs more insight and detail that allow individuals better to explain relevant social behavior. Scholars have for decades produced historical research regarding white men and women as broadcast station owners and content producers and consumers. Researchers use considerable primary data crafting Eurocentric perspectives revealing social trends aiding the launch of theoretical speculations. Research on race and radio must systematically inquire and similarly explore primary data. Scholars must meticulous seek to discover findings of various analyses to enable readers to explain and fairly well predict the outcome of human interactions. This section reviews relevant literature. The next part discusses theories of why whites initially omitted blacks from meaningful broadcast productions. It lays out the mechanisms that coalesced to deny the realistic presentations of African Americans on air.

Some writers of black broadcast history access secondary information and interpret limited amounts of primary sources. Louis Cantor presents personal memories of his experiences in broadcasting, which are instructive but contain little indication of the sources of data.[1] Cantor published *Wheelin' on Beale*, an interpretative history of a southern station and its racial integration. Cantor, a white man, described details of persons, circumstances, and events associated with WDIA, the Memphis radio station that changed its programming in 1949 from white appeal to rhythm and blues, gospel, blues, talk, and other content targeting blacks. WDIA was the first station in the United States to broadcast all of its content for black consumption.[2]

Cantor provides an eyewitness account of some of the events at WDIA, which employed him in the 1950s as a control-board operator and later as host of a gospel and a rhythm and blues show. He concludes that black personalities talked on the air in jazzy jargon about music and culture, produced programming building their communities, provided African Americans with opportunities to gain a measure of status and to promote their activities, and contributed to changing marketing and advertising strategies. The station's black air personalities were local role models, raising black consciousness and helping make black pride a reality instead of simply a slogan. The insight is outstanding, but it is not reliable; in other words, future research intending to replicate or verify the story is impossible because analytical data is not available.[3]

Some other authors paint broad sweeps of images without focusing details, thus limiting opportunities for the construction of a thick historiography. The prolific black radio scholar William Barlow, in his book *Voice Over: The Making of Black Radio*, reveals a national history discussing the blackface radio period, 1920–1939. He wrote concerning federal agencies involved in endorsing scripted programs featuring black issues and historical figures and events, the era of disc jockeys, and black public radio, among other topics.[4] Other scholarship tends to focus on blacks and radio in the North and underrepresent their southern counterparts.

Stephen Roy James Walsh, in his dissertation "Black-Oriented Radio and the Campaign for Civil Rights in the United States, 1945–1975," presents superior scholarship regarding the movement, but his analysis is at the macro level. It does not zero in as does a case study.[5] Brian Ward's book, *Radio and the Struggle for Civil Rights in the South*, also includes considerable primary data in its discussion of African American broadcasters and audio media outlets. Ward looks at Birmingham, Memphis, Atlanta, Charlotte, Washington, D.C., and Nashville.[6] However no significant discussion concerns the role of black-specific radio in New Orleans, the city that drew national attention to the development of jazz, Mardi Gras, the French Quarter, the Mississippi River port, the African slave trade, and local Civil Rights activism.

Barbara Dianne Savage's book *Broadcasting Freedom* is another remarkable work of scholarship. The document advances the discussion of the role blacks played nationally in public affairs programming between 1938 and 1948. The networks diverged from white exclusivity after federal administrators created the Radio Education Project of the Office of Education in 1935. The office employed blacks who wrote scripts, such as "Freedom's People," a series that explored African American history and culture. NBC broadcast the series in 1941 and 1942 after federal officials expressed concern about potential racial unrest in urban areas. Savage also deals with circumstances in which black writers and voice actors delivered programs that originated at radio stations in the North such as "Destination Freedom," a thirty-minute drama series written by Richard Durham and broadcast via WMAQ in Chicago between 1948 and 1950.[7]

Otherwise, white image-makers virtually closed the creation of radio drama to African Americans but reserved opportunities for writers of European descent during the World War II era. Popular arts in the United States relied on negative racial stereotypes and discrimination. In literature, motion pictures, music, radio, and television, racist impediments worked against the production of realistic and equitable depictions of blacks. The mass media portrayed African Americans as stereotypes such as: toms, coons, mulattoes, mammies, and bucks among other typecasts. Media underrepresented blacks in the creative and business aspects of the mass-culture industries. Before the mid-1950s, blacks rarely were news reporters, sportscasters, soap opera actors, and had no substantial roles in romances, dramas, Westerns, or detective shows. No black network executives existed. A few local producers, directors, and writers were on the scene. Theoretical explanations are too limited among works exploring race and radio. The next section explains what is behind the beginning of negative communications perceptions foisted on black people.

◆ ◆ ◆

Theoretical concepts assist with interpreting meanings of actions and inactions associated with racial exclusion and later integration of radio broadcasting. Racism overarches explanations concerning the historical experiences of blacks in the United States. The story of race and radio, as well as African American experiences in general, is a reality in which dominant European peoples took possession of material things; established economic, political, police, and military power; and controlled people of color. The rise of commercial radio, while mostly contributing to continued silencing of authentic black voices, added to the tapestry of negative racial representations already embedded in mainstream print, visual, and audio media.

Traditional racists believed blacks were inferior and whites superior. They favored discrimination based on skin color, cultural representations, and geographic origin. Whites formed racist attitudes toward blacks, by and large, because they held negative thoughts associated with continental Africans and African Americans. Ideas of black inferiority and white superiority diffused through channels such as white opinion leaders, interpersonal communications, and mass media.[8] Racism represented the major factor contributing to white broadcasters excluding blacks from radio in New Orleans until 1946. Even after then, when Caucasians in radio presented black images, they manipulated perceptions of African American experiences by constructing situations wherein they characterized blacks as racially inferior and culturally bankrupt. Such explains state laws, particularly in the American South, that codified white supremacy. State laws concerning public education assigned whites and black to different schools. Public education set aside for whites were adequately funded, while those reserved for blacks were drastically underfunded. White power brokers and the general Caucasian public considered blacks as subhuman. Not only was white supremacy insidious, it had an effect of infesting some blacks with thinking they were indeed inferior. Blacks, before integration, accepted early radio programs and advertisements as serving the needs of mainstream whites and organizations and individuals with social, political, and economic power.

Janette Dates and William Barlow, in their tome *Split Image: African Americans in Mass Media*, credited W. E. B. Du Bois as among black critical explicators of the dominant power and ubiquity of American racism. Du Bois proposed that the collective white mind perceived blacks as members of an inferior race. Racists controlled image making and information and entertainment dissemination and poisoned black self-perception. Du Bois surmised blacks perceived themselves and black experiences through a distorted frame of consciousness.[9] In 1897 he proposed the theory of double consciousness. He said there was a twoness embedded in black people. They were the offspring of the despised Africans who were enslaved in America, and they were Americans infused with European ideals. They had to live in two very different worlds, one black and the other white. Consequently their cultural productions, such as music, differed from that of people of European decent. When black broadcasters integrated radio, they became the disseminators of the products of African American thought. When they emerged as broadcasters, they brought unique cultural expression to their programming.

Dates and Barlow also demonstrate that racism explains images of white supremacy and black inferiority in mass media in the United States. Whites dominated mass media that controlled the portrayal and participation of African Americans in the media. Such control disclosed major cultural contradictions. On the one hand, white station owners and producers appropriated aspects of African American culture to enrich the mass media and themselves. On the other hand, mass disseminated images of blacks, filtered through racial misconceptions and fantasies, denied the existence of a rich and noteworthy black culture. Whenever white image makers developed media products (records, films, radio and television programs, news stories, and advertising campaigns), they did so in terms of "codes and criteria based on their own racial and class background."[10]

The theory of ideological hegemony is another way of thinking about how and why image makers disseminated certain messages. The voices of white people and their ideas helped shore up the status quo. Those white voices presented black people as stereotypes, simplified images of complex realities. White broadcasters omitted realistic portrayals of African Americans. They conjured and distributed negative stereotypes of blacks and controlled access to opportunities for African Americans to create meaningful media images. That control dates back to the colonial period when the founding fathers convinced colonists that Africans possessed no redeemable social values people of European descent might respect. They wrote interpretations of Africans outside of legal protections articulated in the US Constitution. They constructed mechanisms of a developing capital-based economy such that the elite reserved opportunity and privilege for themselves, their progeny, and other approved peoples of European descent.

In *Selections from the Prison Notebook*, Antonio Gramsci articulates intricacies of the concept of ideological hegemony and explains its mechanisms. The concept was associated with white voices and their distorted presentation of black realities. The American elite held onto power, in part, by convincing the masses to accept its versions of reality, among which were images of inferior black people and superior whites. The ideas were diffused in gradual, long-term, and sometimes innocuous ways. Eyes and ears interpreted the ideas as commonplace. Coercion was rare, but the elite availed themselves to it as necessary. Blacks too bought into the ideas, as Du Bois suggested, despite cultural-resistance struggles at the individual and group levels. The white elite continued to remind people that Caucasian culture was superior.[11]

Stuart Hall, in his chapter "Signification, Representation, Ideology: Althusser and the Post-Structuralist Debates," directs thought about ideological hegemony to popular cultural content distributed by mass media. A way to think about Hall's ideas is to consider how proponents of fine art opposed the proliferation of popular art. The distinction concerned class differences and preferences in cultural taste. Mass media professionals produced and disseminated myths about human experiences. The myths or rituals explained, instructed, and justified behavior, systems, processes, and institutions. For example, as mentioned earlier, media content producers created the gravel-voiced Rochester Van Jones, a black servant on the Jack Benny Program, which began in 1937 as a radio show on the NBC network and continued until 1965 after moving to CBS television. The writers imbued Rochester with a black dialect, childishness, and laziness that is indicative of stereotypes whites held of blacks. Media purveyors presented connections among blacks and stereotypical plots, characters, language, and other devices. Rochester's personification presented such connections. Subsequently, mass communicators cued listeners and readers with regard to convention and tradition. They alerted audiences to notions of what was appealing and gratifying. And they showed how Americans established and maintained social order. Presenting blacks as inept and docile eased whites fear that blacks would violently rise up.[12]

Generally, according to Catherine L. Covert in her chapter "We May Hear Too Much," early American listeners feared radio broadcasts would spread communist propaganda, influence their children to dance to jazz music, compromise their choices of what information and entertainment to listen to, and discourage reading. As the medium matured, white middle-class Americans imagined radio made them part of a large, wholesome collective.[13] To them, radio was a boundless source of entertainment, such as for music from great concert halls, and information, such as concerning innovations in farming or news from big cities.[14]

Black people imagined radio too, but differently. To them, it was a closed medium that on slim occasions brought excitement from merely hearing the voice of a black person on air. In the 1930s and 1940s, poor blacks found difficulty gaining access to radio sets. Some blacks first heard electronic media content on a radio set at a neighbor's house, grocery store, or in some public place. When blacks heard an African American talking or singing on radio, for the most part they experienced a sense of racial pride. Michael C. Dawson's *Behind the Mule* conceptualizes the experience as linked fate. African Americans interpreted a black person on air as a major achievement for their race. If whites gave one African American the opportunity to talk on radio, they might give other blacks a similar chance.[15]

As an example, Mark Newman's *Entrepreneurs of Profit and Pride* quotes an excerpt of an interview of a black man who listened to the "King Biscuit Time" radio show on KFFA in Helena, Arkansas, in 1941. The program featured a white host, Sonny Payne, and music performed by Rice Miller, a blues harmonica player and songwriter who later took the name Sonny Boy Williamson. Blacks listened to the show not necessarily because they enjoyed the music. It was the pride they felt because a black man was on the air and that reality signified progress among the race. "We never heard blacks on the radio 'cause Sonny Boy was the first," said J. C. Darnley, a millworker living in West Helena. "He came in representin' the King Biscuit Flour . . . So, then, I was inclined to listen to hem." Darnley had little interest in the blues. But hearing Williamson perform on the air was "something new . . . something we had never been able to witness." As a result, "when Sonny Boy Williamson came on, we would turn that on because he also was black. And that's the only reason we would turn it on."[16]

Walter Lippmann's chapter, "The World Outside and Pictures in the Head," suggests that each man behaved in a certain way because he formed pictures in his mind or someone or something provided the images. The pictures were a pattern of stereotypes, a simple, interpretative model. But people often formed the pictures, or stereotypes, from inadequate amounts of accurate information. If an atlas indicated that the earth was flat, a viewer would not sail near where he believed the edge was for fear of falling off. The way an individual imagines the world determines what he will do; it does not determine what he will achieve. It determines effort, feelings, hopes, but not accomplishments or results.[17]

Lippmann proposes that mass media professionals were among the originators of the messages people used to construct stereotypes used to interpret reality. People formed attitudes or perspectives on issues or events after accessing the stereotypic pictures in their heads. The political and business elite took advantage of the phenomenon. People with similar mental pictures behaved in concert at times. There were always competing and contradictory messages. Nevertheless, the elite hired, subsidized, and otherwise rewarded image makers who constructed and disseminated the desired messages. The orchestrated production of mediated messages, which is the information people use to form mental pictures or stereotypes, helped shape the public's consciousness. The elite used mediated messages for purposes of shaping public opinion toward a national will or specific, social constructions.[18]

In *Politics at the Margin*, Susan Herbst explains the concept of marginalization, which she defines as practices aimed at silencing voices that reside outside of mainstream society. Marginalization encompassed the results of behavior experienced by members of discriminated groups such as women, homosexuals, ethnic minorities, and African Americans. Marginalization explained some of the absence of black voices of intelligence from broadcasting in New Orleans before 1946, yet its usefulness applied beyond racism. Blacks were not the exclusive victims of the elites' hold on opportunity and privilege. Elites attempted to control the art and commentary of members of non-elite social groups, such as poor people and the working class.[19]

Before station managers put black-situated programming into their sight line, significantly beginning in the 1960s, blacks responded to ideological hegemony and marginalization in print journalism, beginning in 1827 with the publication of *Freedom's Journal*, the first African American newspaper in the United States. The *Journal*, published in New York City, responded to anti-black editorial content in the white-owned press. A white newspaper, the *Enquirer*, particularly roused the *Journal*'s founders John B. Russwurm and Samuel E. Cornish. In an editorial that encouraged slavery and opposed people who advocated human rights for the enslaved Africans, the *Enquirer* constructed images of black people as subhuman. The *Journal*'s founders reacted by pooling together resources and creating an instrument to, in their estimation, more accurately define and describe blacks, their experiences and interests. Editorial content in the *Journal* demanded the elite end slavery. The publishers also presented images permitting readers to imagine free northern blacks and their progressive works and activities.[20]

While African Americans challenged hegemony and marginalization in print journalism by launching their own newspapers, they lacked access to enough social, political, and economic capital to establish themselves as broadcasters in any significant numbers until the last quarter of the twentieth century. For example, by the 1970s the number of black-owned radio stations increased to eighty-eight, but that was just 1 percent of the 6,530 stations in the country. In the meantime, one by one and city by city, blacks asked or manipulated whites to provide opportunities to access radio behind the microphone. Gradually and station by station, when sufficient political circumstances or economic pressure intervened, whites responded.[21]

♦ ♦ ♦

Nonetheless, southern broadcasters were less tolerant. When network programmers demonstrated a modicum of racial liberalism, station managers in the South became more adamant segregationists. For example, a radio station in Jackson, Mississippi, affiliated with the Mutual Broadcasting System, in March 1948 silenced the network's feed of the four-part, pro-black series "To Secure These Rights."[22] It was also the urging of civic and Civil Rights Movement organizations that were behind the change that trickled in among the status quo.

The year before WNOE integrated in 1946, the New Orleans branch of the NAACP launched a campaign. While the course of activities was not broadcast oriented, it sought to dismantle obstructions to black equality throughout Louisiana, and it furthered the movement toward integrating WNOE. The branch organized the Citizens Committee to reform state and local laws and practices. Daniel E. Byrd, president and executive secretary of the local NAACP, vice-president Bennett B. Ross, and other members set the Citizens Committee in motion. Objectives included the reduction or termination of racial discrimination in voter registration, education, and National Guard service. Other objectives included fundraising and victory in court proceedings aimed at discontinuing police brutality and other racist activities.[23]

The local branch planned a statewide, multifaceted approach to disrupt systemic racism. The approach targeted in particular voter registrars who denied blacks voting rights. While NAACP lawyers petitioned the judiciary to outlaw public policies and actions that violated tenets of equal protection, blacks who would ordinarily qualify to vote required a better understanding of the workings of American democracy and citizenship. Blacks needed information about the advantages of voting, how to register, principles associated with citizenship, and other ideals. Realizations of the standards in concert would begin the process of lifting the veil of ignorance shrouding African Americans after years of segregation and slavery's legacy. The NAACP concluded that the establishment of voter registration schools and workshops would assist the move toward full citizenship.[24] Even though O. C. W. Taylor's program began in 1946, black broadcasters were not in the calculus. No African American was on air in the state of Louisiana at that time. Besides, station managers would not have allowed such freedom to speak on their airways.

Nevertheless, it is instructive to place in context resistance to white supremacy during a time when blacks were without accessibility to widespread electronic messages. At strategy sessions during the summer of 1945, principals of the organizing effort debated the pros and cons of when was the best time to inform the public of the plans and objectives of the Citizens Committee. Local NAACP officials discussed whether it was prudent to distribute publicity immediately or delay it. They discussed how to coordinate timing of publicity of the local campaign and lawsuits or other activities with the plans of lawyers at the national headquarters. NAACP leaders debated how and when to inform white allies about initiatives of the local campaign.[25]

Despite uncertainties largely centered on the timing of the release of public communication, Byrd shepherded the group, hammered out its statement of purpose, and mailed it to Thurgood Marshall, a lawyer at the national NAACP based in New York City. Marshall would become the first black justice on the Supreme Court in 1967. Byrd also queried Marshall about publicity strategy. The statement also laid out the NAACP's rationale for organizing a statewide civil rights campaign. Branches in Louisiana would combine their efforts and use every legal resource to reach the objective. Newspapers, opinion leaders, flyers, speakers at rallies, and word of mouth were the means by which the public learned details of the organizations' progressive activities.[26]

NAACP leaders determined black newspaper journalists possessed the skills and experience necessary to develop and execute plans of action to publicize the objectives. The officials sought the services of journalists statewide. They assigned them to work on the publicity committee and charged them to work with members of the registration and education committee. The officials also encouraged activists, preachers, and other opinion leaders to inform their constituents of campaign initiatives.[27]

During the period, black journalists worked exclusively at small newspapers or magazines owned by African Americans. The journalists were sometimes employed at the publication full time, as in the case of publishers who also served editorial functions. Often the journalists worked part-time or as freelancers. The NAACP by-laws limited membership on the publicity committee to representatives of the black press. The journalists were responsible for gathering information, writing texts, and disseminating articles, letters, and other forms of printed communications that aided campaign objectives. The committee leadership, however, maintained authority over the release of information. The journalists also collaborated with members of the registration subunit to write letters and submit them to leaders of liberal white organizations. The intent was to remind whites and inform others that the US Constitution and federal statutes prohibited violation of provisions of equal legal protection.[28]

Officers of the national NAACP also employed black journalists to assist the organization with publicity and other strategy formulations. For example, Roy Wilkins studied journalism and sociology at the University of Minnesota. Wilkins worked as a writer and editor at the *Kansas City Call*. NAACP officials learned of Wilkins's leadership activities and the *Call*'s progressive editorial content and hired him as assistant secretary in 1931. Wilkins replaced W. E. B. Du Bois in 1934 as editor of the NAACP magazine the *Crisis*. Wilkins was the *Crisis* editor until 1949.[29]

Daniel Byrd, branch president of the NAACP in New Orleans, wrote letters to national officers and explained the racial scene in the area. In a June 25, 1945, letter Byrd told Thurgood Marshall the Citizens Committee planned a mass meeting in August. The development of fundraising strategy was a principal objective of the meeting. The committee wanted Marshall to invite William H. Hastie to speak at a fund-raiser. Hastie was dean of Howard University's Law School and a federal judge with jurisdiction over the Virgin Islands. The branch's plan was to contact black business owners, labor union heads, and church leaders and solicit financial contributions.[30]

Marshall suggested a goal of raising $100,000 and wrote Hastie on June 27: "...they would like very much to have that venerable gentleman, Judge Hastie, for this purpose."[31] Hastie did not attend. Marshall was the keynote speaker at the mass meeting at the auditorium at Booker T. Washington high school on Sunday, September 10.[32] Marshall described the event in a memorandum. The Citizens Committee of the NAACP of Louisiana established a four-point program: to gain the right to vote in public elections, to equalize educational facilities from elementary schools to universities, to end police brutality, and to integrate the home guard.[33]

Black newspapers were the principal disseminators of information regarding progressive activities among African Americans. Other vehicles included pronouncements by the clergy, leaders and volunteers distributing leaflets and other printed materials, and talking face to face. The integration of radio would eventually compete with black newspapers in the area of sharing public information. This is not to say the integration of radio drastically expanded the black public sphere. It did not. Initially black broadcasters were not allowed to talk in regard to serious issues. Such came years later. During the post–World War II period, African American broadcasters either talked about religious matters, shucked and jived while playing black music, or portrayed negative stereotypes.

The NAACP began a campaign in 1946 aimed at local broadcasters to get them to integrate their stations and programming. In December, Baltimore NAACP executive secretary Addison Pinkney and Leslie Percy of the Washington bureau of the Associated Negro Press news service "conferred with station officials and pointed out radio's responsibility to its thousands of Negro listeners, and the community in general, to offer such a program as a public service feature." They were successful and produced a series of six radio dramas at no cost to their organizations. The programs presented the origin, growth, and activities of the NAACP and portrayed racial discrimination scenarios and other issues evidencing the need for equal rights.[34]

Percy proposed that NAACP branches throughout the country organize radio committees and identify programs trivializing the black experience or otherwise diminishing the dignity of African Americans. Percy proposed branches also challenge radio stations' policies prohibiting the employment of people of color. Percy said the committees should: Oppose local and network programs carrying racial stereotypes and other characterizations obnoxious to minority groups; work to obtain use of black dramatic talent on radio shows and African American announcers and technicians in local studios; protest excessive commercial announcements; advocate for better educational and cultural programs; and ask for free radio time for the NAACP branch to produce progressive programs aired in timeslots other than late nights on Saturdays or Sundays.[35]

O. C. W. Taylor carried the mantel in New Orleans. He chaired the newly formed Negro Citizens Committee, which organized efforts leading to the launch of the radio show first called "Religious Forum of the Air." Later he changed the name to "Negro Forum of the Air." WNOE agreed to allow Taylor to produce and host a fifteen-minute, 10 a.m. Sunday program beginning May 26, 1946. Initially the show did not have a sponsor. "This program has been made possible by the radio station who wishes time given to a worthwhile Negro activity," the *Louisiana Weekly* reported. The schedule of radio programs published daily in white newspapers in the city initially identified the show as the "Religious Forum," but soon, without Taylor's authorization, the dailies began identifying it as "Negro Services."[36]

Before broadcasts began, Taylor and Negro Citizens Committee secretary James E. Gayle promoted the show as one that would appeal to people of all socioeconomic classes. The show would not offend blacks because it would avoid burlesque and other antics ridiculing blacks, according to articles in black newspapers, including the *Pittsburgh Courier,* Houston *Informer,* News Orleans *Informer-Sentinel,* and *Chicago Defender.* Instead, the show would present blacks as dignified people and members of organizations working to solve social problems. The articles promised blacks would be proud of the show.[37]

The plans were quite impressive, but some segments never materialized. For example, a talent search would find singers to perform during broadcasts. Choirs, small-group vocalists, and soloists interested in the opportunities would have to survive auditions. A black newscaster would also broadcast Negro news, but that did not happen. Monthly, the show would recognize outstanding Negro institutions in the state and dedicate specific programs to honor each organization. After two years of broadcasting, all of the ambitions were not realized. But years later, Taylor independently launched new programs on WNOE featuring a talent competition as well as discussion of current events. In addition, the show was to have secured major financial support. Except for sponsorship by the gospel group Soproco, revealed in small weekly display ads in the *Louisiana Weekly,* no such arrangement unfolded.[38]

The Negro Citizens Committee wanted blacks to be able to attend the place where the talk show originated. At the time, broadcasters refused to allow black people inside of their studios. WNOE was no exception. The first of Taylor's quarter-hour broadcasts were at the Almerico Ballroom on Royal Street near Canal Street in the French Quarter. Almerico was among the largest halls in the city. Taylor and the panelists were on the ballroom's stage while members of the public sat in the audience. A white man was also on stage with a set of earphones on his head, a WNOE employee monitoring audio and voicing the station's call letters and city of record. A telephone line was used to convey the signal to the station's transmitter.[39]

Blacks in the audience as well as those listening to their radio heard positive African American discourse on the air for the first time. Discussion among the panelists—three members of the clergy, Rev. W. T. Handy, Rev. A. L. Davis, and Father James Temple—included "Does the Bible Touch Modern Issues of Today?" There was no Negro news, no singing, no black-specific topic. The program simply presented black voices talking about religiosity, a subject to which white conservatives would not object. "The question answered by these ministers bore upon the relationship of the Bible to everyday present issues," the *Louisiana Weekly* reported.[40]

The Citizens Committee distributed materials publicizing the show. *Pittsburgh Courier*, *Chicago Defender*, *Atlanta Daily World*, and (Oklahoma) *Black Dispatch* were among black newspapers throughout the country reporting news concerning the show. They learned the details because black newspapers that were members of the Associated Negro Press received weekly news packets. The Negro Forum was deemed newsworthy among blacks nationally, but some of the publicity was premature. For example, Houston *Informer* reported June 15, 1946, that Taylor and Gayle expected to launch in a few days another black program via WNOE. The program was to be broadcast from the spacious Booker T. Washington High School auditorium in the central section of the city. Taylor would be the announcer, and Gayle was to report five minutes of Negro news. Less than a month later, (New Orleans) *Informer-Sentinel* reported that the program was postponed indefinitely. Organizers could not come to an agreement with officials for use of the auditorium.[41]

A week after the "Forum's" premiere, the public was encouraged to send in questions. During broadcasts, the moderator would ask panelists to respond.[42] Religious topics initially dominated discussion because whites would not object, and black tradition was steeped in spirituality. "For many Negroes the church was the most important social institution in the community. Here the Negro could find a refuge and some hope of escape from his earthly hell," John Blassingame wrote.[43] Blacks readily accepted discussion linked to religion. Although his father was a minister, and Taylor was a member of St. Luke's Episcopal Church, "I don't claim to be that highly religious," he said. As the years passed, African American pastors would be among the major leaders advocating civil rights.[44]

The topic for the second show, "Juvenile Delinquency: What the Bible Says about It and What the Church is Doing about It," continued the theme. Despite the religious angle, the panelists concluded that neglectful parents and teachers contributed to juvenile delinquency. Children needed to be engaged in activity requiring discipline. The best form of discipline involved an adult requiring a misbehaving child to complete labor-intensive tasks.[45]

During the first two months of the fifteen-minute broadcasts, the show was primarily promoted as faith-based discussion. Black newspapers published brief articles, photographs, and captions about the "Forum." The newspapers reported the show's guests discussed topics associated with biblical lessons and religion's applications to social problems. Three members of the clergy were panelists for each of his first three broadcasts.[46]

Beginning with the fourth broadcast on June 16 and continuing through the seventh on July 6, Taylor's guests included a teacher, laborer, physician, mailman, editor, public relations professional, officer of a civic organization, and restaurateur. They talked subtly of their struggles leading to success. Those who were college graduates discussed what they had to do to attend and graduate from an institution of higher learning. Entrepreneurs commented on how the average guy could achieve monetary success. You need to set lofty goals and work hard, one entrepreneur said. Nevertheless, the show continued its religious theme, using the word Bible in the titles of at least six of his first seven shows.[47]

In July, Robert N. Perry Jr., field executive for the Boy Scouts of New Orleans, discussed the organization's fund-raising drive. On July 21, race-specific language appeared in a show's title for the first time, but it was also framed in religiosity. Gladys Jones, head of the music department at Booker T. Washington High School, led the discussion concerning "How the Bible Has Affected Negro Music." The next Sunday, Rev. Glenn T. Settles, the organizer of the Wings Over Jordan Radio Choir, talked about the origin of the group. By the start of the school year, Taylor turned to high school and college football topics. The September 19 show featured Ernest Curry, sports reporter at the *Pittsburgh Courier*; Alfred C. Priestley, football coach at Xavier University; and Peter W. Clark, publicity director for athletics at Xavier.[48]

Taylor also enjoyed hearing comments from young people. "We Children Like the Bible" was a hit among the audience. A newspaper reporter mentioned that one of the children, London Thomas Seals Jr., was exceptionally articulate: "Frankly, Thomas did a better job by way of voice tone than the announcer himself." The show "... was grand from beginning to end." The reporter hoped that Taylor would produce more shows featuring young Negroes.[49]

In October the "Forum" secured a local sponsor who paid for display advertisements appearing in the *Louisiana Weekly*. The group, Soproco Singers, also known as the New Orleans Chosen Five, purchased advertisements announcing the name of the person(s) or organization featured on an upcoming show. The newspaper published the small advertisements, each about the size of a business card, for fifteen consecutive weeks beginning October 5 and ending January 11, 1947.[50] One of the announcements said Rev. H. Thomas Primm, pastor of Union Bethel African Methodist Episcopal Church, would explain the organizational structure of the denomination, the functions of the church's administrative departments, and the responsibilities of its leaders. The church's choir also performed.[51]

On a few occasions women's groups were featured. Mrs. Eloise Thornhill, a representative of the Women's Auxiliary of Flint-Goodridge Hospital, informed listeners that a role of the auxiliary was to organize fundraisers for the hospital owned by Dillard University, a historically black liberal arts institution in New Orleans affiliated with the United Methodist Church and the

United Church of Christ. The hospital exclusively served blacks in the city that mandated in ordinances racial segregation in public places. The women sewed sheets and curtains, repaired other items, and assisted hospital administrators and staff. Thornhill used her appearance to also recruit women and solicit donations.[52] The next Sunday, members and leaders of the Negro Branch of the New Orleans Girl Scouts were guests. They promoted scouting and the Brownies unit, answered questions, and let the girls talk concerning their scouting experiences.[53]

Six months after the "Religious Forum" premiered, Taylor wove discussion of social problems among topics. Representatives of the New Orleans Colored Home for Colored Incurables obtained his support. Taylor announced the dedication of the building and invited the public to attend the ceremony.[54] Later he announced the dedication of a different building of particular significance to local blacks, the Dryades Street branch of the Young Men's Christian Association. Hundreds witnessed the dedication standing or sitting in folding chairs set up in the street in front of the building near Jackson Avenue.

The two-story brick building in Central City was designed by a black architect, Ferdinand Rousseve, and built almost entirely by black workers. The Dryades YMCA operated a school providing men and boys academic instruction and job training. The building, for the exclusive use of blacks, had a dormitory with forty-four beds and housed a gymnasium, cafeteria, conference rooms, and offices.[55] Among presenters at the dedication were J. A. Holtry, president of the Good Citizens Mutual Benefit Association, and James E. Gayle, president of the Dryades YMCA. They announced a membership drive with the goal of signing two thousand. Gayle was also secretary of the Negro Citizens Committee whose efforts preceded the launch of the "Religious Forum."

CHAPTER THREE

Radio Forum Evolved from Religion to Negro

The convergence of the lives of James Albert Noe, a white man who owned WNOE, and Orlando Capitola Ward Taylor, a black man who integrated the radio station, illustrates the disparity between the amounts of access to broadcast opportunities whites had compared to blacks. In 1946 Noe was the first New Orleans broadcaster to integrate his on-air staff. WNOE obtained the services of Taylor, who produced and hosted a non-sponsored talk show, the "Religious Forum of the Air," which name was later changed to the "Negro Forum." The acquisition situated Taylor as the first black person whose voice transmitted via New Orleans radio as a program host. Taylor possessed tremendous energy, talent, and intellect but no major business concerns. His primary employment was as a principal at a black public school in New Orleans.[1]

Noe was a skilled politician and held extensive interests in real estate, oil, and gas. Noe became interested in radio in 1929. He acquired control of the New Orleans radio station WBNO in 1936. In 1939 he purchased the station and gained FCC approval to change the call letters to WNOE.[2]

John M. and Belle McRae Noe gave birth to James Noe on December 21, 1890, approximately one year before Taylor's birth. The Noes reared their son near Evans Landing in Harrison County, Indiana. Noe only attended county schools. He enlisted in the armed forces and was approximately twenty-seven when US troops landed in France on June 26, 1917. The military elevated him to first lieutenant in the 369th Infantry in France during World War I. After the war, Noe relocated to Monroe, Louisiana, and married Anna Gray Sweeney on May 7, 1922. They produced three children between 1922 and 1936.[3]

Noe became active in Democratic party campaigns in Louisiana and developed a close political relationship with Huey P. Long, the governor from 1928–32. Long won election to the US Senate in September 1930 but did not leave Louisiana for Washington until February 1932. In the meantime, Noe won election to the State Senate in the 29th District, representing Ouachita and Jackson Parishes in north central Louisiana. Much of the country was experiencing the Great Depression's economic decline following the stock market crash of 1929. By 1932 Noe was elevated to legislative floor leader of Governor Long's administration.[4]

Long held the governor's mansion long enough to help his boyhood friend Oscar K. Allen succeed him as governor. Consequently, Noe gained an appointment as lieutenant governor. By February 1934, Long was gaining national media attention because of his "Share the Wealth" plan. Long proposed sweeping federal initiatives intended to limit large incomes and inheritances, provide $5,000 grants to needy families, and establish other social programs. But Carl Weiss, a physician, shot Long, who died in Baton Rouge on September 10, 1935. Shortly thereafter, Oscar Allen died in office. Noe succeeded Allen and served the remaining four-month term as Louisiana governor from January to May 1936. Noe failed to gain the nomination to seek a full term. He believed that Long's supporters betrayed him.[5]

Noe wanted revenge. Long's supporters nominated New Orleans Appeals Court Judge Richard W. Leche as their gubernatorial candidate. Leche won the governorship, but Noe played a part in his resignation in 1939. Noe returned to a seat in the State Senate and served until 1940. Noe began exposing corruption in Leche's administration and sparked investigations by the press and the federal government. Noe had obtained a measure of revenge but ran unsuccessfully for governor in 1940 and 1956.

F. Edward Herbert provided insight into Noe's character, saying Noe was uneducated. Herbert, a longtime friend, was the city editor at the New Orleans *States-Item* in 1937. Voters elected Herbert to Louisiana's First Congressional District, and he served in Congress from 1941–77. Herbert wrote about Noe in his autobiography. The excitement of battle during World War I lured Noe from his home at Bear Wallow. "I signed up as soon as the fightin' started," he was quoted as saying. Despite no formal education, Noe nevertheless rose through the ranks from private to lieutenant. After the war Noe went to Kentucky, where he bought oil leases and turned them into profit before migrating to Ouachita Parish in North Louisiana.[6]

Herbert reconstructed a conversation Noe held with a visitor whom Noe entertained at his estate in North Louisiana. Noe's words indicate reasoning informed by observation, not reading or critical thinking. "You take a fine bull and breed it to a scrub cow and you'll have a pretty good calf. You can take a scrub bull and breed it to one of my finest cows and you'll have a scrub calf. It's all in the man—it's in the bull. It's the bull that puts the deal over. It's ninety percent. She's just reproducing the damn thing." Noe said his observation applied to people as well. "What the hell is the difference between human beings and other people?"[7]

Noe attempted to use his lack of formal education as a way to distinguish himself as a hard worker. He testified at an FCC hearing October 7, 1954, in support of his interest in obtaining a license to transmit television signals via a VHF channel in New Orleans. Noe responded several times that he lacked information about technical aspects of broadcasting. An attorney who represented WWL, which was competing for the license, said Noe's proposal promised to air a ceramics show, and asked Noe to define ceramics. Noe admitted he had no idea what ceramics were, but added caustically that he had a long-standing work ethic: "When you were studying law, I was picking cotton and working in oil fields."[8]

In contrast, racists and segregation laws limited O. C. W. Taylor, who had to work as a waiter in a country club in New Orleans in 1915 after graduating from college. His father believed a man with a bachelor's degree should not work as a waiter. Subsequently, Taylor found a job as a teacher that paid $45 a month but $75 to whites teaching he same load. Nevertheless, the teaching profession represented social status in the black community. Despite his father's objection and to supplement his salary as a teacher, Taylor continued to work at the country club and was promoted to headwaiter.[9] Taylor had no chance to obtain a license to operate a radio station or win an election to a public office in the Louisiana, but he added his black voice to the airwaves and helped lay a foundation on which blacks built communities and nudged whites toward racial equality. He never sought public office in postwar New Orleans. Blacks represented no more than 0.4 percent of the city's voters during the 1940s, and whites refused to consider a black person as worthy of their votes. Nevertheless, in 1946 Taylor would produce and host what would become a long-running pioneer radio show at WNOE about blacks in the New Orleans area. He would take on additional responsibilities at WNOE and remain affiliated with the station until the mid-1960s.[10]

Taylor was born November 23, 1891, in Huntsville, Texas, to Rev. David F. and Mrs. Capitola H. Taylor. O. C. W. Taylor earned a B.A. degree at Wiley College in Marshall, Texas, in 1913. He majored in English and Latin. Taylor moved to New Orleans because his parents moved from Texas to the city where his father was pastor of a church. White employers by and large refused to hire blacks to positions paying well or indicating prestige. Teaching positions at black schools were open, but the pay was low. At age twenty-four in 1915, Taylor began nearly forty years of employment at public schools in New Orleans as elementary teacher, principal at McDonogh 35, and other positions.[11]

Teaching, however, failed to satisfy his hunger to chronicle accounts of experiences of his people: "Somehow or other I just wanted to be a newspaper man."[12] At age thirty-four, Taylor encouraged his friend, insurance executive

Constance C. Dejoie Sr. to invest approximately $2,000 and launch the *Louisiana Weekly* newspaper. Taylor cofounded the *Weekly* with Dejoie and was managing editor. The paper's first issue was dated September 19, 1925.

Taylor stopped teaching for three years because he believed he would be fired or experience a worse fate if he continued while managing the black newspaper. Taylor recalled a school board member summoning to his office a black teacher who published a newspaper. The board member told the teacher to either stop publishing the paper or quit teaching. "And if I were you," Taylor said, recreating the comments, "I'd quit the newspaper because if you don't quit the newspaper, there's so many other things you're going to have to quit, and it might be this town."[13]

Taylor did not want to be fired or physically harmed: "I've seen newspaper men run out of town, by the law." He said racists forced some newsmen to publish lies: "And I've seen newspaper men who've been forced to say things that they didn't want to say, when lynching occurred or something like that." To avoid trouble and pursue his passion for mass communication, Taylor quit teaching in 1925 and worked full-time managing the *Louisiana Weekly*. He returned to the New Orleans school system in 1928 and quietly contributed local news and commentary to the *Weekly*, the Associated Negro Press, and other publications. Taylor was also a public relations professional who publicized organizations throughout Louisiana. He retired from the school system in 1957.[14]

To him, Native Americans, whites, and blacks each brought, with varying degrees of success, resources to their people's struggle to survive in America. White men had guns, ammunition, and organized structures, Taylor said. Native Americans had bows and arrows, stolen guns, whiskey, and a fine physique. On the other hand, blacks possessed the ability to work hard but had nothing else. Despite having little or no possessions, blacks held tightly to their religion, while Native Americans did not. Black ministers preached that African Americans should exercise religious values, diplomacy, and turn the other cheek. As a result, blacks were joining the mainstream, he said in 1973. Their population skyrocketed to the point where they are the majority in several US cities. Some are being elected to Congress and the Senate. To the contrary, Native Americans have not developed to such an extent.[15]

While the city, and indeed the state of Louisiana, maintained racially segregated public accommodations, racist traditions went further, prohibiting blacks from walking through the main entrance of some buildings owned by the private sector. WNOE was an example. Despite providing broadcast time to Taylor, the station would not allow African Americans in its studios, except to clean up. A white man, Cosimo Matassa, let Taylor broadcast the "Religious Forum" from his small studio in the rear of J&M Records on Rampart and Dumaine streets on the edge of the French Quarter. Taylor was rather nomadic with the show, broadcasting from the Almerico Ballroom, J&M, Dryades YMCA, and years later from the broadcast studio at WNOE.[16]

Taylor took advantage of opportunities as they surfaced. In 1947 he linked local blacks with an initiative of the Negro Newspaper Publishers Association. Walter White, national executive secretary of the NAACP, organized a meeting of black publishers of newspapers throughout the country in 1943. The publishers subsequently formed the NNPA and elected John H. Sengstacke president. Sengstacke published a chain of newspapers including the preeminent *Chicago Defender*. NNPA's objectives included the establishment and maintenance of services strengthening member newspapers and supporting the dissemination of information targeting African Americans. Negro Press Week was among NNPA's initiatives.[17]

The *Louisiana Weekly* was a member of the organization. NNPA designated February 28 to March 7 as Negro Newspaper Week. Taylor invited all area black publishers to attend the March 2 broadcast. Three black weeklies maintained offices in New Orleans and each sent a representative: John E. Rousseau Jr., editor of the *New Orleans Informer*, who explained the business side of the Negro press; Lucius L. Jones, editor of the Louisiana edition of the *Pittsburgh Courier*, who discussed the role of the Negro press; and Clarence A. Laws, public relations director at the *Louisiana Weekly*, who talked about the origins of black newspapers: "The history of the Negro press is a history of the Negro's struggle for full American citizenship."[18] Laws mentioned circumstances associated with America's first black newspaper, *Freedom's Journal*, founded by John B. Russwurm and Samuel E. Cornish in New York in 1827. They countered the anti-black editorial attacks of the white-owned *New York Enquirer*, which supported slavery. Besides the abolition of slavery, the *Journal* published articles discussing the chastity of women, the northern free blacks' concerns about their enslaved brethren, and other essays debunking African American stereotypes. Laws also talked about the origin of the Negro press in New Orleans as an instrument for reflecting and interpreting current events that influenced the opinion and behavior of blacks. Subsequently, no one, black or white, can imagine a true and complete picture of America without being acquainted with the black press, he said.[19]

For the first anniversary in May 1947, organizers set up five hundred chairs at the YMCA, 2222 Dryades Street. Everyone who had been a guest on the show was invited to attend. Speakers addressed the crowd and vocalists performed, such as the all-male Original Crescent City Singers, the all-female Bykotas, and soloists Juilet Chesterfield Kimp and Gladys Jones. A delegation led by social worker Ethel Young surprised Taylor and acknowledged his professional and civic accomplishments. Those in attendance presented him with more than two hundred gifts including shirts, neckties, handkerchiefs, socks, flowers, and a cake.[20]

The schedule of activities continued after the anniversary broadcast ended. The program featured young people who reached milestones in academic endeavors. More than fifteen from kindergarten through high school, wearing crisp white shirts and dresses, sat on chairs on the YMCA stage and talked about their school experiences. *Weekly* PR director Laws announced winners of the third annual National High School Essay Contest. The *Weekly* managed the local component of the competition sponsored by the Negro Newspaper Publishers Association. Clara Mae Howard, a student at Booker T. Washington High School, won first place and a $75 US Savings Bond; Joyce Lena Clay of Gilbert Academy finished second and took home a $50 bond. Their essays discussed the significance of the Negro press in relationship to the presidential election of 1948. The win advanced them to the national competition.[21]

On July 20 Rev. Moses Pleasure was moderator of the "Forum" and Dr. Rivers Fredericks was a guest. Fredericks, chief surgeon at Flint-Goodridge Hospital and president and principal stockholder of the Louisiana Industrial Life Insurance Company, discussed the significance of new vaccinations for the prevention of tuberculosis. Other guests included Emile Labat Jr., chair of the Tuberculosis X-ray Survey committee; and Marion Baker, health educator of the Tuberculosis Association of New Orleans. She encouraged listeners to go to Craig School July 28–29 and Labanche's Drug Store July 30–31 to answer survey questions to determine their level of risk.[22]

Without much fanfare, Taylor changed the name of the show in July 1947, from the "Religious Forum of the Air" to the "Negro Forum of the Air." Presenting more and more progressive, secular topics, he invited four representatives of life insurance companies to talk about their services, related historical and contemporary events, and issues and problems they faced. Guests included John L. St. Charles, agency and educational director at People's Industrial Life Insurance Company of New Orleans; H. J. Christophe, secretary-treasurer also at People's Life; A. Victor Williams, agency director at Louisiana Industrial Life of New Orleans; and Dr. C. C. Haydell, vice-president and medical director of Standard Life Insurance of New Orleans. The companies were organized as the Insurance Executive Council, the local affiliate of the National Negro Life Insurance Association.[23]

Blacks established their own businesses and organizations in part because racists refused to serve or otherwise accommodate African Americans. People of color established insurance companies and funeral homes after Caucasian intolerance festered such that whites refused to embalm or bury blacks. African American entrepreneurs filled a void. Their insurance companies provided the major form of security in the event of sickness, death, and destitution. The first formal black institutions, churches, labor unions, schools, and other organizations, emerged during the Reconstruction period. These organizations attempted to solve or limit problems brought on by racism, poverty, poor health, death, and social ills. Benevolent associations, mutual benefit societies, and fraternal orders were among complex systems of social interactions blacks created. Membership in these structures also suggested social status. The Good Samaritans as well as the Union Benevolent Association operated cemeteries for their members. The Young Female Benevolent Association charged members $2.50 to $5 to enroll in its insurance program and monthly dues of 25 to 50 cents during the period between 1860 and 1880 in New Orleans. A claimant would receive $2 to $4 per week in sick benefits, $1 toward each doctor visit, $3 for a wake, and $50 for burial expenses.[24]

On his August 10, 1947, show, Taylor interviewed Naomi Borikins, a public relations professional at Jackson Brewing Co, the makers of Jax beer. The Fitzgerald Advertising Agency represented the brewery. Taylor usually invited more than one guest, but not this time. They sat side by side, at a table talking with their backs near the rear wall of the stage at the Dryades YMCA. One microphone with the WNOE flag rested on a short stand on the table. In her seventh year at the brewery,[25] Borikins was one of only a few female professionals featured on the "Forum." She also worked for organizations attempting to uplift African Americans and reduce their suffering, such as the Women's Auxiliary of Flint-Goodridge Hospital. She was director of the Boy Scout fund-raising drive of 1946, co-chairwoman of the Community Chest Drive of 1947, member of the Cancer Drive, active in the War Loan Drives, member of the New Orleans Negro Board of Trade, and member of the secret society Order of the Eastern Star.[26] In less than two years, Borikins would consult with her bosses at Jackson Brewery. To increase beer sales among blacks, the brewery's advertising agency would hire Vernon L. Winslow, whose unprecedented radio show positioned him as the city's first African American disc jockey.

For the first time, Taylor's guests talked about sports during the October 5 broadcast. Nine attended, representing the twenty-five-year-old New Orleans Independent Football League with teams including the Southsiders, Scrubs, Elks, and Brutes. The reps posed for a photograph; half sat at a long table while the others stood behind them. Two microphones rested on the table. An approximately 12x18-inch-long banner, with frills at the pointy bottom, showed off slanted letters spelling WNOE and smaller type identifying the

MBS network. The banner attached to a pole stood guard in the center of the photo, behind the table.²⁷

Efforts to help the physically disabled were the focus for the National Employ the Handicapped Week, October 5–11. The New Orleans planning committee publicized the observation and orchestrated activities urging employers to hire disabled African Americans. Listeners were told companies were "eager to offer employment to the many veterans and non-veterans that are qualified to hold down a job or position, irrespective of their handicaps." It was estimated 1.5 million Americans were disabled.²⁸

Five months later, the black-press theme surfaced again. This time four representatives of area publications shared their views about the significance of the black press: Lucius L. Jones of the *Courier*; John E. Rousseau of the *Informer-Sentinel*; C. C. Dejoie Jr. of the *Louisiana Weekly*; and Louise Willis, publisher and editor of the new publication, *Negro South Magazine*.²⁹

During the same month, local African Americans stepped forward to advocate for WNOE in its dealings with the FCC. Leon Lewis, managing editor of *Negro South Magazine*, organized efforts to influence prominent blacks throughout the state to support the station's interest in more broadcast power. According to the *Louisiana Weekly*, "The increase in wattage will offer to this section a wider range for the informative programs conducted exclusively by Negroes." On August 29, 1947, the FCC announced it canceled the hearing scheduled September 4 but did not schedule a new date.³⁰ The agency, however, acknowledged it received letters of appreciation and commendations on behalf of WNOE for the station's black program.³¹

Three months short of the second year of Sunday "Negro Forums," and six months after blacks corresponded with the FCC on behalf of WNOE, program director Beverly Brown informed Taylor she intended to change the show's start time from 10 a.m. to 12:15 p.m. Brown conveyed the news in a letter Taylor read on Friday, February 27, 1948. The schedule change was to begin in two days. Brown had agreed with executives at Mutual Broadcasting System to assign Taylor's 10 a.m. slot to profitable network programming. After twenty-one months, Taylor knew the listening habits and cultural traditions of his audience. Taylor conducted no systematic survey, but he talked to his listeners. Blacks, regardless of socioeconomic class, attended Sunday church services more frequently than whites, Taylor believed: "We are a religious people. Whether we are a moral people, now I don't [know], but we are a religious people." An affluent white man may play golf or engage in other leisure activity on Sunday, "But you don't find many Negroes, I don't care what position they hold, that don't feel like going to church on Sunday. They want to do that."³²

Taylor abhorred the decision but maintained his usual dignity. He responded in a letter dated February 28: "I do not feel that we shall be able to serve our usual audience at the 12:15 time and so I am advising that at least for the time being we eliminate the 'Negro Forum.'" Taylor tactfully explained his objections and willingness to end the show. African Americans listened to the show, by and large, before departing home to attend church services, the first of which customarily began at 11 a.m. Sundays. Delaying the broadcast until 12:15 p.m. would deprive WNOE of access to its black audience. The change would more importantly deny listeners the opportunity to listen to or attend the broadcasts.[33]

Taylor believed his position was justified. He reasoned that the "Negro Forum" had developed among the largest black audiences of any radio station in the South. Taylor had no hard data. He had a feeling in his gut and indication from listeners his show was better than any other similar program, but the show did not generate revenue from commercials. Profitability did not matter. The show's service to the community was preeminent, so he stood firmly on principle: "[W]e do not feel that we should be proper in continuing the program." Taylor informed Brown he would consider reestablishing the "Negro Forum" in the future, if WNOE scheduled it at a time when his audience was available. Taylor ended his letter by telling Brown that he would announce the decision to end broadcasting on the next day's show. He also said he would inform Negro newspapers about circumstances leading to the decision.[34]

Taylor told his listeners on Sunday, February 29, that the "Negro Forum" would discontinue, perhaps temporarily. Clergy members, civil rights leaders, business owners, and the general black public were saddened, some outraged. They interpreted word of its demise as a loss to the community. People wrote letters expressing support. Others telephoned Taylor at his home to get details and to offer assistance. In a letter, Minister W. Talbot Handy of First Street Methodist Church agreed with Taylor. An afternoon slot conflicted with church attendance. "Thousands upon top of thousands of our people, who listen each Sunday, with so much pride to this interesting presentation will be deprived of this opportunity if the hour is changed." Handy encouraged Taylor to try to convince WNOE to move the show to a weekday evening or otherwise reverse the decision. Handy said he was leaving town Monday, March 1 to attend his mother's funeral services, but he would return in a few days and serve at Taylor's pleasure to save the show.[35]

Additional support from black leaders came swiftly. Paul A. Landix, membership chairman of the local branch of the NAACP, listened to Taylor's radio announcement. He wrote to Taylor: "So many of us look forward on Sunday to your program, but maybe a week day program might suit just as well," and that the NAACP would assist him in negotiations with WNOE. James E. Gayle also heard Taylor's announcement. Gayle, president of First District Baptist Training Union Association and owner of James E. Gayle & Sons, a retail music and bookstore, said the show was too valuable to be discontinued: "This program has created such an interest on the part of the people of Louisiana, that we cannot afford to lose it"; indeed, it was an "institution among radio listeners of Louisiana."[36]

Overwhelming evidence of public support provided Taylor leverage when he took his case to the station management. On Tuesday, March 2, two days after Taylor's discontinuation announcement, WNOE reversed Brown's decision. Taylor was happy. He stood on principle and won, yet he maintained his typical sense of diplomacy. "Their action is proof that they appreciate that this program has developed one of the largest listening audiences of our group in the South," the *Louisiana Weekly* reported.[37]

A wave of public support propelled him into the May 30, 1948, broadcast celebration of the show's second anniversary. For two years blacks had talked about the issues, community services, and accomplishments of local African Americans. The show spoke to blue-collar workers, domestics, entrepreneurs, professionals, leaders of organizations, and young people. Indeed, blacks had within their communities models of achievement, individuals who despite structural barriers maintained high levels of dignity, diligence, and determination. A *Pittsburgh Courier* headline aptly labeled Taylor a "Community Builder."[38]

Officers of civil rights groups, educators, and preachers were also among supporters who wrote letters addressed to Taylor via WNOE, McDonogh No. 37 school, and his home at 2309 Iberville Street. Each thanked him for shepherding the "Negro Forum" to its second year. Alvin H. Jones, executive secretary of the New Orleans Urban League, said he was grateful. The program provided his organization opportunities to discuss issues of supreme interest to the African American community.[39]

Public health was one such issue. Marion P. Baker, health educator at the Tuberculosis Association of New Orleans, reaffirmed the utility of the show as a vital information disseminator: "The program is a civic project worthy of distinction. It aids public relations and gives information that is pertinent to all." J. O. Richards Jr., president of the Orleans Principals Association, expressed hope the program would live on. Richards confirmed the program had informed listeners of "various phases of the cultural and religious side of Negro activity." Similarly, Rev. A. Prince Fortner, executive secretary of the First District Missionary Baptist Association, said he appreciated Taylor's efforts because they encouraged people to attend church.

WNOE ought to give the show more time, rather than fifteen minutes, said Leon J. Bickham, health education supervisor at the New Orleans Health Department. The director of the New Orleans Area Methodist Church, W. Talbot Handy, thanked Taylor for creating opportunities for groups like his to "place its wares in the show cases of the world's market." The show "exposed the community to Negro culture and achievements, like nothing else has.... You have played up the bright side of life," which has helped blacks and whites think positively and realistically about African Americans, their culture, and their social contributions.[40]

Anniversary well-wishers also sent accolades via Western Union. E. Lyons Baker, the leader or Basileus of a local chapter of the black Greek-letter sorority Zeta Phi Beta, sent a one-sentence message May 30 saying Taylor and WNOE officials were goodwill ambassadors. Black racial pride poured from a telegram sent by a representative of the business Saul's Costume Shop: "Congratulations to a product of our race and a rare gem that the nation can be proud of."[41]

Taylor was a collector and understood the value of documentation, particularly of his accomplishments and events relevant to his objectives. He gathered and copied the letters and telegrams supporters sent to him. Some supporters also sent Taylor a copy of their FCC missive. Taylor compiled a set and sent them to James E. Gordon, vice-president and general manager at WNOE. Gordon expressed his appreciation in a June 11, 1948, letter addressed to Taylor. The general manager returned the copies and asked Taylor to keep the communiqués because the station may need them in the future.[42]

The outpouring of praise heaped on WNOE contributed to the FCC finding the station's overall operation meritorious. On January 26, 1949, the agency gave WNOE authority to broadcast at 1060 kilocycles with 50,000 watts of daytime power. The authorization, however, was conditional. Before the FCC would issue a construction permit or license, the feds required WNOE to obtain Civil Aeronautics Administration approval of its transmitter site and antenna system. On June 13, 1950, WNOE began broadcasting with 50,000 watts during days and 5,000 watts at night.[43]

In 1951 two applicants requested FCC permission to use frequency 1450, which WNOE vacated. Royal Broadcasting Corporation as well as Gretna and Lower Coast Radio and Broadcasting Company, in their applications, indicated that each proposed a sole black-aimed program which would concern religiosity. Royal proposed a daily 9 a.m. program "for the Negro churches in the community." Its competitor Gretna and Lower Coast proposed a thirty-minute program of "spirituals by Negro groups in the area."[44]

The applicants recognized the ubiquity of radio but intended to limit its black functionality to spirituality; however, radio increased the potential to disseminate newsworthy information to an otherwise silenced audience. Before blacks emerged and were allowed to broadcast discussion of community affairs, illiterate African Americans obtained information from the sermons of preachers, attendance at rallies, debates among family members and acquaintances, and other non-literate means. News circulated by listening to someone read a newspaper while at a neighbor's house, barbershop, beauty salon, grocery store, or other social gathering. Prior to radio establishing a relationship with African Americans, the illiterate needed to be in an audience or face to face with someone who verbally delivered a message. Broadcasting directed at blacks changed that limitation, and the audience began to interpret radio as a new mode of mass information delivery. Black newspapers began acknowledging the capability of radio to instantaneously reach broad and wide sweeps of members of African American communities. Taylor planned to travel outside New Orleans and find more black voices discussing their achievements.[45]

In the meantime, the third year included broadcasting from small nearby cities. Taylor went to the outlying areas with a microphone and recording equipment seeking more programming ideas and a larger spectrum of expression. African Americans in the metropolitan area were interested in spreading the news of their good works, and blacks in New Orleans were interested in the activities of their brethren.[46] Taylor released to the press the "Negro Forum's" June 1948 schedule. He called the initiative a salute to neighboring cities and communities. He scheduled guests from Slidell, June 6; Kenner, June 13; and Ponchatoula and Hammond, June 27.[47] The first in the series featured residents of Slidell, in St. Tammany Parish approximately thirty-five miles northeast of New Orleans. To promote the shows, Taylor wrote letters to white politicians and other decision makers in the towns. The responses seemed reasonable but were infused with racist ideology. Taylor distributed to the black press copies of the letters he received.

The correspondences intimated that blacks were of the demeanor of children, saying African Americans in their jurisdictions were well behaved and had no reasons to be discontented. A physician and mayor of Kenner, Joseph S. Kopfler, learned Taylor was visiting his city. Blacks in Kenner were law-abiding citizens, unlike their counterparts elsewhere, he said: "Delinquency, both juvenile and adult, is at a minimum in this community."[48] Blacks were happy and prosperous, in part because whites treated them cordially. Some even owned their own homes. "As you know, happy homeowners make good citizens. Interracial relations are good. There is no conflict."[49]

Despite the pronouncements of white officials raving of the quality of life among blacks in their jurisdictions, laws denied African Americans equal legal protection and segregated them to dilapidated parts of residential areas. State and local legislation required segregation in theaters, on public transit, in bars, and in cemeteries, among other places.[50] Taylor was keenly aware of the dire social, economic, and political status of blacks in New Orleans and nearby towns. Major disparities existed between public resources allocated to whites and blacks. The inequality was widespread and long-standing. Whites enjoyed higher teacher salaries and better funding for public schools. When blacks petitioned the Orleans Parish School Board to increase the number and quality of public school buildings assigned to African Americans in 1946, the school board strongly opposed the demands. Board members later acquiesced and appropriated a token increase to the budget for school funding, but it did not budge on teacher salaries. A. P. Tureaud, a local attorney who worked closely with the NAACP, proposed a plan that would equalize the salaries of black and white teachers. Typically, white teachers earned up to $1,000 more annually than blacks with the same credentials. Tureaud's plan called for closing the gap in two years. The school board dismissed the plan.[51]

Taylor used a letter written to him by Slidell Mayor H. G. Fritchie to promote his show. He forwarded a copy to the *Weekly*, which published it as a thirty-one-line article, and he read it on air. The "Negro Forum" contributed to uplifting blacks, Fritchie said: ". . . accept my congratulations on the work you are doing to raise the cultural level of the people of your race."[52] Blacks in Slidell comported themselves well, he said. They were not simply well behaved but were good citizens contented living among white people: "It appears to us that the Negro people of Slidell are entirely satisfied with their work, home life and civic life."[53] Proper black leadership, schools, and churches were responsible for the tranquility.

The sheriff of Jefferson Parish, Frank J. Clancy, was among officials who wrote communiqués warning against broadcasting discourse promoting equal opportunity or calling on blacks to engage in political action. African Americans living in Kenner were among the first black people to serve as jurors in Jefferson Parish. He said equal protection was extended to blacks partly because African Americans practiced Christianity: "Your improvement in citizenship is due largely to your interest in your Churches, regardless of your creed, and your interest in better education for your children." The sheriff admonished blacks not to organize activities denouncing the status quo because there was no reason for discontent.[54] The communists were the troublemakers, he added: "banish from the minds of every citizen of our Community any thought of Communism or any Communistic tendency and forever preserve the Democracy of the United State [*sic*] of America."[55]

FBI director J. Edgar Hoover attempted to intimidate and undermine civil rights leaders by accusing them of being members of the Communist party or being influenced by them. Testifying at a hearing of the House Committee on Un-American Activities on March 26, 1947, Hoover said President Franklin D. Roosevelt in 1939 put the FBI in charge of all law enforcement efforts to obtain information relating to espionage, counterespionage, sabotage, and subversive activities. Included among those investigated were blacks who sought to end racial discrimination, even those like Taylor attempting to use radio to disseminate the progressive activities of African Americans. There is no indication Taylor was a direct target of the investigations. Nevertheless, Hoover said the Communist party no longer depended exclusively "on the printed word as a medium of propaganda and has taken to the air. Its members and sympathizers have not only infiltrated the airways but they are now persistently seeking radio channels."[56]

The communism theme surfaced again. Judge Henry Arnoult, of the First Justice Court of Jefferson Parish, said his roots run deep in the dark soil of the parish. His ancestors owned plantations and employed hundreds of African Americans. His father, the late Judge Louis Edgar Arnoult, maintained good relations with blacks. Arnoult knew thousands of blacks of all social classes over the years, and he claimed every one of them was progressing. The parish's elite improved housing conditions and sanitation services in African American residential areas. No longer did whites stop black children from attending schools. Southern whites and blacks were purported to understand the racial problems. Nevertheless, they held mutual respect. Their relationships were peaceful. Race relations were improving, but Communists would reverse the progress. A small minority of agitators, who do not live in the South, exacerbated dissension between white and colored people. He added: "I have no hesitancy in placing this blame upon the Communists. We all know that in other countries where they have gained control, they first started by confusing the people and causing internal strife...." However, in this country southern black leaders have championed democracy and were not easily persuaded by "agents of a foreign totalitarian power."[57]

Such sentiments were baseless. The letters intended to lessen trepidation concerning the "Negro Forum's" potential to threaten whites' long-standing political and economic control. The officials attempted to convince blacks that their conditions were improving and simultaneously tell Caucasians their leaders had arrested any potential threat to white privilege.

Taylor was no threat. He believed the positive portrayals of blacks would illustrate to whites that African American stereotypes were meritless. He also intended to impress blacks by promoting among them the progress their people had made despite political and social obstacles. Nevertheless, Taylor's efforts also elicited condescension from New Orleans Commission-Council member Theo. O. Hotard,[58] who also said blacks were content and their social conditions were progressing. Hotard addressed his letter to Rev. G. B. Franklin dated July 10, 1948. Rev. Franklin was among four guests of the "Negro Forum" show devoted to residents of Algiers, a neighborhood on the west side of the Mississippi River.

Taylor read Hotard's letter during the Sunday, July 11 broadcast. It congratulated the "Negro Forum" for its loyalty and devotion to patriotism. Black leaders have always been outstanding citizens promoting the welfare of African Americans. Blacks and whites lived happily and contented and would "not allow isms and philosophies contrary to our democratic principles to disturb this condition."[59]

The local white newspapers were largely silent about the "Negro Forum." One small exception was the daily (New Orleans) *Picayune*, which reflected efforts of some whites to isolate and diminish black activities. Racial discrimination dictated that black people and their cultural productions were inferior and at times in opposition to values whites professed. Before the emergence of television broadcasting in New Orleans in 1948, radio held the distinction as America's major mass medium of entertainment and instant information dissemination. Newspaper publishers acknowledged that their readers sought information about names of radio programs and the times stations broadcast music, comedy, drama, and public affairs programs, among other genres.

The *Picayune* demonstrated how the majority press marginalized African Americans. Two other dailies were based in the New Orleans, the *States* and the *Item*. The *Picayune* published a schedule of the programs of the top four stations broadcasting in New Orleans in 1946: WWL, the CBS affiliate; WSMB, associated with NBC; WDSU, linked to ABC; and WNOE, an MBS affiliate. On June 2 the *Picayune* program schedule informed readers WNOE would broadcast Taylor's new show, which it referred to as the "Religious Forum," Sunday, June 3 from 10 a.m. to 10:15 a.m. That was one week after the show premiered on May 26. The paper's radio section included a couple of sentences about some of the scheduled programs. For Taylor's show it mentioned: "'Juvenile Delinquency' will be discussed on the new WNOE 'Religious Forum' at 10 a.m. The panel will be composed of the Revs. H. T. Primm, Morris Burrell and W. J. Gipson, with O. C. W. Taylor as moderator."[60] Seven days later, without prompting from Taylor, the paper changed the show's name from "Religious Forum" to "Negro Services." On June 9, the *Picayune*'s description no longer was neutral. It mentioned the show's guests in racial terms. "Negro ministers will discuss 'What has the Church [done about] Education,' via the WNOE [unreadable word or words] at 10 a.m."[61]

Taylor did not ask the papers to refer to the show as Negro services. To the contrary, he continued for at least fifteen months with the original program title, "Religious Forum of the Air." A black journalist wrote in opposition to the continued use of the title "Religious Forum." In the August 30, 1947, edition of the *Weekly*, reporter Scoop Jones wrote: "Memo to O.C.W. Taylor: That radio program is great. Why why not chop the word 'religious' from the title since you do cover a varied field of events...."[62]

The white newspaper, however, injected the racial label into the show's title and description, alerting Caucasian readers the program concerned issues and opinions of black people. White supremacy ideology cued its supporters to distinguish between black cultural and Eurocentric ideals. Readers of the newspapers generally concluded that white people were the default race of individuals discussed in articles touting accomplishments. If a report referred to a black person, convention required the use of a racial label. White racial bigots viewed blacks and their cultural productions as inferior at least and offensive at best.

On the other hand, one could argue the *Picayune* was alerting blacks to the new show and its featuring of African American guests and topics of particular interest to blacks. The argument stands on sinking ground. The black press nationally alerted its readers to the show's debut before its broadcast. Indeed, the "Religious Forum" was big news. Word spread quickly among blacks in regard to occasions when an African American achieved in endeavors reserved for whites, such as hosting a radio show. As mentioned previously, scholar Michael C. Dawson conceptualized the experience as linked fate, an interpretation suggesting Taylor's accomplishment meant other blacks could also break through racial barriers. If whites gave one black man an opportunity previously reserved for whites, they might give other blacks similar chances.[63]

The marginalization of blacks by presenting them as the racial other was not limited to newspaper accounts of day-to-day affairs. Music was no exception. Jerry Wexler of *Billboard* magazine suggested similar racialization occurred in the popular music industry in the late 1940s. Industry executives decided to affix a black racial label to popular music produced by African Americans. Before *Billboard* adopted the music category rhythm and blues in June 1949, it referred to black songs as race music.[64]

Taylor returned to focusing on the black achievement of New Orleanians in July 1948. He featured standouts in business, art, and other professions. The *Louisiana Weekly* columnist and associate editor Joseph "Scoop" Jones and the New Orleans *Informer* city editor Elgin Hychew represented journalists.

Clement Mac Williams, manager of Laundromat, denoted business ownership. Maxine Holtry, a sculptor and art instructor at Gilbert Academy, and Numa [sic] Rousseve, member of the faculty of Xavier University's Fine Arts Department, signified artistic prowess.[65] In the meantime, Taylor decided to also go into the local community.

In 1949 Taylor took his microphone and a white broadcast engineer into meeting places and business establishments in black communities in the city. He recorded and later broadcast commentary, such as of Mary McLeod Bethune, who in 1904 founded Bethune-Cookman College in Florida. She was also president and founder of the National Council of Negro Women (NCNW). Bethune visited New Orleans to attend the NCNW's Region IV conference April 29 through May 1. She was the principal speaker at the organization's dinner. Bethune wore a dark, formal dress and stood talking into a microphone on a stand. Taylor held another microphone close to her face. The record did not indicate the topic of her talk at the Hayes Chicken Shack Restaurant, 2001 Louisiana Ave., but the occasion was formal. Despite the shack in the restaurant's name, it was "The most beautiful eatery this side of the Waldorf-Astoria."[66]

Hayes also hosted Taylor's new Negro Talent Hour. Beginning on May 17, 1950, WNOE broadcast a fifteen-minute recording from the one-hour live show. The broadcast aired from 10:15 a.m. to 10:30 a.m. Sundays, running directly after the Negro Forum's fifteen-minute slot. As master of ceremonies, Taylor meticulously laid out the order of the components of the broadcast. First he described the show, explaining that he recorded a portion of the Talent Hour and a winner would be selected at the end of the broadcast. After the remarks he slotted audience applause and a short musical transition before his introductions of the acts. On the May 30 show, he introduced I. L. Hardon, a baritone who sang "Chloe" for two minutes. Soprano Joyce Harper followed singing "I Love Life." Her song lasted approximately a minute and forty seconds. After Harper, WNOE staffer "Vic" Williams voiced a commercial. His second and final commercial came near the end of the show. The commercials advertised Hadacol, a patent medicine manufactured by the LeBlanc Corporation. Hadacol was an acronym of the Happy Day Company. The L was added to represent LeBlanc. When asked how he thought of the name, LeBlanc replied, "Well, I hadda' call it something."[67] Hadacol contained vitamins B_1 and B_2, iron, niacin, calcium, phosphorous, honey, diluted hydrochloric acid, and 12 percent alcohol. The liquor was said to be a preservative. It was the most prominent and popular ingredient, especially in dry countries in the South. Between the commercials were performances by a whistler, a nine-year-old tap dancer, and a boogie-woogie trio. Taylor announced the winner among the amateur performers, provided closing remarks, and Williams signed off.

In October 1950, WNOE extended broadcasts of the show to thirty minutes beginning at 10:30 on Sunday mornings. The name was changed to the "Hadacol Talent Hour and Jamboree." Taylor continued as the emcee, but commercials were announced by Larry Wilson. Taylor also acknowledged producer Eldon Durand. Wilson and Durand were white. A six-piece stage band, Houston's Jamborites Orchestra, played the feature music. WNOE also lengthened the "Negro Forum" by thirty minutes, offering a total of one hour of black programming from 10 a.m. to 11 a.m. Sundays. To provide additional performers for the broadcasts, the Hayes portion of the talent show was extended to two hours and held on Saturdays between 6 p.m. and 8 p.m. Performers at the Saturday shows were auditioning for the opportunity to perform on the radio program. People who wanted to attend the nighttime show were required to present one Hadacol box top.

Blacks corresponded with Taylor telling him the extended broadcast of the talent show was entertaining, another facet the Negro radio audience could be proud of. John E. Rousseau, legal redress chairman of the local branch of the NAACP, listened to the show: "We were particularly impressed with the trumpet renditions of Herbert Permillion, the postman. Such lively programs are desired by the general public and, too, they give a much-needed outlet of expression for our talented youths. Again we congratulate you and station WNOE."[68] Taylor's first radio program the "Religious Forum" was sustaining. It did not have a sponsor. Later listeners noticed the sponsorship of the tonic maker. "May I extend congratulations and best wisher for the continued success of the Negro Talent Hour which is aired weekly through the channels of radio station WNOE and sponsored by the makers of Hadacol," Dorothy W. Wiltz said in a letter to Taylor.[69]

In terms of the talk show, Taylor advanced the programming by adding more politically conscious topics than those he broadcast in the days of the "Religious Forum." He stepped forward when the New Orleans Committee on Race Relations invited Ralph J. Bunche to the city to speak at a public meeting. Bunche, director of the United Nations Trusteeship Department, visited New Orleans December 14 and 15, 1949. Taylor, whom WNOE had promoted to public relations director for the station's black programs, interviewed Bunche at the home of Albert W. Dent, Dillard University's president. Dent and his wife Ernestine Jessie Covington Dent frequently hosted black public officials and figures who visited the city. Taylor recorded Bunche's comments and broadcast the interview on the "Negro Forum." While in New Orleans, Bunche said freedom and equality are birthrights: "There can be no

Table 2
New Orleans Radio Station Frequencies in 1950

call letters	frequency
WWL	870 kHz
WNOE	1060 kHz
WSMB	1350 kHz (1999)
WJBW	1230 kHz (1947)
WDSU	1280 kHz
WJMR	990 kHz
WWEZ	690 kHz
WTPS	940 kHz (1949)
WMRY	600 kHz

Sources: *Federal Communications Commission Reports*, vol. 15 (Washington, DC: US Government Printing Office, 1950), 935–37. Other volumes as well.

side doors for minority groups. No person can enter a position of human dignity except by the front door. Until then we will have an imperfect, dangerous world." Bunche would win the Nobel Peace Prize in 1950 for mediating an armistice ending the Israeli-Arab war in Palestine.[70]

Under Taylor's leadership, by 1950 WNOE broadcast four programs disseminating information or entertainment targeting blacks: 1) "Negro Forum," a four-year-old talk show airing 10 a.m. on Sundays; 2) the Soproco program, spiritual music show, 1:30 p.m. Sundays; 3) "Negro News," a two-year-old program sponsored by the Monarch Life Insurance Company, which was owned by the local International Longshoremen Association. Taylor reported news and rewrote reports appearing in the *Louisiana Weekly* and the Associated Negro Press. It aired at the conclusion of the "Negro Forum;" and 4) The one-year-old "Negro Talent Hour," an amateur-entertainment show Taylor hosted at Hayes Chicken Shack on Tuesdays evenings. The broadcast portion aired on Sundays. Taylor produced all of the shows except the Soproco program.

CHAPTER FOUR

Black Culture, Music, and "Hep Phrasing" Permeated Radio

The emergence of black announcers in talk formats transformed radio, making it a better servant of the interests of African Americans. When recorded music formats were added to the mix in the late 1940s and early 1950s, blacks on the air fashioned radio into a resource emphasizing African American thought, music, language, style, soulful rhetoric, and consumerism.

The rise of blacks in radio occurred during a milieu in which whites, because of the profit motive and political activities, began to experiment with African American voices behind their microphones. As a result, a new discourse representative of more inclusive social structures contributed to transforming the medium into a community-building mechanism. In other words, new mediated conversations about components of black society contributed to uniting African Americans.

Prior to the World War II era, white managers at radio stations in New Orleans (and nationally, for the most part) prohibited blacks from entering their studios, offices, and in some cases, the buildings housing the broadcast and production studios. When allowed to enter a multi-story building, for example, blacks had to go through a back or side entrance, walk through the kitchen, take the back steps, or ride the service elevator to get to the station. As blacks entered broadcasting as hosts of programs, whites continued barring them from the studios and denying them opportunities to train for jobs as broadcast, audio, or maintenance engineers.

In New Orleans, when O. C. W. Taylor and Vernon L. Winslow Sr. got their chances, they were also subjected to treatment as second-class broadcasters. In 1946 Taylor was barred from WNOE's broadcast studios. He used the auditorium at the Dryades YMCA and a small independently owned recording studio owned by a white man, Cosimo Matassa. In 1947 WJMR hired Winslow to write scripts in the vernacular of a hip-talking black man, but prohibited him from speaking on air. During station breaks or while a record

Table 3
New Orleans Radio Stations in 1947

call letters	year established	watts	network
WWL	1922	50,000	CBS
WNOE	1925	250	MBS
WSMB	1925	5,000	NBC
WJBW	1926	250	
WDSU	1928	5,000	ABC
WJMR	1946	250	
WWEZ	1947	5,000	
WTPS	1947	1,000	

Sources: Tom Farrell, ed., *Working Press of the Nation* (New York: Farrell Publishing, 1950), 140–41; *Broadcasting & Cable Yearbook 1999* (New Providence, NJ: R.R. Bowker, 1999), D-194; C. Joseph Pusateri, *Enterprise in Radio: WWL and the Business of Broadcasting in America* (Washington, DC: University Press of America, 1980), 223.

was playing, he sometimes whispered in the ear of a white disc jockey the authentic articulation of slang words and phrases. In 1949, after a brewery hired Winslow to promote Jax beer, its advertising agency negotiated with WWEZ and placed him on air to host his own show. Thereafter, stations slowly began their racial transformation, allowing chocolate voices to begin coloring the airwaves. Religion, social affairs, and music dominated the individual broadcasts.

Exceptions cropped up here and there. WJBW broadcast a thirty-minute on-site remote of the dedication ceremony of the racially segregated Dryades YMCA on November 17, 1946. The remote provided WJBW listeners a one-time opportunity to hear local black nonreligious discourse. WJBW was the second New Orleans radio station to permit blacks to talk on air.

WJBW arrived on the scene after Charles C. Carlson, a self-employed electrician, obtained a broadcast license from the FCC in 1926. He employed his wife, Louise Elsie Carlson, as program director and announcer, and operated the station from his home. Louise became the first woman radio announcer in New Orleans. Louise and Charles divorced, and she became owner and operator of the station in 1947. WJBW transmitted a 250-watt signal. During that time WNOE and WJMR also broadcast at 250 watts. The three stations transmitted the weakest signals among the eight licensees broadcasting in the city in 1947 (see Table 3). WJBW was the least popular station among listeners, a position that led it to attempt to attract black listeners.[1]

CBS, WWL's network, hired Price, Waterhouse & Co. in 1932 to conduct a nationwide survey of the popularity of radio stations in major markets. The accounting firm randomly selected names from telephone directories of seventy-two cities. The staff mailed questionnaires asking respondents to identify the call letters of stations they listened to regularly. Only 1.9 percent of respondents identified WJBW as a regularly listened-to station. NBC affiliate WSMB led with 86.1 percentage of respondents reporting regular listenership. ABC affiliate WDSU was second with 82.5 percent.[2]

In 1943, Louisiana State University published results of the first comprehensive survey of radio listening in the state. The survey indicated the listening habits of whites. None of the Louisiana radio stations transmitted significant programming respecting the special needs and interests of blacks. Indeed, few Louisiana blacks owned radio receivers in 1943. The LSU survey interviewed 1,740 radio families and grouped respondents into seven regions. New Orleans respondents were designated region seven, comprising the southeastern part of the state. Five radio stations transmitted programming in New Orleans at the time. WJBW ranked last again. Only 4.7 percent of respondents indicated WJBW was their "most frequently listened to" station. This time WWL was first with 26 percent of the positive responses. WSMB was second with 24 percent, followed by WDSU, 22.4 percent; and WNOE, 11.8 percent. The remaining 11.1 percent of respondents identified other.[3]

The most listened-to local radio stations did not play race records before the 1950s. Some whites publicly said they detested black music, and white parents did not want their children listening. Mainstream stations rarely played black music, but when they did the audience heard the "acceptable" sounds of entertainers such as Nat King Cole and Duke Ellington. Instead of the pounding, emotion-laden music, at times with risqué lyrics, white stations played Caucasian musicians, such as Pat Boone's version of Little Richard's "Tutti Frutti," singing the tame versions of black R&B musicians. White owners of bars and restaurants played the cover versions of black songs on their jukeboxes, and record stores experienced brisk sales. It was common for an R&B record to reach Number One on the black charts but only 50 or so on the white charts. When a Caucasian singer rerecorded a black song, it frequently reached the Top Ten on the white charts. As time passed, whites began buying, listening, and enjoying the records featuring black musicians.[4]

In last place, WJBW had to change its business model. To increase the size of its audience, and hence its profit, the station partnered with Frank Painia, a black man whose Dew Drop Inn was open seven days, twenty-four hours, and operated as a hotel, nightclub, cafe, and barbershop. Located at 2836–40 LaSalle Street near Washington Avenue, in a poor and working-class neighborhood in central city, the Dew Drop was a major establishment. Carlson had to adjust to the market within which competitors effectively captured white listeners. In addition to the four network-affiliated market leaders WWL (CBS), WDSU (ABC), WSMB (NBC), and WNOE (MBS), three new independent stations had launched operation by 1947. WJMR, licensed to Supreme Broadcasting Company, operated out of the eighteen-story Jung Hotel, 1500 Canal Street at Claiborne Avenue beginning in 1946. In 1947 two new entrants thickened the mixture of signals. WWEZ, owned by WWEZ Radio Inc., established its studio in the Hotel New Orleans on Canal Street. Lastly, the *Times-Picayune* launched WTPS for a second time. The newspaper was the largest and most influential in the state. Non-affiliated stations did not have access to the popular standard programs such as soap operas, dramas, and game shows produced and distributed by the major networks. The independents found music to be cheap programming that attracted listeners. The white stations played pop music, while stations marketing some of their programming to blacks played race music.[5]

New competitors WWEZ and WTPS attracted advertisers who targeted white consumers. The partnership with Painia brought live remote broadcasts to the Dew Drop that featured black musicians, female impersonators, comedians, and other entertainers. WJBW began broadcasts of Dew Drop Inn fare at 11 p.m., Thursday, August 14, 1947.

Painia was shrewd. Over the years he saw entrepreneurial opportunities and responded. In 1938 he rented space in the building and operated a two-chair barbershop. By 1942 he purchased the building.[6] He relied on display advertisements in the *Louisiana Weekly* to publicize his performers. Between August 23 and December 6, 1947, he purchased twelve display advertisements, each approximately one column wide and five inches long. The first ad contained large text announcing the performance of blues man Smiley Lewis, Dave Bartholomew's orchestra, and others. Small print at the bottom mentioned that WJBW was broadcasting performances live every Thursday beginning at 11 p.m. Among other performers were Roy Brown, Baby Irene, and Patsy and Bob Parker. By October, the remotes had moved to 11 p.m. Saturdays. The October 11 show was a held-over performance of touring vocalist Tina Dixon. Painia charged 75 cents for admission to see her perform in the Groove Room. He also gave patrons a food and drink voucher worth 75 cents redeemable at her final shows on Saturday and Sunday. Clarence "Gatemouth" Brown, a guitarist who played swamp blues, swing, country, and Cajun music, followed Dixon, playing a five-week engagement.[7]

Despite the broadcasts, Painia wanted individuals to patronize the club instead of staying home and listening to the performances on the radio. He had nothing to worry about. His acts were so entertaining and at times outrageous that customers flocked in. The *Weekly* ads and WJBW exposure added to Painia's prestige in the black community.

For months, WJBW broadcast the live music originating at the Dew Drop, but there was no survey to indicate definitively whether the station's ratings increased. On October 25, Painia departed temporarily from the routine of broadcasting songs and music targeting blacks. Unheard of on radio previously, Daniel E. Byrd, executive secretary of the New Orleans branch of the NAACP, spent a few minutes talking about the NAACP's voter registration drive and the benefits of voting. Byrd stood at a microphone, topped with WJBW's call letters. Near him were recording artists Joe Turner, Painia, and Bob Parker, the master of ceremony at the Dew Drop's Groove Room. WJBW listeners were hit with progressive yet measured black political discourse that had been absent from broadcasts in the city. Indeed, even O. C. W. Taylor, who integrated radio in New Orleans, avoided political topics during the first couple of years of broadcasts of the "Religious Forum" on WNOE.[8] Except for a picture in the *Louisiana Weekly*, the brief talk about the voter registration drive was not emphasized in the black newspaper, an unusual occurrence considering the vast extent to which the paper championed African American causes.

Earlier Scoop Jones, who wrote an entertainment column at the *Louisiana Weekly*, critiqued Dew Drop's announcer Bob Parker, whom he described as a "rising young baritone." Painia had recently hired Parker as emcee. "Bob's first night performance was rather pitiful because he had a hard time phrasing his speech." But Parker improved significantly by listening to the city's creative masters of ceremony and paying close attention to their innovations. "He studied the culture of black people and spotted the new social trends, and out of it came original Parker, who established unique 'hep phrasing.'" In a few years, Parker would become a local radio deejay.[9]

The Dew Drop was also one of the black hotels accommodating African American performers who visited the racially segregated city. Emcees and promoters chaperoned nationally known black musicians to the Dew Drop after concert performances. Sometimes the musicians performed jam sessions, and they usually ate, drank, socialized, and slept overnight at the hotel. Entertainers, such as Buddy Johnson, Billy Eckstine, Nat King Cole, and Lionel Hampton sometimes stayed overnight in the city. They slept at black-owned hotels such as the Page, Patterson, and Gladstone. Some spent the night at the homes of their hosts.[10]

In mid-May 1947, after WJBW found some success with the Dew Drop broadcasts, the station moved its remotes to the cocktail lounge of the

Gladstone Hotel, 3435 Dryades Street, where it held a twice-a-week music variety show. It aired Thursday and Saturday from 11:30 p.m. to midnight. The Dew Drop also lost its rapid-fire emcee Bob Parker, whom Scoop Jones praised:

> Bob learned how to emcee. He watches the trend of times and keeps his modern version of master of ceremonies right on the ball. What customers like best is Bob's unique hep phrasing, for instance, when he introduces shake dancer Baby Irene, he says "Get on the beam with Baby Irene." Some of his jive emceeing may go like this, "Keep it groovy with Ruby" . . . "Keep it straight, Gate, don't be late." Bob is a hustling family man, who would like to go places in the entertaining world.[11]

Two years later, in May 1949, the same nightlife columnist wrote again about Parker's vocal dexterity, "Your jive is still tops." This time Parker teamed up with white announcer Richard Riesling at WJBW remotes at the Gladstone Hotel. Riesling opened the show briefly talking about inconsequential local events. He and Parker also discussed jazz music from time to time. After that, Parker took over, sometimes interviewing special guests.[12]

By the end of July, Parker moved on and George Joseph Emery Stephens Jr., who used the stage name Tex Stephens, replaced Parker as co-emcee at the Gladstone broadcasts. He appropriated the nickname Tex because he visited relatives who wore cowboy hats in Houston. When he returned to New Orleans wearing those big hats, people began calling him Tex. He was also fond of his five colorful long-coat, baggy pants called zoot suits. Stephens had been a regular listener to the WJBW remotes which were extended from 9:30 p.m. to midnight. He called Riesling on the telephone to ask the announcer to play a record by Woody Herman. Tex's bass voice was smooth. Riesling played the song and invited Tex to visit him during the next show. After two to three visits in as many weeks, Riesling asked Tex to replace Parker. Tex was interested and the station owner agreed but said Tex would have to sell commercial time and find another venue.[13]

Initially Riesling and Tex handled the show similarly to the format used by Riesling and Parker. Riesling opened the show, after which they talked about jazz and other race music. Tex eventually moved the show to the Hayes Chicken Shack on Louisiana Avenue. The live shows at the Shack, which was black-owned and a fine eating establishment, were held once weekly but expanded to three times a week. Tex played a Woody Herman record as the theme song.[14]

In May 1949, with the start of WNOE's talent show, which was also held at the Hayes restaurant and partly broadcast on Taylor's second radio show, there had been eight programs with some content targeting blacks. Seven were strictly entertainment (see Table 4):[15]

Table 4
New Orleans Radio Stations with Black-oriented Programs in 1949

call letters	program	format	date launched
WNOE	"Negro Forum"	talk	5-26-46
WJBW	Dew Drop	live music remote	8-14-47
WJMR	"Jam, Jive, & Gumbo"	recorded music	12-47
WWEZ*	title unannounced	recorded music	12-47
WDSU	"Gospel Train"	recorded music	4-49
WJBW	Gladstone	music variety	5-49
WNOE	"Negro Talent Show"	amateur talent	5-17-49
WWEZ	"Jivin' with Jax"	recorded music	5-29-49

*One or more white men hosted the WWEZ program.

WWL, the station with the most powerful signal and largest audience, in September 1947 was not among its counterparts airing programming targeting blacks. Station management made a halfhearted attempt to change, but it never materialized. Program directors Ray McNamara and Henry Dupree announced the station would begin broadcasting a series of talent shows featuring local blacks. The first broadcast was scheduled October 6. *Louisiana Weekly* reporter Clement MacWilliams was to act as talent scout. Hundreds of talented colored vocalists and instrumentalists were said to have dreamed of accessing opportunities to perform on air. Starting October 1, judges were to begin daily 3 p.m. sessions to evaluate the quality of competitors. WWL would schedule people selected at the auditions to perform during Monday broadcasts. Professionals were to accompany individuals who needed musicians. A *Weekly* article said those interested should contact MacWilliams at the paper. Unlike initial public announcements of new radio shows targeting blacks, no advertisements, articles, photographs, or commentaries appeared in the *Weekly* after the September 27 announcement. No rationale was publicized.[16]

◆ ◆ ◆

As television arrived and siphoned white audiences away from radio, some executives at local stations began easing their custom of whites-only on-air talent. Stations, such as WJBW, WJMR, and WNOE began to no longer ignore the commercial possibilities of black music, culture, and creativity. The small independent broadcasters bought into the new paradigm and included rhythm and blues, inventive black language, spirited emotions, and stylized personifications among their on-air repertoires.

Vernon Winslow was one of those who could no longer be ignored and who would become a major player in black music radio. He would become the first full-time black disc jockey in New Orleans. Winslow was born in 1911 in Dayton to parents who were educated at Wilberforce University in Ohio. Racism prevented his father from landing gainful employment, despite being college educated. His father moved the family to Chicago to find better opportunities, but he only found work as a porter and as a stockroom clerk. Winslow's parents shielded him from much of the harsh life of the massive inner city. They require him to read fiction, nonfiction, and poetry. He had to engage in activities stimulating intellectual development. But he had to keep secret his love of reading. Otherwise, his hoodlum peers would tease him and start fights. Winslow graduated from Lindblom High School in Chicago; the Art Institute of Chicago, where he earned a bachelor of fine arts degree in advertising design in 1937; and the University of Chicago, where he earned a master's degree. In 1938 he accepted an appointment to the faculty of the art department at Dillard University in New Orleans, where he earned $44 a week.[17]

The desire to enter broadcasting germinated during his stay in New York City in the mid-1940s when he discovered a magnetic announcer who happened to be white and mainstream. The opportunity surfaced while Winslow taught at Dillard. The Rosenwald Fund awarded him a one-year fellowship to study industrial art design with Norman Bel Geddes, a renowned author who designed cars, stage sets, buildings, and other elements exuding futuristic and artistic aesthetics. The fund provided grants to African American artists, writers, researchers, and intellectuals. Winslow's ambition was to be a painter. He would walk through Rockefeller Center, the home of the NBC Studios, to get to and from the design studio on the twenty-fourth floor. Winslow heard David "Dave" Garroway, an NBC announcer whose easygoing, relaxed vocalization would later influence Winslow's on-air presentation. Winslow did not actually meet Garroway. He simply made mental notes of his style and delivery, sometimes while standing at the window looking into the broadcast studio, other times while walking past. "He had a very wonderful magnetic kind of voice," Winslow said. He imagined himself as a radio broadcaster: "Why can't I be an announcer" and use radio as another vehicle for disseminating aspects of black culture?[18]

Winslow, nevertheless, was influenced by Chicago's street life and music, of which his parents disapproved. He envisioned radio as a medium to spread popular black music and cultural expressions. In New Orleans, Winslow formulated a plan to get into radio, which remained off limits to blacks. He wanted to host a hip radio show but realized he was not very hip. Winslow convinced the *Louisiana Weekly*'s editor, C. C. Dejoie, to let him write a nightlife gossip column. He used the pseudonym Browneyes as his byline instead of his real name because Dillard president, Dr. Albert Dent, would not approve of his faculty writing a gossip column laced with black slang. Dillard was affiliated with the United Methodist Church and the United Church of Christ.[19] To better understand life in the entertainment world and also obtain news/gossip for his column, Winslow grabbed his notepad and ink pen and visited the city's most popular black nightclubs, including the Dew Drop Inn. He did not take copious notes inside of the establishments. When he didn't have his notepad, he clandestinely wrote phrases onto a brown paper bag or napkin. He needed to establish a vocabulary epitomizing the latest slang to use in his column and later on the radio. Winslow visited the clubs regularly and paid attention to the names of musicians and song titles played most often on the jukeboxes. He analyzed the most listened-to selections. With light brown skin and straight hair, a handsome man with an easy personality, Winslow had no trouble getting introduced to people connected with music, hospitality, and entrepreneurial activities. Winslow placed his fingers on the pulse of the people's perceptions of what was new, up-to-date, and forward moving.

> The Dew Drop was a good place to be. It was just the sprouting up of new terms like, ... Things like, "Come on, Ruth, get out of that phone booth, drinking that strong vermouth...." Those phrases I would listen to and new languages just seemed to spring up. New meanings for a combination of ideas and metaphors: this rhyming pattern, which everybody took a little bit of....
>
> It was, as I could figure it out, a kind of urbanity they were reflecting, not knowing too much of the prepositions and Latin derivation of words, and the Latin connection of word structures ... They would just develop their own hip talk. I would interpret those phrases and put them into the script, like "Don't act foggy or I'll make you jump." It was laced with neighborhood inflections.[20]

Armed with a much better sense of the social peculiarities of a subculture of black New Orleanians, in 1947 Winslow decided to make his move. He wrote radio scripts based on his experiences and submitted them to station managers along with a proposal to produce and host a hip show featuring jump blues, boogie woogie, New Orleans music, and other "jive" recordings. He wrote letters to station representatives at WWL and WJMR explaining his proposition. Winslow's proposal was distinct in part because he would create a trickster character who would tantalize listeners with his vocal dexterity. He would play records by local black musicians who otherwise did not get airtime, and spin some nationally known artists. Among locals were Annie Laurie's "Since I Fell for You" and Paul Gayten's "True," both singles recorded in 1947 on the DeLuxe label, which would later record James Brown and other popular black musicians. No station was broadcasting local black artists, interspersed with a mischievous persona, and hosted by an African American.[21]

WNOE aired two white programs featuring recorded music in 1946. Both were produced by Cosimo Matassa, the J&M Music Shop owner. "J M Session" aired fifteen minutes weekly starting at 11 p.m. Tuesday and "Jam Session," a fifteen-minute Friday night show also starting at 11 p.m. Just the same white voices and their pastel sentiments were on the air with an occasional song by an acceptable black artist, such as Nat King Cole, thrown in the mix.

In December 1947 WWEZ aired a show including recorded music by black artists daily at 2:35 p.m. Those artists played music with predictable mainstream lyrics and sentiments, such as Louis Armstrong and Count Basie. The station launched its signal earlier in the year. *Louisiana Weekly* columnist Scoop Jones characterized it favorably: "For a real treat tune-in on the new radio station WWEZ daily at 2:35 p.m. for hep time." But, again, white men selected the music and voiced their interpretations of African American slang. For a very brief time in December 1947, the *Louisiana Weekly* broadcast "Jazz, Jive and Gumbo" on WJMR, Wednesdays at 1:45 p.m. The next month, January 24, the show was hosted by a white man whom Winslow coached to speak in black hipster dialect.[22]

In the meantime, from Winslow's perspective, whites had limited opportunities to develop an understanding of how black people interacted in social environments. At first, Winslow too was deprived of familiarity with black vernacular and the unfiltered taste of grass-roots African American music. His college-educated parents influenced him to avoid much of the black artistic culture, so in New Orleans he had to play catch-up. Unlike whites, he could visit economically poor black neighborhoods and linger in the nightclubs without attracting attention. Winslow envisioned broadcasting black-laden music for African American consumption because radio overlooked the preferences of the city's most culturally creative community.[23]

Winslow prepared to make his move, deciding to first woo WWL, the local 50,000-watt station owned by Loyola University. He mailed a cover letter, proposal, and script to WWL's manager, who responded saying the station once considered producing a black music show but rejected Winslow's proposal. The letter said several years would have to elapse before the station would further consider "anything in that line." Winslow also mailed his packet to WJMR, located in the Jung Hotel downtown. This time he did not indicate his race in the letter. He mentioned only that he was from Chicago and an instructor who earned a degree at the Art Institute of Chicago. WJMR was independent and cofounded by George Mayoral and a Puerto Rican, Stanley Ray. It did not have access to broad-appeal network programming. The management recognized the proposal represented a fine business opportunity. WJMR played some black music performed by proper Negroes. The disc jockey did not play the black music Winslow proposed, which he heard on nightclub jukeboxes. One of the cofounders invited Winslow to the station on Canal Street, the city's principal thoroughfare in the central business district.[24]

When Winslow arrived at the station, an owner, most likely Mayoral, listened to the ideas and asked a few questions about the show's commercial potential. Winslow said the show would bring in new black advertisers. The owner was definitely interested in increasing revenue. He wanted to bring Winslow aboard and asked how he would present the show. Winslow returned in a few days with more text of a funky disk jockey talking about records and inconsequential events. Winslow was an excellent writer. He named his character the eccentric deejay Poppa Stoppa who used slang, such as the rhyming three-line couplet: "I saw a chick and she really was slick, but I tell you what, she swings a powerful mitt."[25] Despite the jargon, Winslow pronounced words as the station owner expected of whites. The owner liked the presentation but looked suspiciously at Winslow's winning smile, short straight hair, and light-brown skin, which resembled the complexion of his Puerto Rican partner. Mayoral suspected Winslow might be black. He asked, "By the way, are you a nigga?"

"I'm not a nigger, I'm a Negro."

"I'll be goddamn," he said as he slammed his hand against the desktop. He jumped up from the chair and leaned forward as though he could pierce through Winslow's conciliatory eyes. "I'd tear my station down before I'd put you behind the microphone. Get the hell out of here."

Winslow was discombobulated but calm. His spirit fractured as he turned toward the door. The owner quickly came to his senses and composed himself. The idea was novel and could potentially open new markets. He said wait a minute, and paused a bit. Could you teach white men to voice the language in the script?[26] Winslow had never thought of such an arrangement. He and his wife could use the extra money. Dillard University paid him less than $2,500 annually. Besides, Winslow wanted to be in radio, but could he fit his artistic and entrepreneurial vision into a race-conscious, white-dominated hegemony? WWL had flatly rejected his proposal. WJMR would hire him as a consultant. Maybe when he proved himself, the gentlemen would be willing to hire him full-time and give him his own show. Winslow agreed to produce the program and train white announcers how to talk convincingly in hip, black dialect.[27]

For WJMR, Winslow developed a radio persona he called Poppa Stoppa, a fictitious black male trickster. The name suggested identification with a brash aspect of black culture. Poppa Stoppa was slang for a condom; it stops pregnancy and therefore prevents a man from becoming a papa. Later, in the 1970s, rappers appropriated the term to refer to the windscreen in front of a studio microphone that softened the puffs of air when the vocalist pronounced certain sounds, especially words that begin with the letter "P." Poppa Stoppa's character emulated the rhyme and rap of entertainers, emcees, and the chatter of everyday blacks as expressed on street corners and in bars and barbershops throughout the chocolate city. Such language was for insiders: "Look at that gold tooth, Ruth" and "Wham, bam, thank you ma'am." Whites didn't understand it because it was uniquely associated with black people in a racially segregated but somewhat autonomous milieu. The progenitors of the expressions were proud of it because it was a way to show solidarity or brotherhood. Winslow wrote his scripts in such language, and Poppa Stoppa was his mouthpiece.[28]

Winslow worked part-time at WJMR, writing scripts and commercials, selecting records, selling airtime, and vocal-training white announcers. Duke Thiele was the first white man to play the role of Poppa Stoppa and host the program "Jam, Jive & Gumbo," an alteration of the name of the *Weekly*'s short-lived show "Jazz, Jive & Gumbo." Winslow coached Thiele to verbalize words and act out the personality of the fictional hip-talking black man. During practice sessions, Winslow taught him to splatter words, phrases, and use double entendre such as: "Man, she's so fine, I don't come through the door, man, I come through the window." He picked up such expressions at the Dew Drop and other nightclubs. Winslow would sit down with Thiele and read to him: "This is the way you got to say it." Thiele repeated what he heard until Winslow was satisfied. Winslow would also stand behind Thiele looking over his shoulder: "Wait now, slow down on that, you're going too fast with that." Sometimes the coaching would occur while a record was playing.[29]

Winslow's creativity led him to invent a female character, a "chick" he called Browneyes. She did not speak; nevertheless, no such scenarios had ever been on local radio targeting blacks. Winslow would get Thiele to say things like, "Browneyes don't leave me like that. I tell you I could get a beer come back and talk to you, if I could really make the play." In the late 1940s it was unacceptable to make reference on air to any type of sexual activity, such as "make the play." In spite of such conservatism, the show continued with Poppa Stoppa referencing a condom and a repertoire including sexual euphemisms flying under the radar.[30]

Airing daily at 1:30 p.m., "Jam, Jive & Gumbo" became the talk of the black community. Three months later, on March 4, 1948, an ad in the *Louisiana*

Weekly announced the show had expanded to sixty minutes daily. Blacks began to tune in to hear the familiar music and language of the humid streets, despite the fact that a white man was attempting to sound black. William Barlow calls it racial ventriloquism, a circumstance when whites try to sound black by appropriating street culture and cool talk. With Winslow in the streets selling the show, advertisements such as from tailors, insurance companies, drug stores, and owners of other types of black businesses wanted in. Winslow maintained the arrangement. He wrote scripts, picked records, coached Thiele, sold ads, and performed other duties. During his one-year stay at WJMR, he trained four Poppa Stoppas. One day in June 1948, Winslow was in the broadcast studio coaching one of the trainees. The guy went to the restroom while the record was playing. Winslow sat down at the turntable, put on the set of earphones, turned on the switch, and talked. He forgot there was a speaker in the main office, and the staff heard him. The manager stormed in saying, "Get the hell out of here. If you ever try to do this for any other station, . . . I'm going to tell all the stores to kick the shit out of you." "Jam, Jive, & Gumbo" continued without Winslow, yet New Orleans would hear from him again. In the meantime, blacks and whites thought Poppa Stoppa was black, and WJMR's listenership grew.[31]

Louisiana Weekly columnist Scoop Jones was aware Poppa Stoppa was characterized by a white man, and Winslow was the creator and coach. Radio stations in Alabama and other southern states utilized black disc jockeys. The music blacks created was among the most popular of radio shows exclusively featuring records. Even the language of jive talk was gaining popularity. Jones expressed his observations in general terms, avoiding mention of a particular station. Therefore, who was the most qualified to work as a disc jockey? New Orleans is the seat of jazz and the birthplace of Louis Armstrong and several other exponents of swing. New Orleans has the background to give color and flavor to a music show more so than any other place in the nation: "When somebody stops thinking so religiously of 'color' line, maybe radio in New Orleans will get hep."[32]

After a year at WJMR and being fired, on January 15, 1949, Winslow's nightlife/entertainment/gossip column, "Boogie-beat Jive," debuted in the *Louisiana Weekly*. He played off the writer as the rhetorical figure Browneyes, the female character he created at WJMR. Winslow also sold ad space for the paper. He maintained his connections with the retailers to whom he sold airtime while working at WJMR. Four months later, the paper announced it hired Winslow as assistant advertisement director. In the meantime, he continued teaching at Dillard, selling ads, writing his nightlife column, and visiting nightclubs.[33]

His dream was about to materialize. Naomi Borikins, a black woman who was a public relations professional at Jackson Brewing Company, knew of Winslow's success at attracting listeners via Poppa Stoppa at WJMR. She was also aware of his salesmanship at the station and the *Weekly*. She told her superiors Winslow would be an ideal person to head a new marketing campaign to target blacks among Jax beer consumers. Executives at the Fitzgerald Advertising Agency, whose principal client was the brewery, conducted a study of black beer-drinkers in the city and determined the market was wide open. Historically, major brands of virtually any product or service avoided advertising featuring blacks or in black newspapers because condescending whites would consider the brand inferior. Fitzgerald had no such trepidation. The statistics indicated a high sales potential trumping any threats from disapproving whites. The agency sent Winslow a telegram: "We understand you are the person who initiated Poppa Stoppa. If you can think of another name, and think of another name." They said it twice, according to Winslow. "Come down and talk to us." The agency offered $5,000 a year, nearly twice the salary he earned as an art instructor. This time Winslow would personify the on-air character. His duties included creating a radio show featuring black music and marketing Jax beer among African Americans. Winslow finally found the opportunity to host his own show. He intended to make it better than "Jam, Jive & Gumbo," but he needed a name, an original character for this new show.[34]

The end of the spring academic semester neared. Winslow, at the rank of assistant professor, went to the office of Dillard's president and told him about the offer from the Fitzgerald agency, his intention to accept the job, and his plan to teach until the end of the semester. Dent asked whether he tendered his resignation because of money problems. Winslow's answer was yes. He asked how much the offer was. After Winslow mentioned the $5,000, Dent said the university could not afford to match that and wished him well. Subsequently, he formally accepted the offer.[35]

In the meantime, Winslow had to give rise to an inventive, jazzy character with a catchy name. His choice needed to signify a crafty figure similar to Poppa Stoppa but also to reflect polish and dignity. One day, he thought about the time the singer Louis Jordan visited New Orleans. Jordon, aka the King of the Jukebox, was a bandleader, songwriter, singer, and saxophonist popular with black and white audiences between the 1930s and 1950s. Among his headlining titles were: "Is You Is or Is You Ain't My Baby," "Caldonia," "There Ain't Nobody Here but Us Chickens," and "Saturday Night Fish Fry." A white promoter brought Jordan to town to perform at the Municipal Auditorium. At the time, whites sat on the main floor and blacks occupied the balcony. One night on stage Jordan looked up toward the balcony and said, "I'm playing this number for everybody, including my buddies up there. . . . And one of these days you gonna' be down here with me." The white people were not amused.[36]

Later that night Winslow encountered Jordan at the bar at the Dew Drop. Winslow had a popular reputation in segments of the black community because he created Poppa Stoppa, which newspapers publicized. Winslow also devised "Jive, Jam & Gumbo," wrote a nightlife column that became widely known after he resigned from Dillard, and sold ads for radio and print. One night after Jordan performed at the auditorium, he and Winslow sat next to each other at the bar. Jordan told him racial segregation, pointing to the practice as it played out at the auditorium, was on its last legs. "You know, the next time I come in town, Daddy-O, you're gonna sit down on the main floor, and I'm gonna sit down on the main floor." It was not so much what he said, but the term Daddy-O stuck in Winslow's mind. He had never heard it before. He loved it, but something wasn't right. Daddy-O did not seem as though it could stand alone. Poppa Stoppa had two parts. Daddy-O needed something else. Later, he remembered what guys said at the Dew Drop. When you sat at the bar and nursed a drink, the fellow next to you might say, "Doc, you got a match?" It dawned on him: "Doc was a way of extending camaraderie so I just put it together, Dr. Daddy-O. So it would fit right in on the heart, a kind of language, this acceptance that I heard around town."[37]

In mid-1949, word was spreading about Winslow's acceptance of the opportunity to host his own recorded music show. The *Louisiana Weekly* published a story on page one with a headshot of Winslow handsomely smiling next to a microphone sporting the WWEZ call letters. "The Jackson Brewing Company today announced that on May 29, New Orleans will listen to its first colored disc jockey, 'Dr. Daddy-O.'" The article also said he would continue writing his nightlife column and selling ads for the *Weekly*. Winslow called the show "Jivin' with Jax," which aired Monday through Saturday, from 5 p.m. to 6 p.m., and soon became the top-rated radio program in the city. The *Weekly* described it as "sepia 'jive.'"[38]

WWEZ permitted the brewery to use its frequency to launch the African American music show despite receiving threats from white supremacists. While the decision was progressive, the Hotel New Orleans, where the WWEZ studios were located, refused to allow Winslow to enter the hotel through the lobby. He had to go in through the rear of the building and ride the freight elevator to the studios. Cosimo Matassa learned of the situation and let Winslow broadcast from his small studio in the rear of his record shop. The rather liberal white man recognized Winslow's significance and loathed the hotel's policy. In the meantime, WWEZ did not train Winslow to operate the broadcast equipment. Instead the station sent an engineer who sat in a chair near Winslow as he interviewed guest entertainers at Matassa's studio. The engineer played the records and operated the audio equipment. Winslow announced the records, conducted interviews, read the commercials, and provided other commentary. Guests sometimes packed the small record shop.[39]

Winslow's show played boogie woogie, swing jazz, New Orleans music, bebop blues, and other genres performed by Smiley Lewis, Fats Domino, Dave Bartholomew, and others. As dawn broke, mass media was broadcasting black records spun by an African American disc jockey. Jukeboxes and live performances were no longer the only game in town. As Dr. Daddy-O, Winslow introduced records to his listeners and created demand. He played and helped popularized "The Fat Man," written by Domino and Bartholomew in December 1949 and subsequently performed by Fats. Winslow's "Jivin' with Jax" also included short interviews with singers who became public figures, such as Roy Brown and Chubby Newsome.[40]

In July 1949 Winslow added a new component to his show, thirty minutes of "popular recordings and local jive" including interviews specifically with recording artists and entertainers who performed at the Dew Drop and other local nightclubs. He interviewed Lil Ella, a blind singer who sounded similar to Ella Fitzgerald; shake-dancer Bertina Jackson; singer Larry Darnell; members of the comedy team Lolly Pop and Ethel; and singer and pianist Camille Howard, who performed with Roy Milton's orchestra. During the interview, Howard tickled the ivories between Dr. Daddy-O's smooth, stylish utterances.[41]

Winslow also exhibited an opposite version of racial ventriloquy, an intentional manipulation of stereotypical cultural norms of verbal expression. For example, in late 1947 Winslow trained white disc jockeys to talk like the black hipster character, Poppa Stoppa. In his gossip entertainment column, Winslow wrote comments from Alvin Richardson, who listened to "Jivin' with Jax." Richardson thought Winslow was white. "You don't have a 'colored' voice," he told Winslow, who wrote a brief query in response: "Say, is that good or bad?"[42]

Jax brewery ran advertisements in the *Louisiana Weekly* announcing the show. The initial ad, a quarter of a page, appeared July 2, 1949, at the lower right side. It illustrated Winslow's gymnastic advertising verbiage. The ad pictured two black men including a young man with a big smile holding a glass of beer. He's identified as Mr. Madlee Griffith of 6309 Madmen Street. "This Jax is a real gone brew! It's mellow and light . . . tastes just right, morning or night. It's got me asking' for Jax every time." The other man, middle-aged

Ulysses Jones of 1928 Louisiana Avenue, held a bottle of the beer. "Sure, I'm proud to work for Jax Brewery. I know that the Jax beer I'm talking about is the finest there is! And all my friends agree." The subtitle read. "Listen! JAX 'Doctor Daddy-O' WWEZ, Monday thru Saturday 5 p.m."

The ads appeared nearly every week between July and November. On October 29 a large head-and-shoulders photo of the handsome Winslow dominated the ad. It announced Dr. Daddy-O would begin a second "Jivin with Jax" Monday through Saturday, 10 p.m. to 10:30 p.m. "Now there are two frantic 'Jiving with Jax' shows. One at 5 p.m. and the other at 10 p.m." Dr. Daddy-O would also host a special two-hour Halloween show from 10 p.m. to midnight on October 29.[43]

The Jax marketing strategy worked so well that Jax's rival American Brewing Company, makers of Regal Beer, copied the approach. American Brewing sought to expand its black beer-drinking market in the city by launching a music radio program and purchasing advertising space in the *Weekly*. In July, American Brewing began broadcasting "Music of New Orleans," an all-Negro show on the *Times-Picayune*'s WTPS.

American Brewing distinguished its show by hiring producer Elwood Smith, a New Orleans actor, singer, and writer. Smith worked as master of ceremony at social events, sung with the Xavier University Opera Guild, studied at the Julliard School of Music, and performed on Broadway in *St. Louis Woman*, in which Pearl Bailey and Rex Ingram starred. Instead of recorded music, the premier program featured live musicians. Geraldine Patterson, who studied at the Kansas City Conservatory of Music and Howard University School of Music, directed the Regal Singers, consisting of four females and three males, all young adults. Their selections included Cole Porter's "Night and Day" and "There's a Meeting Here Tonight." Marie Moten accompanied on piano.

The program also included New Orleans music and traditional jazz performed by Oscar "Papa" Celestin and his Original Tuxedo Orchestra. Veteran musician Celestin played trumpet and had been performing since 1923. The Tuxedo Orchestra performed "Way Down Yonder in New Orleans," with Celestin singing the lead; "Basin Street Blues" and "High Society," which featured Alphonse Picou on clarinet. Octave Crosby played the piano and occasionally sang lead. The *Weekly* reported the musicians were outstanding: "They 'went to town.'" The "Music of New Orleans" show aired Sundays at 3 p.m. to 4 p.m. In August the program included a thirty-minute pre-broadcast show in the Booker T. Washington High School auditorium, including Celestin and the Regal Singers. "Listen in, 'Music of New Orleans' with an all-star all-Negro cast, Sunday–3 p.m., WTPS- 940 on your dial," a *Weekly* ad read.[44]

By late 1949 writers at black newspapers circulated word, without specificity, of a station planning to hire Bob Parker. Vernon Winslow, in his Dr. Daddy-O column (originally sporting the byline Browneyes), instigated the Parker gossip. "Rumor says that fast-talking Bob Parker will be New Orleans' second colored disc jockey (congratulations!!)." Parker hosted a WJBW music and variety show in the lounge of the Gladstone Hotel in a working-class neighborhood on Dryades Street. He also emceed at the Dew Drop Inn's non-broadcast shows. Parker did not become the second black jockey, but he would eventually join the staff of WMRY. Winslow wrote as though he were Parker's cheerleader, inserting himself as the authority who evaluated the quality of the performances of blacks as they emerged in local broadcasting. Articles also mentioned that a black female announcer, as well as a new all-colored station, would enter the market. The prognostications had some validity but were somewhat off the mark.[45]

Weekly reporter Scoop Jones mentioned that a third player, a wine distillery, would sponsor a new show introducing the city's first black female announcer, but the entity backed away. "That wine company that was out hunting for a female disc jockey suddenly discovered that its budget couldn't afford another radio show so they temporarily tabled the idea." By the end of 1949, Jones was again advocating for more blacks on air. "Give some more local lads a chance on the radio, including the fems."[46]

Dr. Daddy-O continued in the fray in his column in December: "What's this we hear about two new radio stations moving into Crescent City? One: entirely colored and the other may operate with colored announcers and ofay management." Two weeks later Winslow was at it again: "And when that new colored radio station gets going, why not consider A.V. (Vic) Williams as one of the announcers."[47]

In his job promoting Jax beer, Winslow was creative in the way he approached branding the brew among blacks. His contract required him to market and advertise the beer. One approach he implemented was the Jax block party. Winslow entered into agreements with owners of nightclubs whose patrons were black and offered to produce a party at their location. Jax would supply complimentary beer the day of the party, but the owners had to agree to sell Jax in the future. The block party was one of Winslow's innovations. The parties were held in the street outside of the neighborhood lounge. The police department put movable barricades at each end of the street to divert vehicles and allow people to dance in the street, mill around, or relax sitting on chairs. A distributor would stock the bar with Jax. Sometimes Dr. Daddy-O hired musicians such as Smiley Lewis or Fats Domino. The bands played perched on the bed of a big truck with speakers blaring the rocking sounds of rhythm and blues, which could be heard blocks away.[48] To publicize the festivities, Winslow announced the location of the parties on his show. He also mentioned details in his column.

> Say chere, ya shoulda heard Cha Cha Hogan blast those blues at the Sunset Tavern (Roman and St. Louis) ... pops, the place went up in smoke ... (If I'm lyin,' I'm flyin') ... with a WWEZ microphone we had a party that just wouldn't don't [sic] ... The music (and, babe, it was solid stuff!) came from Handy and his Rhythms: S. Handy, bass: Curtis Godchaux, trumpet: Harold Antoine, drums ...[49]

Winslow served as the master of ceremony at the parties, often holding a bottle of Jax in his left hand and a WWEZ flagged microphone in his right. He even held Jax parties, sometimes called Dr. Daddy-O parties in small towns such as Napoleonville, sixty miles west of New Orleans.[50]

The events also provided material for his radio show. He took recording equipment and briefly interviewed tavern customers. He used some of the interviews on his show. In the process, he drew more attention to Jax beer, his show, and himself. Editors at community newspapers were long aware that more people would buy their paper if the publication contained pictures or even names of residents, their family, or friends. Winslow was among the innovators who applied the concept to radio and therefore milked African Americans' fascination with the newly integrated medium. Winslow provided laymen brief opportunities to hear their own voices and those of acquaintances on radio. "I hope Dan Rousseve finally heard his name on the air ..." The strategy worked so well that swindlers surfaced claiming association with Winslow. For a fee, they said Dr. Daddy-O would mention the name of their business during a broadcast.[51]

Also in 1949, WDSU radio station "just signed up" the black-owned Louisiana Undertaking Company as sponsor of a new recorded gospel music show. The show, "Louisiana Gospel Train," was broadcast on Sundays at 8:30 a.m. and featured recordings by Sister Rosetta Tharpe, Marie Knight, and Mahalia Jackson, among others. WDSU production director Ray Rich further announced that the station had signed an agreement to hire "Papa" Celestin as a disc jockey. The show featured primarily Dixieland jazz, which was typically performed in the city by white musicians, but it also included European art music such as Johann Sebastian Bach. WDSU announcer Roger Wolfe, a white man identified as a jazz authority, provided commentary. The show aired Saturdays from noon to 1 p.m.[52]

In April WNOE added a new black show to its lineup that would become hugely popular. On July 19, over seven hundred people crowded into the

Hayes restaurant to witness the broadcast of the "Negro Talent Hour" aired on WNOE Tuesdays beginning at 8 p.m. O. C. W. Taylor was the emcee. Organizers of the "Talent Show" set up auditions at the Dryades YMCA at 1 p.m. Saturdays. Music and dance teachers coached the prospects. Hayes had recently installed air conditioning and was among the city's most comfortable black-owned restaurants. The lack of an admission charge contributed to the standing-room-only crowd. To reduce the congestion in the future, the management set up more tables and chairs, but cut the maximum attendance to 400. Subsequently all patrons were seated during the performances.

The "Negro Talent Show" also moved forward the transformation of the racial barriers in broadcasting. Blacks in the community were discovering more evidence of a reduction in constraints foisted on them by a racist social structure. For the first time, black owners of insurance companies, among the wealthiest sector of the African American community, joined together and sponsored a program, the "Talent Show." Blacks had more reason to think full access to the American dream was approaching. African Americans were finding more entry points from which to imagine themselves in new ways and as meaningful community participants. The building blocks of broadcast dissemination of racial solidarity and advocacy of full and immediate equality were being put in place. *Weekly* staffer John Lee Neely expressed the sentiment of racial solidarity: "It is encouraging to note that it was not a white business that is sponsoring this effort, but three colored establishments which enjoy the confidence of the public."[53]

Representatives of the insurance companies collaborated with other local black business owners and provided cash and other prizes to winners. Among participants were the Creole Ritz Hotel, Creole Trade Schools, Wylon Beauty Products, Groff's Hosiery, King's Food Store, Teddy's Shoe Repair Shop, McLain's Studio, Lorenzo Robinson Studio, Haydell's Florist, and Dejoie's Florist. Dr. Rivers Frederick, president of the Louisiana Industrial Life Insurance Company, contributed $100 toward a $200 first-place prize. In early July Fird Eaglin, a twelve-year-old blind boy, played "The Twelfth Street Rag" on guitar and took first place. Eaglin was a student at the Blind Institute at Southern University, Scotlandville. Xavier University student Anthony Green sung an aria and finished in second place.[54] (He later had a long musical career as Snooks Eaglin.)

In similar manner, African Americans began retooling radio when whites in broadcasting or advertising commenced hiring them as hosts, disc jockeys, or salesmen. Radio had been a medium of predictable content celebrating Euro-centered images and ideals. Then came African Americans, but only after the independent stations found themselves otherwise unable to compete with the network affiliates. An experiment here and there, with the creativity of black music and language, led to the discovery of the commercial potential of African American music, language, style, emotions, and consumerism.

CHAPTER FIVE

The Pioneer Mixed a "Batch of 'Congrats'"

In December 1949 Vernon Winslow, in his Dr. Daddy-O column "Boogie-beat Jive," published once a week in the *Louisiana Weekly*, hinted an "entirely colored" radio station would broadcast in New Orleans and a second station would employ some "colored announcers" along with "ofay management."[1]

As white listeners migrated to television as it transitioned into the dominant player in broadcasting in post–World War II America, radio stations not network-affiliated increasingly sought black audiences. Similarly, to attract African Americans, between 1948 and 1952 new radio broadcasters increasingly aired programming including the music genres rhythm and blues, gospel, jazz, and traditional blues. They began employing black talent, scheduling black entertainment programs, broadcasting African American talk shows, and advertising the services and products of black entrepreneurs. The options presented themselves clearly. Independents either targeted a nontraditional audience or went out of business.[2]

Drastic conversion in the color of radio in New Orleans was about to unfold in the winter of 1949, when new licensee WMRY began broadcasting from the Court of Two Sisters restaurant at 615 Bourbon Street in the French Quarter. The station, on the property of one of the most elegant white courtyard eating establishments in the city, targeted Caucasians and was failing financially. General manager Mort Silverman had to take his station in another direction. WJBW, as early as 1946, broadcast live music performances from the black Dew Drop Inn nightclub. Silverman hired WJBW's program director Jim Warren. At the time, two additional local stations aired shows targeting African Americans. WJMR had "Jam, Jive & Gumbo," a recorded music show featuring white disc jockeys playing race music and trying to mimic black street-talk. Vernon Winslow trained most of them. WWEZ was the other station broadcasting African American music. Its singular show, "Jivin with Jax," hosted by Winslow, propelled him to fame. The appointment placed Winslow as the city's first full-time African American deejay, aka Dr. Daddy-O.[3]

After only three months on the air, on March 4, 1950, WMRY brought listeners Ernest Bringier and his daily black music record show, "Tan Timers Club." Bringier became the city's second full-time African American disc jockey. Days later, Silverman hired another African American, George "Tex" Stephens, who assumed the name "Mr. Cool," and hosted "Tippin' with Tex," a daily midday show featuring mellow tunes.[4] Bringier and Stephens were not simply disc spinners. They were brought in to attract black listeners, advertisers and, subsequently more revenue. Stephens, for example, was affiliated with Caire Associates, an advertising and sales promotion agency.[5] Four months later, Silverman moved his station from Bourbon Street to the black-owned Louisiana Industrial Life Insurance Company building, 2107 Dryades Street, approximately one block from the Dryades YMCA, in the heart of a working-class African American community. On May 28, WMRY began fully broadcasting from Dryades Street.[6] Silverman said, "Before 1950 we were featuring good music and failing. May 28th of that year we switched to a solid Negro format. In a month we paid our way, and revenue has increased steadily ever since."[7]

The relocation of the station and its new black format were unprecedented in local broadcasting on three levels. First, WMRY fired its white staff of on-air personalities, replacing them with blacks but keeping the white engineers and management personnel. Second, the station converted its "good music" format to black-oriented programming. Third, white-owned Southland Broadcasting Company, which owned WMRY, entered into a long-term lease agreement with a black corporation. Dr. Rivers Frederick, a surgeon, was president and principal stockholder of the Louisiana Industrial Life Insurance Company. The insurance company owned the building in which WMRY relocated. The lease provided WMRY control of the entire second floor of the multi-story building.[8]

The city's second black full-time disc jockey, Bringier, was a verbal gymnast. He highly impressed Winslow, who was on the air only eight months before Bringier. Winslow used his "Boogie-beat Jive" column in the *Louisiana Weekly* to comment on and critique vocalizations of the city's first black disc jockeys. He heaped praise on them during the infancy of their arrival but later assumed the position of critic.

> And here's another batch of congrats to Ernest Bringier (The Whip) for his flashy, razzle-dazzle program, "Tan Timers Club" (WMRY; Everyday) ... (Ernie is New Orleans' newest sepia wax-twirler!! ... And congratulations to Tex Stephens, soon to be our third colored disc jockey ... (It couldn't happen to a better person!)[9]

Bringier incorporated a long whip into his persona calling himself Ernie "The Whip." From time to time he thrashed his whip making a loud pop. WMRY publicized in December that general manager Silverman had promoted Bringier to chief announcer, after one year on the job. Silverman said more than 2,300 letters and cards arrived monthly addressed to Bringier, whose show he said rated at the top of local counterparts at non-network stations.[10]

Tex Stephens's success with his jazz show on WJBW in 1949 found its way to the attention of Silverman. Bringier and Stephens were high school and college classmates. Silverman hired Tex to host a show featuring jazz by Count Basie, Duke Ellington, Lionel Hampton, and other nationally known artists. He also played New Orleans music by Fats Domino and Roy Brown, among others. Playing the role of critic, Winslow tactfully unpacked Stephens's delivery. But first, in the early broadcasts, he spoke nothing but praise: "Everyday at 12:30 'Tex' Stephens knocks me out with his highly original patter over WMRY . . . (nice going, Tex . . . your pet phrases and razzle-dazzle are strictly your own!!!)."[11]

As WMRY hired more black disc jockeys and announcers before its full-blown launch at the new location, the station intermittently placed ads in black newspapers, fed press releases to print reporters, and otherwise provided the names of the new air personalities and the titles of their shows. Jim Warren, former program director at WJBW and new assistant manager and director of production at WMRY, said the station added Malcolm LaPlace, who hosted "Sweet Talkin' Time," targeting housewives Monday through Saturday from 10 a.m. to 11 a.m. LaPlace also reported news, edited releases and announcements, and performed other duties. The station hired Rev. Percy "Windbag" Simpson Jr., who hosted the six-day-a-week program "Southern Melodies," which opened the broadcast day airing 5:30 a.m. to 6:45 a.m. LaPlace also hosted recorded religious music programs. WMRY hired a woman, Herminie Baham, to host the program "Tan Town Homemakers," 9 a.m. to 9:30 a.m., and to work as station receptionist.

WMRY released a full program schedule days before the May 28, 1950, inaugural broadcast. The station transmitted programming via 500 watts at 600 on the dial, Mondays through Saturdays, 5:30 a.m. to 7 p.m., and Sundays 7 a.m. to 7 p.m. The full schedule tweaked the lineup somewhat, such as changing the name "Tan Town Homemakers" to "Sepia Homemaker" (see Table 5).[12] Bringier was also selected to host a daily program sponsored by a Milwaukee brewery, the "Blatz Radio Show" from 5:30 p.m. to 6 p.m. the Blatz assistant district manager of sales, Paul A. Gray Sr., joined Bringier in the studio and read commercials during the debut show. Gray's interest was to convince nightclub owners, sports organization officers, social club leaders, and others to purchase or sell Blatz beer.[13]

Meanwhile, Winslow used his nightlife column to pass on a rumor of a second black-oriented station emerging in the city: ". . . and what's this we

Table 5
WMRY May 1950 Program Schedule

Monday through Saturday	
5:30-6:45 a.m.	Southern Melodies
6:45-7 a.m.	Morning Gospel
7-7:55 a.m.	Tan Town Club
7:55-8 a.m.	Tan Town News
8-8:30 a.m.	Tan Town Club
8:30-9 a.m.	Sepia Spirituals
9-9:30 a.m.	Sepia Homemaker
9:30-9:45 a.m.	Singers to be announced
9:30-9:45 a.m. [sic]	Talent to be announced
10-11 a.m.	Malcolm's Corner
11-12 p.m.	Tippin With Tex
12-12:30 p.m.	Warm up Time
12:30-3:30 p.m.	Major League Baseball
3:30-4 p.m.	Sepia Merrymaker
4-4:30 p.m.	Rev. Percy Simpson, Jr.
4:30-4:55 p.m.	Tan Town Tea Time
4:55-5 p.m.	News
5-5:30 p.m.	Deacon Lollipop
5:30-6 p.m.	Sepia Star Parade
6-6:15 p.m.	Sports
6:15-7 p.m.	Sundown Supper Club
Sunday	
7-8 a.m.	Coffee Cup Club
8-8:15 a.m.	New Orleans Chosen 5
8:15-8:30 a.m.	Hymn Time
8:30-8:45 a.m.	Sunday Thoughts
8:45-9 a.m.	The Consolators
9-9:30 a.m.	Masonic King Gospel Singers
9:30-9:45 a.m.	Rev. Simpson
9:45-10 a.m.	Marion Carter
10-11 a.m.	Sunday Morning Rockin'
11-11:15 a.m.	Gloryland Singers
11:15-12 p.m.	To be announced
12-12:30 p.m.	Warm Up Time
12:30-2 p.m.	Major League Baseball
12:30-2:40 p.m. [sic]	Sports Intermission
2:40-4:30 p.m.	Major League Baseball
4:30-5 p.m.	Record Parade
5-5:30 p.m.	Sunday Pulpit
5:30 p.m.	Sepia Serenade
7 p.m.	Sunday Sepia Serenade

hear about another colored radio station??" Six months later he said, "It's only a rumor, but a little bird told us that a certain Jim-Crow radio station may change its plans and hire a staff of sepia announcers!!"[14]

One year after ascending as the city's first full-time black disc jockey on June 11, 1949, Winslow began asserting his authority as the dean of New Orleans black radio. In his Dr. Daddy-O column, he discreetly criticized some deejays and praised others. He detected various levels of quality in their delivery and provided constructive criticism.

On May 20, 1950, Winslow criticized the vocal performances of disc jockeys Bringier and Stephens.

> Congratulations to WMRY on that opening!!! . . . But here's a tip: In talking to a blind fella the other day I asked him his opinion of sepia radio talent, and his reply was this . . . "God took my sight, but he gave me extra wonderful hearing, and I'd like to hear better Negro voices on the air!!!" . . . Mebbe he's right!!![15]

A week later, Winslow advised WMRY's staff to be intelligent in their presentations. His advice was published one day before the station went full-blown as the city's only outfit with all-black on-air talent.

> The biggest thing uptown this week is that WMRY deal . . . yeah, pops, that Sunday opening oughta wake up the dead . . . and if the WMRY boys play it smart, they've got a gold mine!!! . . . But I warn ya: it's gotta be plenty SMART!!! So a warm handshake to Mort Silverman, Mike LaPlace (your voice is groovy!!), Jim Warren, Tex Stephens, Ernest Bringier, Rev. Percy Simpson, Jr. and Luscious Hermine Baham!!![16]

Winslow also highlighted the man whom he predicted would follow himself and become the second black broadcaster. In fact Bringier did become the second, but in Winslow's opinion, Bob Parker was the best.

> Around the Lincoln Theater, everybody's talkin' about those Wednesday night shows handled by Bob Parker. Yeah, Bob you're still the nimble-witted emcee . . . and lemme tell ya one thing: your radio show (WMRY: 6:00 Everyday) is the best show on that station . . . no lie!!! . . . Mebbe it's because you're completely original . . . mebbe it's because you're working with those "Spider" Bocage boys . . . mebbe it's because Carlton Pecot's voice is great, too!!! . . . Anyway . . . keep it up!!![17]

The next month, Stephens and the others conceded, in so many words. Winslow was the dean. They publicly acknowledged his supremacy, and Winslow thereafter only published praise.

And my deepest thanks to Denton Jefferson, Malcolm LaPlace, Norman Dunlap, Tex Stephens, Bob Parker, Jimmy Willis and Lucius Jones for surprising me with that beautiful plaque; incidentally, those are the fellas who are fighting for a higher level of broadcasting among Negroes . . . Thanks!!! . . . Thanks a million!!![18]

Stephens took to heart Winslow's critique.

Listening to "Tex" Stephens handling of his radio show, everyone is impressed with the improvement that has occurred. Yeah, Tex, your pace is swell . . . your resonance is getting there and that new warmth is mighty nice to lissen to!!! . . . Keep it up!!![19]

Winslow's watchful ear continued listening to the neophytes and drawing attention to their foibles. Instead of outright criticism, he camouflaged it by accentuating their quality performances.

The commercials at WMRY sound much, much better . . . mebbe it's because Mal LaPlace is doing the thinking (and writing) on those copy-problems! . . . Say, Mike, you and Tex ought to do a great job with those games (here's waiting for the kick-off!!)[20]

In 1951, Winslow was still drawing attention to the delivery of his colleagues at WMRY: "and have you noticed the great improvement in Tex's announcing? . . . (keep goin', fella!!)"[21]

Before then, in 1950, the Jackson Brewing Company noticed an increase in sales and appointed Winslow sales director for the Negro market. Duties included selling the brand, promoting the product, researching the market, and training disc jockeys in other cities to impersonate the Dr. Daddy-O character. Winslow wrote scripts for beer commercials.[22] His scripts sometimes employed the hip language of the streets. At times it proved to be too daring. One client said, "I can't play that." It was customary for the agency to have a white writer check the language and sign off on the scripts. However, one of the white censors was hip and right at home in black neighborhoods. Winslow's storytelling and phrasing impressed him so much, the gentleman said, "I wish I could write these moth' fuckin' things."[23] Some of Winslow's commercials were short film presentations, advertising Jax beer in black movie theaters. The commercials were filmed in a studio and included musicians such as Smiley Lewis, Henry Roeland Byrd (aka Professor Longhair), and Antoine "Fats" Domino. The shorts were also shown in black theaters in Houston, Jackson (Mississippi), and other cities.[24]

The Fitzgerald agency continued acknowledging Winslow's versatility and his effectiveness at marketing Jax beer by way of his Dr. Daddy-O character. In June 1951 the company aired Dr. Daddy-O at 10:30 p.m. Mondays on WSMB broadcasting from the Maison Blanche building on Canal Street. Ironically, Winslow's new broadcast replaced the show of Dave Garroway, whose smooth voice Winslow had long ago decided he would pattern his own style after. Winslow, however, was a skilled code switcher. He could talk the jive and settle down into a smooth pace with a professional intonation. He presented both types of delivery in the new show. "The Jackson Brewing Company announced that Winslow's show will be handled in the very same manner as always, with studio audiences and special guests." Fans were asked to arrive by 10:15 p.m.[25]

The Fitzgerald agency agreed to expand the influence of Dr. Daddy-O by establishing Winslow's marketing strategies in other southern cities where Jax was sold or places with sizable black populations where the beer should be sold, cities such as Baton Rouge, Louisiana; Jackson, Mississippi; and Houston. The agency purchased airtime and Winslow traveled to the cities and recruited black disc jockeys who attempted to imitate Dr. Daddy-O. He wrote a Dr. Daddy-O training manual instructing them of the intricacies of the persona and how to present themselves professionally on and off air. "They would learn my format, my way of talking and my selection of music, and I would write their scripts."[26]

During the period, it was popular for black disc jockeys to open the mike while a song was playing. They would lower the volume a bit and yell a rhyme or some clever phrase. In the process they developed unique personalities but, to Winslow's taste, they were garish and uncouth. He rejected yelling especially while a song played and evaluated his trainees in terms of whether they had "... a sense of theatrical kind of feeling at the same time not going overboard with any kind of filthy kind of slang that would be something against the brewing company..."[27] Of course the ultimate objective was to push Jax beer into African American communities. If a competing brewery, such as the makers of Falstaff, had a significant share of the beer-drinking market in a particular location, Winslow engaged block parties and hired bands to draw attention to Jax beer. Falstaff was using Jackie Robinson as a spokesperson and putting tremendous pressure on the Jackson Brewing Company.

Cesta Ayers, who also recorded with Imperial Records, was one of the first deejays Winslow trained. "Jivin' with Jax," the same name as the New Orleans program, debuted in Houston on February 20, 1950. The brewery purchased time on station KTHT and Ayers was allowed to broadcast from the station studios. He also broadcast live remotes from the Bronze Peacock and the

Eldorado Ballroom.[28] The brewery ran ads in a black newspaper, the *Houston Informer*, touting the arrival of Dr. Daddy-O, but did not mention the names Ayers or Winslow. The ad was in all text except for a small picture of a bottle and a can of Jax beer. It read:

> Here it is. The radio show you've been waiting for from Dowling Street and Lyons Avenue. Doctor Daddy-O Jivin' with Jax, Monday, Wednesday, Friday, Bronze Peacock Tuesdays, Thursdays, Saturdays Eldorado Ballroom. KTHT, 790 on your dial. Starting at 4:55 p.m. Rock 'n' roll with this solid half hour of jam 'n' jive. Jackson Brewing Company, New Orleans, La.[29]

At the time, Houston had four black deejays. In addition to Ayers were Lonnie Rochon at KNUZ, beginning in February 1948; Vernon Chambers on KCOH, who began later that year; and Trummie Cane, who came along a little later.

Back in New Orleans, in 1952, Winslow picked-up a 10 a.m. to 10:15 a.m. slot announcing news on WMRY, the station that would become WYLD in 1957. In 1953 Winslow continued announcing news at WMRY and on the same station, he began hosting a recorded music show from 11 a.m. to 11:15 a.m. In 1953 and 1954 he announced news at WWEZ from 3:30 p.m. to 3:45 p.m. He continued playing popular music as a deejay at WWEZ but introduced a genre new to him, gospel. He called the program "Goodnight Mother" airing from 8:30 p.m. to 8:45 p.m. and again from 9 p.m. to 9:30 p.m. A half-hour later, he returned to playing secular music from 10 p.m. to 10:30 p.m.

From 1955 to 1957 he was on air exclusively at WWEZ. In 1958 Winslow moved from WTPS, the station owned by the *Times-Picayune*, to WYLD. WTPS and WYLD switched frequencies. WTPS was at 940 on the dial, while WYLD broadcast from 600 kHz. WYLD took over the 940 spot. Winslow played gospel music on WTPS at 10:05 p.m. on Thursdays, Fridays, and Sundays. A few months later, WYLD hired him as announcer for three gospel shows: "Glory Road," 7 p.m. to 9 p.m. Mondays through Fridays; "Goodnight Mother," 9 p.m. to 9:30 p.m., Mondays through Fridays; and "Old Ship of Zion," 8:45 a.m. to noon, Saturdays. Jack Willman hosted the morning installation of "Old Ship of Zion" from 8:45 a.m. to 11 a.m., Mondays through Fridays. Winslow continued that schedule until 1959.

He worked as Jax's sales director for the Negro market for nearly seven years until 1957, all the while hosting "Jivin with Jax" on WWEZ. Toward the end of his tenure, he got permission from the agency and played a gospel song here and there during "Jivin with Jax." Part of the reason was he heard another local disc jockey playing gospel on Sundays and determined he was not doing it right. As was his propensity, he wanted to demonstrate how to properly host a show.[30]

When Winslow decided he no longer wanted to sell beer and instead pursue other opportunities, he notified Jackson brewery executives, who said they were pleased with his work and wished him well. Unlike WJMR, which kept the rights to the Poppa Stoppa name, even though Winslow coined it, the brewery gave Winslow full control of the Dr. Daddy-O moniker. Jax ended the WWEZ "Jivin with Jax" in 1957.[31]

Winslow broadened his career by working for Lester Kabacoff, who was a principal player in the building of Pontchartrain Park. Kabacoff hired Winslow as an advertising consultant for the subdivision. Built in 1955, it was the first subdivision for blacks and one of the first in the country.[32] It contained an eighteen-hole golf course, picnic areas, tennis courts, a playground, and lagoon. Residents included doctors, lawyers, teachers, nurses, postal workers, business owners, and individuals in other professions. One of Winslow's ads in the *Times-Picayune* in 1962 read: "If you missed the big opening with Dr. Daddy-O and all the gang, you can still see these magnificent big split-level homes completely furnished to a king's taste in beautiful Rosemont Place."[33]

Winslow also emceed concerts at the Municipal Auditorium. He introduced performances by Duke Ellington, Nat King Cole, Joe Turner, and other nationally known performing artists. Winslow continued working as a salesman at the *Louisiana Weekly*, and developed sales and promotional relationships with a myriad of businesses, including the United Federal Savings and Loan Association, which was the first black financial institution in the city. The state of Louisiana refused to grant a black business a charter to operate a financial institution. To get around the state barrier, the association applied to the US Department of Treasury which awarded a charter. Winslow purchased advertising space and airtime for United Federal.

Winslow continued working as an air personality at WYLD in 1958 and further developed his signature recorded gospel show "Goodnight Mother." For the program, he maintained the Dr. Daddy-O character but discarded the hipness, replacing it with his smooth, rich, conversational, and hypnotic voice. On the show, he had a running dialog with his fictional mother. It was exceedingly popular. "I know old women used to just like get off on his voice," said Mable John, aka Dr. Mable John, a Louisiana gospel and later blues vocalist who was the first female to sign with Barry Gordy's Motown Tamla label. "I know that he had one of them like, I guess you'd say romantic, mellow, baritone voices that just would do a number on you."[34] Winslow loved gospel but also wanted to go against the grain: "Although the record companies insisted that hip music was the only thing, the real music that I felt most toward, and the music that really had the psychological input as far as the black market was concerned, was gospel music."[35]

At times Winslow created sound effects during broadcasts. A company that produced bacon bought airtime on one of his shows. Winslow mentored a young Art Neville, who with his siblings would later form the popular Neville Brothers funk band. In the studio at WYLD, Winslow demonstrated how to vocalize, how to operate the audio board, and even tutored Neville in the Spanish language. Neville would listen to Dr. Daddy-O during nights before bedtime. He heard Daddy-O simulate a conversation with the mother telling her he was frying bacon for breakfast. Neville said, "It sounded like he was actually frying bacon in the studio, and I just knew that's what they were doing." One morning Daddy-O allowed Neville to visit the station. To his surprise, Daddy-O was not frying bacon. The deejay was holding the cellophane wrapper from a pack of cigarettes, holding it about an inch from the microphone, and crumbing it in his hand.

Sacred music became his newly discovered lover. "Gospel music provides for a different kind of introspection," Winslow said. "You begin looking a little bit deeper, and you say, 'Gol-lee, you mean to tell me I wasted those four hours, and all I did was talk about myself?' It makes you question yourself." Sacred music was different. "While gospel is rhythmic, it has a different purpose than other highly percussive popular music. I know that they listen to this hand-clapping music. This up-tempo music is nothing new. You can turn on any station and get up-tempo music." Conversely, if you listened to gospel for a while, it said something. "It definitely makes me happy that, with all that can be heard on the radio, they listen to gospel. I'm always pleased."[36]

❖ ❖ ❖

Larry McKinley provided insight regarding Winslow. McKinley over the years was a disc jockey, announcer, civil rights reporter, and station manager at WMRY, WYLD, and WNNR, He said Winslow would say something like: "Did you enjoy your meatballs and spaghetti tonight, mama?" As Winslow perfected the role of the gospel deejay, "He had no peer. I mean he was non-parallel. He was just great, a great voice, and he knew how to deal with people. Smooth, smooth, smooth. And I think he, more than anyone else, turned the gospel disc jockey sentiment to another level, brought it up to another level, which has never been reached by anyone else either. I mean, he's just, he would just talk to people."[37] And then, he interspersed the tone and timbre with appropriate gospel tunes such as from the quartets the Soulsters or the Dixie Hummingbirds. Winslow said the spiritual messages in their songs embodied what gospel meant to the black population.

Winslow's emphasis changed from secular to sacred music because of an epiphany. When he was playing secular records, his routine included dropping in at bars and nightclubs, such as the Tijuana and Dew Drop. He needed to maintain a presence in the neighborhoods as well as collect nightlife gossip and news for his "Boogie-beat Jive" column. While walking at night to and from his car, he sometimes passed black churches where gospel music spilled out of the buildings. He began paying more and more attention to the gospel singing, shouting, and spirit-filled sermons. One night he stopped and listened, not wanting to draw attention to himself or offend anyone. After all, he sold beer for a living, organized block parties, hung out in bars, and rubbed shoulders with all sorts of rowdy characters. Despite his initial reluctance, he could not resist that aspect of black cultural expression. His curiosity got the best of him, and he would venture inside and sit on a rear pew. Winslow's only knowledge of gospel music was from the choir at Morehouse College in Atlanta. Before he finished his master's at the University of Chicago, he took advantage of an opportunity to attend for a year an HBCU (Historic Black Colleges and Universities).[38]

During Winslow's formative years, his father and mother, who were college educated, despised gospel and other traditional black music. He was never introduced to those art forms. Subsequently, he was unfamiliar with the traditions of the churches that the lower-class and working-class African Americans attended. He was impressed, however, with what he heard and saw in the neighborhood churches down the street from the city's popular nightclubs. Those church services contrasted with his upper-middle-class religious experiences in Chicago and even in New Orleans. "When they would get happy," he said, "they would just do all kinds of dancing, and they had more feeling about their sermons and their reactions then I did in my church." He was fascinated by the way they sang prayer songs and exuded a feeling of community. "It was something about the way in which church music said something that jazz wasn't saying. Dr. Daddy-O as a beer salesman wasn't saying it." Once again, he became aware of his lack of knowledge of an intricate component of black culture. This time it was African-American church music and preaching instead of black slang, rhythm and blues, nightlife, and other black cultural and subcultural idiosyncrasies. Years ago, his interest in black street life blossomed. Presently, his curiosity about gospel flourished.[39]

◆ ◆ ◆

The new racially integrated radio station Winslow mentioned in his column came to fruition on February 1, 1951, the day WBOK began broadcasting programming simultaneously to blacks and whites. White owners Jules J. Paglin, president of WBOK, Inc., and Stanley W. Ray Jr., vice president and general manager, hired a racially integrated staff, attempting to distinguish the station from the competition. "WBOK will have an integrated staff of announcers and featured artists," Paglin said. "They will include specialists both white and Negro who will be featured artists in their field."[40] The approach was progressive considering a local ordinance allowed white owners of bars and restaurants to deny service to blacks. It was not until December 23, 1969, that the New Orleans council passed the Public Accommodations Ordinance. The anti-discrimination law guaranteed equal access to public places in the city not previously covered by federal civil rights legislation. WBOK, located at 505 Baronne Street at the corner of Poydras, near the central business district, broadcast at 800 on the dial with 1,000 watts.[41]

WBOK was the tenth station in the market and used disc jockeys to play "popular and jive type" records as well as hillbilly music. Sunup to sundown found the station broadcasting gospel singers and news, including national reports from the United Press. In addition, the station broadcast church services, musical concerts, civic events, and other important public service programs. Over the years it used the slogans "Sunshine 1230," "Love you can listen to," and "Where the Message is the Music." WBOK branded itself as a multicultural, multi-genre medium. In the 1970s, it was in competition with WYLD, but the two stations nevertheless cooperated on public service events, such as the 1972 Sickle Cell Pledge-A-Thon, which raised more than $27,000, some $2,000 over its goal. In 1983 WBOK changed format from rhythm and blues to full-time gospel interspersed with paid preaching.[42]

The station's disc jockeys and announcers did not escape Winslow's scrutiny. Winslow praised WBOK's air personality John "Honeyboy" Hardy: "Honors for the perfect radio voice goes to 'Honeyboy' Hardy! (WBOK)." He said Hardy did not sound like a hollering Sambo: "Without a trace of 'Sam' in his voice, he handles his announcing like a net-work ace!! . . . (and girls, he's cute, too!!)" Winslow ended his columns with the phrase: "Ever' time . . . Ever' time . . . Ever' *Louisiana Weekly* time."[43]

WMRY would retire its call letters and replace them with WYLD. In December 1957 the FCC approved Robert W. Rounsaville's application to purchase WMRY from Lester Kaman, the principal owner of the holding enterprise, the Southland Broadcasting Company. Rounsaville paid $250,000 for WMRY, changed the station's call letters to WYLD, and used the 600 frequency. On October 17, 1958, it was reported that Rounsaville sold WYLD to Connie B.

Gay for $200,000. Rounsaville acquired WTPS, the radio station owned by the Times-Picayune Publishing Company. On November 30, 1958, WTPS, which used the 940 frequency, transmitted its final programming under the ownership of the *Times-Picayune*. On the next day, Gay moved WYLD from the 600 frequency to the 940 spot. The 600 frequency was granted to a new radio station, WYFE of the Town and Country network which established it studios at 4006 Canal Street and began operation on December 1.[44]

◆ ◆ ◆

Earlier, in July 1948 a *Pittsburgh Courier* commentary had encouraged program directors to broadcast a Negro sports roundup. Sports coverage was about to come forth for the first time in radio that narrowcast to African Americans. Jim Hall was the first announcer. "Jim Hall's Louisiana Weekly Sportscast" was launched October 29, 1949, airing Sundays on WNOE. The next month, WDSU announced it was broadcasting "Negro Sports Roundup," hosted by *Pittsburgh Courier* editor Lucius Jones. WMRY scheduled a fifteen-minute, six-day-a-week sports broadcast beginning May 29, 1950. In July WMRY announced a special series of baseball game broadcasts with announcers Malcolm LaPlace, Tex Stephens, Jim Warren, and Bob Parker. WMRY announced in a July 22 *Weekly* ad that it would cover five days of the National Baseball Congress Games.[45]

WMRY also inaugurated broadcast coverage of home football games hosted by the two local black collegiate institutions, Xavier University and Dillard University. The games started at 2 p.m. on Saturdays. Among their competitors were Alabama State University, Wiley College, Lane College, Tuskegee Institute, Le Moyne College, and Philander Smith College. Malcolm LaPlace announced play-by-play, while Tex provided commentary. Good Citizens Life Insurance Company financed the broadcasts in exchange for advertising time during the broadcasts. Sports broadcasting represented a new direction for the black-aimed medium that previously had focused on civic talk and music.[46]

On May 30, 1959, WYLD teamed with the Indianapolis Motor Speedway Network and broadcast live coverage of the Indianapolis 500 race. Full coverage began at 9:30 a.m. A delayed airing of the time trials was also broadcast.[47] Sports reporting also included professional boxing; however, the coverage was unorthodox. One of the station's announcers, Joe Walker, called the blow-by-blow action of the Ralph Dupas vs. Emile Griffith match. Walker was totally blind and did not attend the Las Vegas fight. He sat in WYLD's control room with a headset on, listening to an announcer who sat on the third row at the arena. Walker repeated with flair what the announcer fed him over a telephone. *Times-Picayune* sports writer Bob Roesler was not impressed: "We listened to the tape Monday . . . the reception was poor, but even poorer was Swan's commentary. Swan, who was at ringside, would go thirty seconds without a word. Walker, therefore, had to ad lib until Swan decided to say anything."[48]

CHAPTER SIX

Some Black Broadcasters Spoke Concerning the Civil Rights Movement

Early black radio broadcasters in New Orleans were unable to protest on air the various forms of inequality African Americans endured. Station owners prohibited them from commenting in earnest or conveying information that suggested advocacy for equal rights. Racism in America was institutionalized, and it plagued blacks nationally. Radio stations, however, were in business to make money, not to make social or political statements.[1] It was the African American press that boldly expanded the black public sphere and advocated for ending segregation and degradation. The US armed forces were among the targets of this effort. To attack discrimination, black newspapers, led by the *Pittsburgh Courier*, established a Double V Campaign, victory for equality for blacks in the United States and victory for democracy abroad. The military prohibited blacks from obtaining the training and placement into positions as infantrymen, pilots, tankers, medics, and officers. Instead, blacks were most often assigned to work in the mess hall as dishwashers or cooks.

During the 1940s and 1950s, the *Louisiana Weekly* published articles and editorials drawing attention to the need locally for better schools, playgrounds, health services, jobs, business opportunities, and integration in the public sector. Black broadcasters would have been immediately fired for such vociferous endorsements. White supremacists threatened domestic terrorism aimed at station operations if disk jockeys were courageous in voicing opposition to injustice. The *Weekly* and other black newspapers could write commentary boldly resisting oppression because financially they were relatively independent. The newspapers received its revenue from blacks who purchased subscriptions, display advertisements, and the sale of individual copies. The *Weekly* charged 7 cents per issue in 1945. Newspaper employees did not have to worry about being fired for espousing pro-black ideology. By no means were the newspapers immune from violence. Racists threatened the *Weekly*, but no physical attacks were carried out.[2]

Black broadcasters faced a very different reality. They generally feared violence from segregationists or were protective of their jobs. They did not want to be fired. Therefore, black radio did not in earnest broadcast news or commentary aiding the struggle, at least not until Larry McKinley arrived at WMRY. It was the first station in the city to target blacks with an entire format of African American programming. The station was four years old when McKinley decided to accept employment there in 1954. He was initially an intern but management quickly hired him, and he worked as an announcer, disc jockey, civil rights reporter, and would become the station's program director. McKinley was only eighteen when he arrived in New Orleans to serve an internship at WMRY in August 1953. The speech and drama major had an ambition to become an actor. At the internship the station manager put him on air at 1:30 a.m. His show was called "Listeners' Choice." He responded to requests from callers to play particular songs. The show included tape-recorded telephone conversations with listeners. He planned to return to Chicago in January and complete his coursework at Roosevelt University and earn an undergraduate degree, but that did not happen. He kept postponing his return until he realized he had become caught up in the traditions of the muggy, riverfront city. Before McKinley realized it, he was calling New Orleans his home: "Yeah, one drink of that Mississippi water and a plate of red beans and rice, and I was hooked. Well Mardi Gras and these very lovely New Orleans ladies had a little bit to do with it too."[3]

At the station, all of his coworkers had full-time jobs, such as auto mechanic or postal worker. None except McKinley had experience in news reporting, so he also took on that responsibility. Shortly thereafter, and since he was the only black staffer with some relevant college credits, management promoted him to program director. McKinley did not tell his colleagues he was a teenager nor did he let much time elapse before further distinguishing himself. One of the first changes he made was to affiliate the station with the new National Negro Network, which featured African American programming. WMRY's first NNN program was the popular soap opera "The Story of Ruth Valentine" starring Juanita Hall. It aired Mondays through Fridays at 11 a.m.[4] In 1954, after four years in business in the black-owned Louisiana Industrial Life building on Dryades Street in midtown, the station moved to 2904–06 Tulane Avenue, near the central business district. A two-hour celebration packed with all-star performers punctuated the move. Among performers were Huey Smith, Ernie K-Doe, Bobby Mitchell, Smiley Lewis, the Xavier University choir, and the New Zion Baptist Church choir.[5]

One of McKinley's most auspicious roles was to announce news and commentary concerning the Civil Rights Movement. Black leaders met to formulate strategies to end segregation in public accommodations and disrupt discrimination in the private sector. They organized rallies, marches, pickets, sit-ins, and various civil disobedience actions. Local and national civil rights figures discussed ending segregated seating on intra-city buses operated by the New Orleans Public Service Inc. Among locals in that struggle were Rev. A. L. Davis, president of the Interdenominational Ministerial Alliance, and medical doctor William R. Adams, president of the New Orleans Improvement League. Organizers established the League to clandestinely stand in the place of the NAACP, which a state court order banned in 1956.[6]

A major push to end segregated seating on New Orleans public buses and streetcars was coming to the Crescent City. The Rev. Dr. Martin Luther King Jr., president of the Montgomery Improvement Association and pastor of the Dexter Avenue Baptist Church in that city, led blacks to a successful conclusion of a 381-day boycott of the Montgomery city buses. The boycott ended December 21, 1956. WMRY reported news of the victory. Local keyboardist Art Neville, who would become a member of the R&B group the Neville Brothers, remembered hearing news reports on WMRY: "I used to be in the kitchen when my mother was cooking and doing something else in the kitchen and this news thing came over the radio that Rosa Parks was arrested because she wouldn't get up to give this white man her seat."[7]

The US Supreme Court, on November 13, 1956, agreed with a lower court, and declared segregated transportation was unconstitutional. Subsequently, Montgomery passed an ordinance permitting African American passengers to sit anywhere on city buses. Blacks in other cities experienced racial segregation in public transportation. One of them was New Orleans. King and associates moved in. On the night of Friday, February 1, 1957, King spoke in the city at the Coliseum Arena at 401 N. Roman Street. McKinley was there. The local United Clubs organized the program, which concerned black New Orleanians' fight against segregated public transportation and its push against racism in general. The United Clubs formed in 1953 and represented four social aid and pleasure clubs, such as the Zulus, Bon Temps, and Plantation Revelers. Membership also included the local musicians' union.

United Clubs changed their focus from purely social activities to include the fight against racism in all of its manifestations. One impetus was Earl K. Long's statement about blacks. Long's second stint as Louisiana governor was from 1956 through 1960. During a stump speech, Long told a white audience that blacks should not enter white society: "Oh yeah. Let me tell you good people something. Niggers got no business in our schools. Why, a hundred years ago they were eatin' each other."[8] For that and other reasons, the non-profit Clubs turned their attention to improving conditions in voter registration, education, recreation, and transportation. In 1957 they organized a boycott of the Mardi Gras season, asked Clubs members to cancel carnival balls, and urged African Americans not to attend parades. They urged blacks to save money typically spent during the Mardi Gras season and instead donate it to a civil rights organization. Publicizing such strategy was off limits to black broadcasters, but not newspapers.[9]

One of the Clubs' initiatives was to bring King to the Crescent City to fire up the black community. King accepted the invitation and his eloquent speech, espousing political involvement, rejuvenated the 2,500 in attendance. His expression of keen observations from an emotional standpoint fired up McKinley.

> We are still confronted in the North with hidden segregation and in the South with glaring segregation. But I say that if Democracy is to live, segregation has to die. It is an evil we must seek to eliminate.... Unfortunately, we are a race that has been betrayed by both the Democrats and the Republicans. The Democrats have betrayed us to the Dixiecrats and the Republicans have betrayed us to the radical northern Republicans. But I tell you we are not going to be a political football any longer. The most decisive step we can make is that walk to the voting booth, and we've got to continue to give big money to the cause of freedom.[10]

The *Louisiana Weekly* and the *Times-Picayune* reported details of the speech, which was McKinley's first major reporting assignment. He listened closely, mesmerized. The message transformed him.[11]

> The tension in the South can be traced to the Negro's determination to suffer, sacrifice and even die if necessary for his freedom. We will be able to see old man segregation come to his death-bed in spite of the fact that many will mourn the passing of dear old brother.[12]

McKinley said he did not remember what King said: "It was just his delivery ... but I just know I left there with goose pimples, and I knew I had to be a part of this."

In the meantime, on February 14, 1957, nearly a hundred leaders of the Movement held a meeting in New Orleans in Central City at New Zion Baptist Church, pastored by the Rev. Abraham Lincoln Davis Jr. Organizers called on the forty-two-year-old Davis to accept the position as chairman of a new organization formed a month earlier in Atlanta called the Southern Leadership Conference on Transportation and Nonviolent Integration. Davis declined, saying the organization needed a younger leader. King, who was twenty-eight, was elected, and the group shortened the name to the Southern Christian Leadership Conference. Tex Stephens, who was a disc jockey and also presenting news at WMRY, said he was at the meeting at New Zion, sat next to King, and interviewed him. The station broadcast the interview. Tex also wrote a story about his talk with King and regularly contributed news and a column to the *Louisiana Weekly*.[13]

King's speech so moved McKinley that he wanted to join the Movement. He found leaders of the local branch of the national civil rights organization the Congress of Racial Equality. Representatives told him to come to a meeting at 7 p.m. at the office of the law firm Collins, Douglas, and Eli. They said he would be interviewed to determine whether they would allow him to participate in the sit-ins, pickets, and other types of demonstrations. McKinley arrived at the office and sat in one of the wooden folding chairs which were neatly arranged in rows. He waited and waited. He was the only person in the room and thought he arrived too early. The law firm was a half block from the former studio of WMRY on Dryades Street. As McKinley waited, growing impatient, a white man silently entered the room behind McKinley and hit him hard on the side of his head. "Bam. I mean, really slapped the piss out of me." The man hit him several more times and knocked McKinley out of his chair and onto the floor. "Nigger, get out of here." McKinley jumped up and grabbed him. "It was my Chicago coming out. I was grabbing, so they broke it up."[14]

One of the CORE representatives said, "'No Larry. We can't use you. You would get somebody killed if you reacted like that. And that's what's going to happen. But here's where you can help us. Go on the air. We'll feed you stuff. You relay it to the public.' And that's how I served."[15] McKinley failed the test but maintained tremendous respect for the civil rights workers who engaged in the dangerous activities. They had to act with dignified discipline. While McKinley operated as a subtle broadcast messenger of the affairs of local civil rights leadership, he also conducted original reporting from the field, covering sit-ins and other demonstrations. One such field report was of a meeting of the Orleans Parish School Board as it ruminated school integration.[16]

As the late 1950s and early 1960s arrived, McKinley somewhat tenuously captured the lead in civil rights commentary on air. The historical record is quiet about exactly what other black personalities said on air during the Civil Rights Movement as it played out in New Orleans. At best, it is known that disc jockey Vernon Winslow, aka Dr. Daddy-O, directly remarked on air about protesters participating in sit-ins. Tex Stephens reported activities such as a conversation with King and events of the extraction of a civil rights foot solider from City Hall, and James "Okey Dokey" Smith of WBOK talked about some of the events and issues concerning the Movement.

Mort Silverman, WMRY's general manager, gave McKinley a measure of freedom to announce civil rights news and commentary, which were mostly informative, telling the public the location of marches and sit-ins and some details of what happened. Nevertheless, no indication surfaced suggesting he told his audience how to interpret events and issues. Some of the information aired came from conducting interviews of participants in the marches and sit-ins. Civil rights leaders did not ask him to solicit over the air individuals to join their organizations. "I was never asked to tell people, don't fight, don't do this, don't do that. If you recruit over the air, you don't know what you're going to get."[17] The leaders were very selective in terms of who they took in as members, as McKinley witnessed.

McKinley attended several events concerning the cause for integration. One was a meeting of the Orleans Parish School Board. The members discussed whether to integrate grades kindergarten through high school. Specifically, the purpose of the June 20, 1960, meeting was to determine what to do concerning James Skelly Wright's desegregation plan. Wright was a liberal judge at the US District Court for the Eastern District of Louisiana. A month earlier he ruled that the schools must be integrated by September, but the school system challenged the order. A raucous overflow crowd showed up at the modest-sized room at the school board building. To accommodate more spectators, the board moved the meeting to the nearby auditorium of Rabouin High School at 727 Carondelet Street. At the auditorium, segregationists hollered and booed while a small group of white parents cheered as board president Lloyd Rittner read a letter from the Archbishop Joseph Rummell of the New Orleans archdiocese: "The moderate form of gradual integration proposed by Judge Wright is a sound temperate interpretation of the American way of life and, incidentally of the Christian way of life."[18] Rittner read a few other letters from pastors at small congregations that also asked the board not to close the schools to avoid desegregation.

McKinley was fully aware of the issue. At the time, Orleans Parish operated two separate public school systems. African American students outnumbered whites, who disproportionally attended private and parochial schools. The school system dragged its feet, failing to introduce a procedure for desegregation. Instead, Wright put forward a plan. Starting in September, parents of first grade students would be able to enroll their children in any school in the city regardless of race. Young children were color-blind, Wright intimated. In 1961 the second-graders would also be able to enroll in any school near their homes. The system would apply to one grade every year until all grades were integrated.[19]

McKinley never made it inside of the Rabouin auditorium. It was too crowded, but he stood outside tape recording and observing. Thongs of people were in front of the auditorium shouting obscenities and vitriol against school integration. US marshals in riot gear stood like a chain-link fence arm in arm between the mob and the building. Two of the marshals were black. A white guy was standing in the crowd shouting at one of the black officers: "Hey, Nigger this, and talking about the marshal. Yeah, you know, blah, blah, blah." The crowd gradually surged forward. The white guy was getting closer and closer to the where one of the black marshals stood. McKinley found the vociferous white spectator amusing. "I was laughing because he didn't realize he was getting closer and closer, and he was yeah, yeah, yeah. Next thing you know he's looking this guy eyeball-to-eyeball, and he wacked him." McKinley, catching environmental sound from the crowd, saw the black marshal hit the white guy. "The marshal took like a little slapjack; I guess they call them, you know, the little, not a billy, like a billy club but it was small, and hit him, hit him like about five times, bap, bap, bap, bap. Like nailed him. And then he reached around and grabbed hands again and just formed that link again."[20]

McKinley also reported the affairs of the collaboration among the Urban League, NAACP, the Consumers League, and CORE, among other groups challenging the racist status quo. During the 1960s, local civil rights leaders such as Oretha Castle Haley, Revius Ortique, and Ernest "Dutch" Morial met weekly at the Dooky Chase's Restaurant on Orleans Avenue. They discussed strategies to advance voter registration and other approaches to combat injustices. Don Hubbard, a CORE foot soldier and movement organizer, attended the meetings: "And so we met and we planned the strategy, and McKinley would take the strategy and bring that strategy to the minds of black people as to what was going on, how we should participate, and what the next move was." Before then, Hubbard was a member of the NAACP youth council, but moved to CORE because the NAACP was too conservative. It preferred to file lawsuits to dismantle segregation instead of focusing on street protests. The white print media and Caucasians broadcasters most often framed protesters as unruly. Therefore, black announcers were supremely important, because civil rights leaders did not communicate with their constituents through mass mailings. "There would be no civil rights movement with any success if we didn't coordinate with black radio and the black press," according to Hubbard.[21]

Dooky Chase restaurant was a meeting place and respite for nationally known movement stalwarts who visited the city during of the 1960s. It was one of perhaps two white-tablecloth, black-owned restaurants in the city. Andrew Young, Thurgood Marshall, Ralph Abernathy, and Martin Luther

King were among the visitors. McKinley allowed the national and local leaders to talk on air concerning their activities.

New Orleans had a rather unique civil rights leadership structure compared to other cities during the period. African American New Orleanians sometimes divided themselves into two camps, light-skinned and dark-skinned blacks. Joseph Logsdon and Caryn Cosse Bell termed it "cultural duality."[22] Historically, the light-skinned blacks, called Creoles, were born in Louisiana by way of miscegenation between white men of French or Spanish origin and African women, who were initially enslaved or daughters of free people of color. Sometimes a slave owner, who procreated with an enslaved woman, would free her and their children from bondage. Some Creoles had physical features of whites, such as a light skin tone and straight hair. Some were mistaken as being Caucasian. In the early 1800s, the Civil Code prohibited the enslaved from marrying free persons of color.[23] Nevertheless, later Creoles sometimes acted as intermediaries between the white and African American communities. Creoles often communicated across racial lines because the city's white leadership respected them more than the dark-skinned leaders. In other situations, some Creoles were able to be in the presence of whites discussing pro-segregation rhetoric. Those inclined would pass along the information to the darker leadership brethren. Creoles typically did not immediately embrace direct action to change racist laws and customs. Instead, they favored lawsuits, such as filings against segregation of the Orleans Parish School System. The renowned local NAACP attorney Alexander Pierre Tureaud Sr. was one of the Creoles who preferred to file lawsuits against racist impediments.

Fundamentally, dark-skinned African Americans were procreated from the union of enslaved Africans. They did not evolve from the union of a white man and a black woman and had no chance of being mistaken as white. African Americans lacked access to the advantages available to some Creoles or free persons of color, such as manumission of mother and/or child, access to trade and academic institutions, wealth accumulation, and financial support from white fathers to their mixed-race children. During the period of enslavement, the darker blacks' principal duties were to pick cotton or other crops grown on a planation. They performed mostly unskilled labor. Blacks were denied opportunities to attend formal educational institutions, unlike some Creoles. It was illegal to teach blacks how to read. Slave owners in urban places such as New Orleans allowed the enslaved with marketable skills to spend their days working off-site. They would earn money that would go to their owner. Creoles occupied more skilled jobs such as metalworking.

During the movement, darker blacks were more likely to advocate and engage in public demonstrations of opposition to discrimination. They were more likely than Creoles to march, picket, boycott, and attend rallies. Nevertheless, both public protests and legal battles attacked the core of unequal legal protection. Work of rights victories were often communicated by way of churches, leaflets, students, and the black press. Some reports were broadcast on radio specifically meant to inform blacks.

McKinley told black listeners where meetings would occur, such as at New Zion Baptist Church that evening or at Greater St. Baptist Church tomorrow morning. Some of the news he reported came from the pages of the black press, such as the *Weekly* and the local section of the *Pittsburgh Courier*. Once he made a veiled threat directed to white New Orleanians: "Well our kids are going to be at Woolworth sitting in today ya know. And I would hope that our white brothers and sisters don't put their hands on our kids."[24]

Once, disc jockey Winslow talked directly to his black listeners about demonstrators who participated in an action. In the early 1960s, in his articulate baritone voice, he had the effect of calming the nerves of parents and others who were worried about the safety of the protesters. Don Hubbard recalled Dr. Daddy-O would say, "Ohhh let me play this number here for the young people who are involved. You know our young people sat in today at Woolworth. Oh no, no, no there was no incident. You know they were just sitting in for the right thing. Nobody got hurt."[25]

New Orleans R&B recording vocalist Irma Thomas, who began her career during the period, had a positive take on civil rights reports. She said news reports were not limited to a few select air personalities: "They all did. . . . In the 50s and 60s, especially the late 50s and early 60s, all the DJs who did the record spins also did the news, and whatever news that was to be told, as far as the Civil Rights Movement, was done by all the jocks because they didn't have a newsman per se."[26] Local and national news were included among the programming of radio stations geared toward blacks, but the reports were likely snippets taken from black newspapers, news syndicates, and wire services. The record did not indicate a widespread distribution of civil rights news locally.

McKinley interviewed movement foot soldiers, activists who risked personal safety by occupying whites-only public accommodations and engaging in other civil disobedience. McKinley let demonstrators tell their stories on air and announce their next meetings. He also played inspirational music and messages suggesting that change was coming. Jerome Smith, one of the young co-founders of the New Orleans chapter of the Congress of Racial Equality, sat through several of the interviews. The local CORE unit duplicated the sit-in tactics of four students in Greensboro, North Carolina, who on February 1, 1960, initiated a gambit that activists employed throughout the South. The young people sat on stools at lunch counter restaurants and refused to leave despite employees declining service. The New Orleans CORE unit duplicated the maneuver. Local police officers arrested Smith and his fellow protesters on several occasions. One arrest occurred in September 1960 during a sit-in at the F.W. Woolworth's store at the corner of Canal and N. Rampart.[27]

In May 1961 Smith visited McKinley at the WYLD studio after participating in the Freedom Riders campaign, during which sixteen African Americans and whites rode on Trailways and Greyhound buses starting in Washington, D.C., with the intention of traveling to New Orleans. They were testing the Supreme Court's ruling in *Boyton v. Virginia*, which said racial segregation on interstate buses and rail cars was unconstitutional. The trip began on May 4 and was to end on May 17. The buses never made it to New Orleans. Ku Klux Klansmen organized other hate groups to stop the demonstration. In Birmingham and Anniston, Alabama, they viciously beat the riders and burned the buses. The group made it to New Orleans by airplane. After the beating, Smith visited the radio station. They talked on air: "He came into the station . . . head bandaged, jaw broken, arm broken, and head twice the size of his normal size. And that's just one incident."[28]

In September 1961, the police arrested Smith and five other CORE members for refusing to end their picket on the sidewalk at the rear of Woolworth and McCrory stores on Iberville Street. They were protesting the practice of not serving blacks at their lunch counters. McKinley covered several such challenges, but he did not witness any violence against blacks. "I didn't see any, a lot of violence here. Lots of noise, but not any physical violence, even at the lunch counters. There were a lot of demonstrations, but I didn't see a lot of bloodshed here."[29]

On September 30, 1963, the black press, and atypically the mainstream press, covered a massive march that flowed through Central City. The white press at the time most often portrayed demonstrators as troublemakers, but not this time. There was no indication that black broadcasters were present; however, some likely were. A. L. Davis, Lolis Elie, Avery Alexander, and Oretha Castle Haley were among organizers leading 10,000 marchers from Shakespeare Park to City Hall, approximately two miles. With the cool blue sky darkening as dusk made it presence, the procession extending eight blocks was punctuated by a lone marcher carrying an American flag at the front of the calm, slowly moving mass of humanity. Placards reading "We Shall Overcome" and "This Little Light of Mine" were sprinkled here and there.[30]

At some Movement events, McKinley and Stephens said they tape-recorded speeches, broadcast the information along with observations, and provided commentary. Stephens said on some occasions, when a protest occurred downtown near WYLD, he would cover the action and run to the station to get his report aired. One of his most notable dispatches was from a demonstration at City Hall. Reporters from radio, television, and print outlets captured audio, video, and still photographs of a spectacular scene of police brutality against Rev. Avery Alexander who, with CORE members, sat in at the City Hall whites-only cafeteria. Stephens went on air drawing attention to the October 31, 1963, demonstration. Stephens said in an interview that a cafeteria worker refused to serve the group and told Alexander, "'I don't serve niggas,'" Alexander replied, "'I don't eat niggas. I want food.'"[31] Police officers ordered the protesters to leave, but they refused. CORE member Doris Jean Castle was one of the protesters who did not move from her chair. Infamous photographs published in newspapers showed four officers carrying her out of City Hall, each holding one leg of the chair. The officers used the same method to remove Sondra Nixon who was also African American. But Alexander was a big black man. Officers wrestled him to the floor. Two of them each grabbed one of Alexander's ankles and in unison dragged him as he lied on his back. They dragged him up a flight of stairs from the basement cafeteria, through the lobby, and down the steps of the front of City Hall. Alexander's head bumped several of the steps and his back was severely injured. They stuffed him in the back of a police vehicle.[32]

CHAPTER SEVEN

Entertainment Content Required on Black-Focused Radio

In the 1960s, US Supreme Court decisions invalidated several state and local laws requiring the separation of blacks and whites in public places. Among key decisions were the 1962 finalization of a previous decision outlawing racial segregation in interstate and intrastate transportation facilities. In 1964 the Court prohibited white businesses from racially segregating places of public accommodation, such as restaurants and hotels. In 1968 it made housing discrimination illegal in the public and private sectors. More progressive decisions were announced, each finding that segregationist public policy violated the US Constitution's provisions for equal legal protection. Details are widely published concerning the roles played by the Rev. Dr. Martin Luther King Jr. and his organization, the Southern Christian Leadership Conference, as well as the Congress of Racial Equality, the Student Nonviolent Coordinating Committee, the National Association for the Advancement of Colored People, and the Urban League, among others engaging in strategic activities to end racial segregation and other injustices. In New Orleans black on-air radio messengers played a significant yet mixed role in advocating nonviolence and issues of morality and constitutionality regarding how the power structure treated African Americans.

◆ ◆ ◆

As King's popularity approached a pentacle in the mid-1960s, the voices of black opinion leaders were increasingly needed. After his murder in Memphis on April 4, 1968, civil revolts erupted in 126 cities nationwide. No riots occurred in New Orleans. Only one or two instances of minor arson were reported to the press.[1] African American broadcasters in New Orleans were not directly responsible. Other factors included broadcast information suppression, conservative leaders, and unusual housing patterns. Broadcasters at

WYLD and WBOK did contribute a calming effect in the wake of the assassination. The stations interrupted regular programming and played gospel music and hymns. Announcers implored listeners to remain peaceful. They asked people to ruminate on the nonviolent rhetoric King championed during struggles for racial equality. Announcers referred to King as a "gentle lamb."[2]

Collusion, however, between local broadcast management and law enforcers as well as self-censorship contributed to the nonviolence. Broadcasters suppressed the spread of news of civil disobedience playing out across the country. New Orleans police officers visited television newsrooms and asked managers not to televise the uprisings. The stations blacked out the news so that local African Americans would not mimic the riots.[3] Moving pictures were more powerful at communicating traumatic events than audio, yet radio had its power. A St. Louis news director at radio station WIL said he ignored network reports in order to avoid copycats. He did not want "kids running around with transistor radios" duplicating the disturbances.[4]

In New Orleans, eyewitness Edwin Lombard, who headed the Voter Education Project in 1967, surmised that opinion leaders needed to be sincere to effectively articulate messages to the masses.[5] Some of the rhetoric from opinion leaders against a violent response to the murder appeased whites and demonstrated that African Americans were not a threat. Conservative black leaders, who had more to lose than young hotheads, were among those speaking to the power structure on behalf of blacks. Included among intermediaries were podiatrist Dr. Leonard Burns, attorney A. P. Tureaud, Dillard University president Albert Dent, and the Rev. A. L. Davis. In this case, opinion leaders needed channels to distribute messages widely and immediately. Broadcast radio could do so, but it did not happen to any major extent in New Orleans in the mid- to late 1960s.

Structural realities such as housing patterns also contributed to the relative calm. The city had one of the largest percentages of black homeownership in the country.[6] Blacks would not burn down their own property. The widely dispersed communities of blacks in the city were in contrast to housing patterns in other cities in which unrest materialized, where blacks were clustered into dense ghettos. In 1960, 223,344 blacks lived in New Orleans, representing roughly 37 percent of the 627,525 total population.[7] During the 1960s blacks gradually crept into the once segregated public housing projects, while whites began moving to affordable residences in working-class suburbs. Thousands upon thousands of the city's poorest blacks migrated to the ten mega-projects spread throughout the city.[8] Black broadcasters in New Orleans had the luxury of several factors contributing to the absence of riots.

The radio experiences of blacks in New Orleans in the 1960s, colored by repressive state and local laws, differed only slightly from those in counterpart cities elsewhere in the South. Birmingham represents a convenient comparison. The extent of segregation in a locality affected radio commentary. In both places, racist state laws were the principal rationale segregationists used for subjugating blacks. Louisiana state laws on segregation were a tad less restrictive than Alabama's. Louisiana codified segregation in transportation, hospitals, prisons, cemeteries, schools, and hotels. Blacks could not marry whites, and racist customs impregnated segregation in parks, theaters, restaurants and other places of public accommodations. Alabama state law in addition prohibited integrated libraries, churches, and residential areas. Alabama outlawed blacks from serving on juries and engaging in intimacy with whites.[9]

During the Civil Rights Movement, there typically was not very much difference in reports conveyed by announcers in the two cities. Protest leaders in both cities employed similar actions: sit-ins, boycotts, rallies, and marches. Birmingham foot soldiers, however, met much more brutality from homegrown terrorists, police officers, and firemen. To stop child-marchers, firefighters turned on powerful water hoses, fierce enough to tear bark off of trees, and aimed them at the protesters, sweeping some of them off their feet. The police employed aggressive dogs to intimidate blacks and send messages that segregation was supreme. In New Orleans, the police and fire department were not as brutal.

Based at the Gray Hotel in downtown Bessemer, a small city some ten miles west of Birmingham, WJLD initiated a regular gospel music show in 1943, approximately one year after the station's launch.[10] WJLD changed its format to all-black content in 1954 and became the first Birmingham-area station to devote all programming to African Americans.[11] In the 1950s WENN in Birmingham broadcast a regular diet of religious radio. In New Orleans, broadcasters did not play much gospel before 1950 when WMRY reconfigured into the city's first station with all-black programming. The first black show, the "Religious Forum of the Air," began as a talk show on WNOE in 1946.

Air personalities in Birmingham in the 1950s and 1960s showed little inclination of obvious support on air for the demonstrations of leaders such as the Rev. Fred Shuttlesworth and his Alabama Christian Movement for Human Rights.[12] In comparison, some New Orleans black broadcasters spoke on air to whites, saying no one must not harm the CORE young people who sat in at lunch counters in the early 1960s. McKinley implored the "white brothers and sisters" not to touch the young protesters. Vernon Winslow also voiced on-air support for the CORE demonstrators.

Prevalent in both cities were on-air black creative linguistics. Some deejays rapped at machine-gun speed, rhyming and chiming words, and busting clever sayings, sometimes while a record was playing. However, there was a class of air personalities who took a different route, one of refined articulation and smooth delivery. Beginning in 1949, New Orleans's Dr. Daddy-O, presented himself on air as an educated, self-controlled, silky baritone. Later, Tex Stephens developed a distinctive voice with a beautiful bass intonation. In the early 1950s, Eddie Castleberry and Jesse Champion in Birmingham eschewed the flamboyant style and adopted the persona of Jack L. Cooper, the preeminent Chicago talk show host in 1929 who migrated his polished vernacular to the airways.[13]

In terms of journalists, Larry McKinley distinguished himself as a newsman and commentator, while George "Tex" Stephens also covered civil rights activities in the city. In Birmingham air personalities Paul "Tall Paul" White and the Rev. Erskine Faush were among those who reported local movement news.

◆ ◆ ◆

The integration of African Americans into radio between 1945 and 1950 provided a potential market for a movement resulting in establishing a small number of black radio networks nationally. This led to radio offering a fuller array of discourse, entertainment, news, and other programming created and consumed by blacks. As early as 1954, Leon Evans founded the short-lived National Negro Network. He also published the African American radio trade magazine *Tuesday*. NNN's syndicated programs included news and the black soap operas "The Story of Ruby Valentine" and "The Life of Anna Lewis." The network also distributed variety shows with entertainers such as Cab Calloway and Ethel Waters. A total of fifty radio stations nationwide with black-oriented formats purchased bargain-basement subscriptions. It proved not enough, and the undercapitalized operation soon shut down.[14]

In the 1970s, two black national radio networks entered the field, the Mutual Black Network in 1972 and the National Black Network in 1973. At that time, there were approximately twenty-two black-owned radio stations in the United States, less than 1 percent of the more than seven thousand white-owned stations.[15] NBN produced and distributed programs including "NBN Shorts," a woman's program; "Night Talk," a late-night call-in program; "NBN Stage Door," a feature on black entertainers; and "One Black Man's

Opinion," social and political commentary hosted by journalist Roy Wood. By 1988 the network had ninety-four affiliates nationally.[16]

◆ ◆ ◆

In the South in the post–World War II era, it was not common for radio station executives to sell time to African Americans to produce programs placing blacks in a positive light. Just as rare were white-owned businesses that purchased airtime to sell their goods or services on programs produced by blacks. Nationally, in the mid-1940s only sixteen African Americans were air personalities among approximately three thousand white disc jockeys.[17] In New Orleans in the late 1940s, Vernon Winslow joined the cadre as a disc jockey on WWEZ, making him the first regular black jock in the city. The Fitzgerald Advertising Agency hired him because of his expertise in marketing, sales, and knowledge of the spending habits of African Americans.[18] Winslow exclusively marketed Jax beer made by the Jackson Brewery. In the early 1950s, African Americans sold advertising time to local black entrepreneurs operating life insurance companies, drug stores, funeral homes, restaurants, hotels, taxicab companies, and other businesses operating in a segregated milieu.[19] Among mainstream businesses that advertised their wares on programs targeting blacks beginning in the early to mid-1950s were the sellers and makers of food products, household goods, packaged drugs, and appliances, among others.

The evolving sophistication that African American advertising agents brought to commercial radio was a factor leading to black consumer acceptance of sales pitches. For example, in the North, David Sullivan, an advertising agent in the mid-1940s, who was previously advertising manager for the New York *Amsterdam Star-News*, advised white agencies of what to do and not do when approaching black consumers. For example, Sullivan advised the use of grammatically correct English in ads and avoiding dialect such as "yas suh," "dem," or "dat." In another case, Pabst beer in 1941 in Harlem hired William B. Graham to increase sales among blacks. Graham talked to bar owners and patrons asking for their opinion of Pabst beer. They held no particular views regarding the beer. Graham's suggestion to hire black salesmen and marketers increased beer sales. To maintain the success, as did Jax beer in New Orleans, the company sponsored an entertainment radio show hosted by an African American.[20]

◆ ◆ ◆

In the meantime, in 1962 WBOK in New Orleans changed its broad-appeal music format. It became the second local radio station that specifically targeted African Americans. Nevertheless, the station did not broadcast civil rights news nearly as much as WYLD, according to Hubbard. When news was heard on WBOK, disc jockey James "Okey Dokey" Smith was usually making such announcements.[21] A 1962 WBOK program schedule in the *Times-Picayune* says it broadcast news on Sundays from 6:55 a.m. to 7 a.m. and from 10:25 a.m. to 10:30 a.m. The station devoted time specifically to announce the results of athletic competition on Sundays from 10 a.m. to 10:25 a.m. Otherwise disc jockeys played records from 6 a.m. to 5:50 p.m. Mondays through Saturdays and 6:55 a.m. to 5:30 p.m. Sundays. Spirituals were heard Mondays through Saturdays from 6 a.m. to 6:30 a.m. and 10 a.m. to 11 a.m. On Sundays, the station broadcast religious programs during four segments: 7 a.m. to 8:30 a.m., 8:45 a.m. to 10 a.m., 11 a.m. to 1:15 p.m., and 4 p.m. to 5 p.m.[22]

♦ ♦ ♦

In terms of national programming, WYLD broadcast two weekly fifteen-minute shows in 1965 produced by Sherwood Ross, the news director of the National Urban League. One of the shows, "The Leaders Speak," contained audio of Ross interviewing prominent spokespersons such as Bayard Rustin, an advisor to Martin Luther King Jr.; Whitney M. Young Jr., head of the NUL; Roy Wilkins, executive director of the NAACP; and Cleveland Robinson of the Negro American Labor Council. Ross also wrote the "Civil Rights Roundup," which WYLD carried, but Pat Connell of WCBS in New York City voiced the information regarding activities of the front-running organizations. Scripts extolled stories of national politics and local controversies. A June 8 script, for example, reported on President Lyndon Johnson's pro–equal rights speech at Howard University; the newly created federal commission on equal employment; the Deacons of Defense, which advocated that blacks use firearms to protect themselves from violence by white terrorists; a strike by cotton workers at a Leland, Mississippi, planation; and summaries of other relevant national issues and events.[23]

The Urban League shows represented the first time a major civil rights organization created its own radio programs for nationwide syndication to African American broadcasters. By 1965 more than seventy-five stations across the country, including the South, aired the shows. The NUL distributed the shows to its local branches on 33 1/3 rpm records. The league had agreed with the Audio Recording and Manufacturing Company to produce at least a thirteen-week series of the shows. However, Ross informed Vince

Mallardi, president of Audio Recording, that the broadcasts had been indefinitely postponed after producing eleven shows. Mallardi was not pleased. His company had already stocked the materials necessary to complete the agreement. He wrote Guichard Parris, the director of public relations at the NUL, calling on the League to produce the remaining two programs. Parris replied saying the postponement of the productions was temporary and would last only a few weeks.[24]

◆ ◆ ◆

In 1970 there were sixteen black-owned stations in the United States. The number increased to fifty-six in 1976 and eighty-eight in 1980. Nevertheless, black-owned stations accounted for only 1 percent of the country's radio stations.[25] Inequality did not stop with black radio station ownership. For example, WYLD, when it was purchased by Inter Urban Broadcasting, found itself the leading station among listeners but had to fight for commensurate advertising. Black ownership of a radio station hit New Orleans in 1980 when James Hutchinson, a tall, stocky black man who was a former football lineman at Dartmouth College, purchased a part ownership of WYLD-AM and the 100,000-watt WYLD 98.5-FM. Hutchinson was the executive vice-president of Inter Urban Broadcasting, an African American firm based in Chicago. Inter Urban owned six other radio stations nationwide. Hutchinson moved to New Orleans and continued operating with an all-black staff. The format included adult black music hits, news, and commentary. Besides promoting African American artists, the station aired grievances from the public and sometimes advocated for change. New Orleans had a 55 percent black population. Beginning in 1982, WYLD maintained the highest listenership in the city and continued its lead for the next four years. Its audience rating was 16 percent in the summer of 1986.[26]

Despite occupying the summit of the rating statistics in the city, WYLD's AM and FM stations earned revenue of approximately $5 million annually, which was $500,000 to $1 million less than similarly rated white stations, Hutchison said.[27] White advertisers, including computer companies, suburban shopping malls, and Japanese electronics companies, would not purchase time on the WYLD stations. Some white companies also shunned advertising nationally on black radio stations.

Kofi Ofori suggested reasons. Ofori is the former director of research for the Civil Rights Forum and Communications Policy. According to his report, "When Being Number One is Not Enough: The Impact of Advertising Practices on Minority-Owned & Minority-Formatted Broadcast Stations," certain firms think blacks cannot afford their products, and therefore limit advertisements on stations targeting black consumers. "When it comes to delivering prospects not suspects, the urban stations deliver the largest amount of listeners who turn out to be the least likely to purchase. Very young and very, very poor qualitative profile."[28]

Those who purchased commercials on WYLD wanted to pay less than they paid white stations with the same or similar ratings. Delta Airlines, which previously advertised on WYLD, discontinued because it said the station's rates were too high. Delta maintained a separate black advertising budget. The station management lobbied Delta and when that did not work, complained to the Federal Communications Commission. Subsequently, WYLD reduced its advertising rates, Delta eliminated its black budget, and the airline resumed purchasing commercial time.

Yet success brings competition. A local white radio station, WQUE-FM, aggressively sought WYLD listeners in the mid-1980s. WQUE hired a mostly black on-air staff of seven and maintained two whites. It marketed itself as playing nonstop music. No news. No talk. No commentary. It included rap among its playlist but no rock or other white-oriented music. WQUE also spent money on promotions such as a $1,000-a-day giveaway and a $5,000 Scavenger Hunt. The station purchased a $54,000 mobile broadcasting booth built like a giant portable radio, which it set up and blasted at promotional events around the city. The tactics worked. In just over a year, by the fall of 1987, WQUE attracted the city's largest audience, nearly 16 percent of black listeners, while WYLD's percentage fell to nine.[29]

In the meantime, blacks increasingly turned their attention to entertainment shows on broadcast television, satellite television, and cable. Growing black participation in an expanded economy contributed to less need for civil rights and other progressive information, particularly among sixteen- to twenty-two-year-old blacks, who wanted music and other mediated entertainment. Nevertheless, WYLD decided it was going to have a news team offering socially and politically conscious information and commentary on the issues of the day. Major civil rights activities were not being championed in the 1970s and 1980s in the city.

◆ ◆ ◆

Before then, revolutionary Robert Williams said radio must have a major entertainment component to reach African Americans. Williams, from Union County, North Carolina, opposed the NAACP's stand on nonviolence. As early as 1959, before the Black Panther Party, Williams said black people must use deadly force to defend themselves from the Ku Klux Klan and other white hate groups. The NAACP kicked him out of the local branch. After being wrongly accused of kidnapping, Williams fled to Cuba in 1961 and broadcast Radio Free Dixie, a thirty-minute radical program aimed at African Americans. During one broadcast, he said, "Our people must stop allowing themselves to be beaten like common dogs in streets. We will never receive protection until we return violence for violence."[30] He said blacks tuned in to a particular radio station or their favorite air personalities in the mid-1960s to mid-1970s because audiences sought access mostly to entertainment. African Americans tuned in to radio first to be entertained, to hear popular soul, rhythm and blues, and jazz. They were likely to "recoil from an unrelieved diet of social documentaries, political treaties, news reports, and calls to arms—figuratively and literally—if they were not offered within an entertaining context."[31]

CONCLUSION

Black broadcasters squeezed onto the airways information that was socially, culturally, and morally relevant to the nonviolent approach to the struggle. No overt political communiqués were evident, such as from black nationalists or others not subscribing to a turn-the-other-cheek philosophy. Then, it was revealing but not surprising that once again segregationists believed whites were supreme, and Caucasians who were liberal tactically augmented segregation. This study made it clearer that blacks historically had to form their own organizations and businesses to serve their needs. Otherwise African Americans had to wait for whites to decide when to allow blacks opportunities to pursue the American dream. Black emergence in radio in New Orleans seemed altruistic but instead was profit-driven and political. WNOE station owner James Noe sought FCC approval to expand his market. He also ran for governor in 1956.

Blacks in the city in the 1940s could hardly afford to purchase radio sets. Perhaps African American businessmen in the city did not believe radio station ownership was a good investment. Be that as it may, it was not until 1949 that a black man, Jesse B. Blayton Sr., amassed enough capital to invest in the purchase of a radio station in Atlanta. He was the first in the nation. In general, blacks had to wait for federal law or court rulings to prod state legislators into allowing African Americans to enter the social, political, and economic mainstream.

Announcers such as Jack L. Cooper at WCAP in the late 1920s in Washington, D.C., and Hal Jackson at radio station WINX in the late 1930, also in Washington, had to use subterfuge to air their programming. For example, Jackson pretended his proposed show was sponsored by a white business. The station managers in Washington considered Cooper's and Jackson's shows as having the potential to immediately increase revenue.

In New Orleans, O. C. W. Taylor instead was a part of an organization that appealed to WNOE owner James Noe who saw future profit from integrating his station. Noe gave Taylor, without charge, a weekly fifteen-minute time slot on Sunday mornings. Instead of using the time to play gospel or spirituals, Taylor eased into the time slot by scheduling men of the cloth to talk about issues such as the relevance of the Bible to contemporary problems facing blacks. One of his topics on the "Religious Forum of the Air," later changed to the "Negro Forum," was "Juvenile Delinquency: What the Bible Says About It and What the Church is Doing About It." Taylor was a pragmatist. He said, although black people were very religious, he was not. Taylor programmed topics that would attract blacks and appease station management.

The "Forum" initially seemed as though Taylor was looking through the lens of the *Black Bourgeoisie*, a book by sociologist E. Franklyn Frazier published in 1957. Frazier said the old middle-class blacks who began emerging in the middle to late 1800s showcased their marginal successes masquerading as exceptional achievements. They had strong cultural and community traditions such as fraternities, debutante balls, and the display of conspicuous consumption. The pretensions attempted to place them on a pedestal above blacks living through widespread underachievement. Frazier said the bourgeois class was living in "a world of make-believe" trying to imitate whites who would not accept them. He also threw darts at black publications, such as *Ebony* magazine, for overstating the successes of African American businesses and other endeavors. Any pretense of respectability no matter how slight gained more recognition in black publications than warranted.[1]

Taylor's broadcast content also featured blacks who were successful in business, the clergy, or a civic organization. His content, however, commanded a different meaning. Taylor gave black leaders the opportunity to talk, such as the Rev. A. L. Davis, who in 1957 was nominated to lead the Southern Christian Leadership Congress but declined, to make way for the younger Dr. King. Among other categories of notable guests were professionals such as print journalist John E. Rousseau Jr., editor of the *New Orleans Informer*, and entrepreneur Dr. Rivers Fredericks, chief surgeon at Flint-Goodridge Hospital and president and principal stockholder of the Louisiana Industrial Life Insurance Company. Taylor's guests not only talked about their individual and organizational successes, they discussed problems affecting black communities and approaches to solutions. Other than the *Louisiana Weekly*, the Louisiana edition of the *Pittsburgh Courier*, and other local black publications, no other mass media outlets existed that presented a platform that highlighted accomplished African Americans whose intent was to uplift the underprivileged.

Taylor entered radio without having to hide his Afrocentricity and pretend he represented a white interest, unlike other pioneers such as Cooper and Jackson. Taylor and other major New Orleans air personalities, such as disc jockey Vernon "Dr. Daddy-O" Winslow, announcer and newsman Larry McKinley, and record spinner and reporter George "Tex" Stephens were hired precisely because they were black. Winslow's proven sales abilities attracted

WWEZ, McKinley's broadcasting knowledge and skills attracted WMRY and WYLD, and Stephens's voice, knowledge of jazz, and potential to sell commercials attracted WJBW.

◆ ◆ ◆

In 1946 and 1947 no advertisements were heard on the "Forum." No evidence surfaced indicating that black-owned businesses or organizations brought time on the "Negro Forum." Indeed, the program was made possible by the political interest of the WNOE management. The "Forum" was the only regularly programmed show in Louisiana meant for a black audience.

The first black commercial sponsorship of an African American radio program came in October 1948. A caption in the *Louisiana Weekly* announced Monarch Life Insurance Company would produce a weekly news and sports broadcast aired on WNOE. It is not surprising. Monarch was an affiliate of the International Longshoremen's Association, Local 1419, one of the country's largest black unions. Black life insurance companies were among the largest and most profitable black-owned businesses in the nation. That distinction applied to New Orleans as well, where sixteen life insurance companies operated in 1947. Their combined total revenue was estimated at $26 million annually.[2] Similarly, black-owned funeral homes represented a dominant industry among businesses advertising on African American targeted radio programs.

In 1947 WJBW launched broadcasts of local and nationally known rhythm and blues artists performing live at the Dew Drop Inn, one of the city's premier black nightclubs. On August 14, the station began broadcasting an hour of performances beginning at 11 p.m. Radio was slowly moving to black content. To survive, non–network-affiliated stations had to attract people of color. Radio programs targeting blacks initially established an audience simply by having an African American on air. In the beginning, the presence of a black person on radio essentially was more important than the content. Blacks were enamored by the arrival of any successful African American in the public sphere. Such recognition translated into pride for the race and the notion that white America was opening doors for black advancement.[3]

In 1947 and 1948, commercial announcements were not heard on radio programs that featured African American content. It was not until the arrival of Winslow, who became the first black disc jockey in the city. He landed the job because principals at the Fitzgerald Advertising Agency and its client the Jackson Brewing Company in May 1949 determined that blacks represented a profitable beer-drinking market. Winslow had the expertise they sought. He created the radio persona Dr. Daddy-O. The agency bought time slots on radio station WWEZ, on which Winslow's rhythm and blues show was launched. Winslow named the show "Jivin' with Jax," which was broadcast daily, Monday through Saturday, from 5 p.m. to 6 p.m. Jax beer was the only product advertised on the show. Rhythm and blues, the inventiveness of black language, and interviews of local black music artists were among the innovations Winslow introduced to the airways. Nevertheless, WWEZ did not allow him to enter its broadcast studio. Instead, the broadcasts originated from a makeshift studio in the back of Cosimo Matassa's J&M Record Store. Despite the racial disparity at the station, the brewery became the first white-owned concern to advertise on a radio program with a black announcer targeting African Americans.

In April 1949 WDSU premiered a radio program featuring recorded gospel music Sunday mornings. The show was sponsored by the Louisiana Undertaking Company, a black concern that operated a funeral home. WNOE expanded its offerings of black-targeted programs in July 1949, which brought in advertisers, most of whom were African American life insurance companies and funeral homes. For example, Louisiana Undertaking, Peoples Industrial Life Insurance Companies, and Good Citizen Life Insurance Companies bought time on a new program, "The Negro Talent Show," which Taylor hosted on WNOE on Tuesdays from 8 p.m. to 8:30 p.m. In July 1949 WDSU brought a new black radio show to the airways. It was called the "American Way of Life," broadcasting Mondays from 9 p.m. to 9:30 p.m. Commercial announcements from the Longshoremen's Association, Monarch Life, and Geddes Richards Funeral Home were broadcast on the show. WNOE's "Negro Talent Hour" picked up another sponsor in July 1949, the Louisiana Industrial Life Insurance Company.

However, scholars have pointed to the overabundance of advertisements aiming beer, cigarettes, and skin lighteners at African Americans. In 1948 radio began the process of promoting beer and alcohol-laden concoctions to blacks. In 1950 Phillip Morris, one of the first cigarette manufacturers to advertise in black newspapers, was criticized for disproportionately targeting African Americans. Producers of skin bleaching/lightening preparations have a long history of advertising on black-content media. Imperial Whitener, Black Skin Remover, and "Madam" Turner's Mystic Face Bleach targeted blacks. Treva B. Lindsay has said such advertisements represent white cultural hegemony suggesting that Caucasian-centered physiology is the standard of beauty.[4]

In 1946 during Taylor's WNOE program, however, no ads for alcohol appeared, likely because the program, "Religious Forum of the Air," initially discussed sacred topics. Besides, the station sustained the show. While

Conclusion

WNOE, at 1060 kHz, did not advertise beer on air during the period, it advertised a 15 percent alcohol–laden product called Hadacol. The makers of the elixir attached it to the "Hadacol Jamboree and Talent Hour" held every Saturday from 6 p.m. to 8 p.m. at Hayes Restaurant at 2101 Louisiana Avenue. An audio transcript was made of the performance of the Oscar "Papa" Celestin Orchestra, part of which was broadcast on WNOE on Sundays at 10:30 a.m. Taylor was the emcee, and prizes were given to the best contestants as well as members of the audience. Admission was free, but entrants had to bring in the top from a bottle of Hadacol.[5]

On May 29, 1949, Jax beer began advertising on Dr. Daddy-O's show "Jivin with Jax" on WWEZ. Jax was the sole sponsor of the recorded music show, which Vernon Winslow, as Dr. Daddy-O, hosted twice daily. Winslow went further than just airing radio ads for the brewery. For example, he hired Porter photography to take pictures he set up in a newly opened tavern named Boogie Beat Cafe. The owner named the tavern out of homage to Winslow and his *Louisiana Weekly* nightlife column called "Boogie Beat Jive." The picture showed three individuals and Winslow, each holding a bottle of Jax with the label facing the camera. Winslow was seen shaking the hand of the owner, Mr. Turner, while the proprietor's attractive wife looked at the camera and an unidentified young woman looked at Winslow. That was typical Winslow marketing strategy. Besides his broadcasts he went to nightclubs and held Dr. Daddy-O parties at which he gave patrons free Jax beer and held block parties wherein the street was cordoned off so that a band could play while people sat on chairs or danced in the street.

On July 30, 1949, Regal beer's first ad in the *Louisiana Weekly* announced that the beer was also being advertised on WTPS, 940 on the radio dial. The ad further announced that Regal, produced by the American Brewing Company, with breweries in New Orleans and Miami, was sponsoring "Music of New Orleans," an all-Negro radio show featuring an all-star lineup of musicians. In August, the ad appeared with the slogan: "Hurry, Hurry-Time's a'wastin'! Drink the beer that's finer tasting."[6] Regal announced more details concerning "Music of New Orleans" in late August. The free show was staged at the Booker T. Washington Auditorium. The doors opened at 1:30 p.m., a pre-broadcast started at 2:30 p.m., and the actual broadcast began at 3 p.m. Regal "Invites you to a big special hour and a half long show packed with the best acts in New Orleans!" which included Papa Celestine, Elwood Smith, and the Regal Singers. Regal also aired the performances.[7]

Blatz beer initially took a different approach: No music. In order to sell beer to African Americans, it used black actor Eddie Green to perform on the NBC affiliate WSMB. Green was a star of "Duffy's Tavern," a popular situation comedy. A May 1950 *Louisiana Weekly* ad quoted Green: "'I get around a lot as an entertainer, and in all my travels, I've never tasted a finer beer than Blatz, Milwaukee's favorite—and my favorite—beer!'"[8] The show was broadcast at 8:30 p.m. on Thursdays. In late May, Blatz ran a commercial on WMRY which, on May 28, 1950, was the first station in the city to broadcast an all-black program format. The newspaper ad announced the Standard Sales Distributor sponsored deejay Ernest "Ernie the Whip" Bringier, daily from 5:30 p.m. to 6 p.m. on WMRY, 600 on the dial. The next month the caption of the Blatz beer logo and a picture of Paul A. Gray Sr., an assistant district manager of sales, said Gray was responsible for the $5,000 contract to cement the show. The paper said, "Mr. Gray would like to contact the executives of all social, sports, and entertainment clubs immediately. He can be reached by writing to 501 North Villere Street."[9]

WDSU, the ABC affiliate, joined the blitz, bringing Jackie Robinson on air to sell Regal beer made by the American Brewing Company. Robinson, picked up by the Brooklyn Dodgers in 1947, was the famed athlete who was the first black to play major league baseball. His program was a nationally syndicated three-minute show on which he interviewed celebrities and answered calls from listeners beginning at 9:30 p.m. Sundays.[10] Regal beer in July also advertised a new radio show titled "Music of New Orleans" on WTPS. Later in 1950 listeners heard Blatz beer commercials on WMRY. During the same year, the Church of God in Christ advertised on a black show on WJBW.

◆ ◆ ◆

As black leadership became more assertive in their insistence that segregation end, their efforts ushered in the Civil Rights Movement. Despite disagreement between African Americans and persons of color in New Orleans regarding remedial strategies, opinion leaders met at planning sessions to hash out approaches for direct action campaigns and legal challenges. The groups determined how to get blacks involved in mass action as well as in small groups to desegregate retailers, shopping districts, public education, transportation, and other sectors. The black churches, leaflets, rallies, the black press, and word of mouth were used to tell the masses how they should interpret racial segregation, what they should do to obtain voting rights, and how they would gain the rights to full citizenship. These means of disseminating progressive messages were effective in reaching their objectives, but it was radio targeting blacks that contributed to the delivery of messages that represented immediate and shared experiences among listeners.

Conclusion

Black-focused programming inspired African American New Orleanians to hold their heads high in the face of oppression. The on-air personalities calmed nervous parents and onlookers by reporting that protesters who sat in at lunch counters were unharmed. Radio was not used for recruiting the foot soldiers who directly challenged laws deemed unconstitutional. Instead, it presented information from the black press and movement organizers concerning marches, rallies, and activities of the foot soldiers. Organizers had little or no access to communicating via television, mailing lists, or the white press. Deejays and announcers helped expand the black public sphere.

Some eyewitnesses during the period said African American disc jockeys and announcers did not do enough to inform and inspire blacks. "I didn't think that the black stations were such a very important thing in New Orleans, in terms of rallying the troops as they probably should have been or could, but there was a lot of risk involved in that," according to Edwin Lombard:

> So when it comes time to talk about alerting the general public to what was actually happening in terms of the rights movement, the most often method to communication was probably the churches, the leaflet, the student bodies and stuff like that.... You didn't get your marching orders off of radio. Again, I could be wrong but I don't recall. I don't recall being exulted and stuff like that ... They were trying to sell records and trying to sell products.[11]

Similarly, Art Neville heard some local civil rights news in the city. He said the black on-air personalities did not disseminate enough information and subsequently did not tremendously effect the Movement: "I don't think it was influenced by them. I think they were supporting it. People were getting tired of just being walked on and pushed around."[12]

Several factors contributed to Lombard's and Neville's interpretations. Some black radio personalities believed they could not broadcast content advocating human rights for African Americans. Such announcers believed management would rebuff or fire them. Other air personalities did not routinely come into contact with movement organizers because the announcers had full-time jobs. Some were in fact simply interested in the entertainment value of the medium and their role as entertainers.

Joseph Deighton Gibson Jr. disagreed with Lombard and Neville, but he discussed the effectiveness of black-sponsored radio in general, not specific to an individual city. Gibson was a pioneer disc jockey born in Chicago. Known as Jack the Rapper, he helped create other opportunities to connect communicators and listeners. He pulled together thirteen of the leading black deejays in the country and in 1955 founded the National Association of Radio

Announcers. At its annual convention in Atlanta, August 9–13, 1967, Dr. King spoke about the importance of radio as the principal mediated voice compared to print media.

> I valued a special opportunity to address you this evening for in my years of struggle, both north and south, I have come to appreciate the role which the radio announcer plays in the life of our people; for better or for worse, you are opinion makers in the community. And it is important that you remain aware of the power which is potential in your vocation. The masses of Americans who have been deprived of educational and economic opportunity are almost totally dependent on radio as their means of relating to the society at large. They do not read newspapers, though they may occasionally thumb through *Jet* [magazine].[13]

The major local black newspapers, the *Louisiana Weekly* and the New Orleans edition of the *Pittsburgh Courier*, provided access to the black public sphere. The black press conveyed keystone information and interpretation concerning unequal treatment. To consume the information, however, an individual needed to know how to read effectively or the person needed to hear someone read the paper. The rise of radio gave broadcasters a tool to immediately and simultaneously reach the black masses whose reading skills were underdeveloped. Such functionality created opportunities for listeners to have shared informational and entertainment experiences.

African American inspired radio and newspapers were not the only voices of the Civil Rights Movement. Even though the clergy was among the leaders of the movement, pastors led individual congregations and their messages lacked unanimity. Rallies attracted varying sizes of attendees depending on factors including the keynote speaker, the venue, the amount of publicity, and the purpose. Estimates of crowd sizes range widely from less than a hundred to more than a thousand. In terms of publicity, using word of mouth was factually unreliable and its timeliness uncontrollable. The broadcast communicators, on the other hand, disseminated believable, timely information and entertainment that created a public community of the airways.

❖ ❖ ❖

While this book is limited, in some respects any work of scholarship basically scratches the surface of its subject area. Notwithstanding, this book provides a comprehensive and meticulous historiography of pioneering black broadcasters in New Orleans. Its relevance includes the fact that the insights in race and radio are not available elsewhere. The period of the Civil Rights

Movement was recent enough for the author to obtain relevant memories from interviewees of eyewitnesses: Don Hubbard, a foot soldier in the New Orleans rights battle; Edwin Lombard, the head of the NAACP youth voter's league in the 1960s; Warren Bell, a news reporter at WYLD; Kalamu ya Salaam, an activist and journalist; Raphael Cassimere Jr., a vice president of the NAACP youth council in 1960 and the first full-time black faculty member at Louisiana State University in New Orleans beginning in 1971; Arthur Morrell, an NAACP worker during the period; and Bill Rouselle, the first black TV reporter in New Orleans, beginning in 1968. Obviously, a study of this magnitude needs the author to interview more eyewitnesses to ascertain additional memories of events, issues, and personalities of the period. Nevertheless, substantial insight came from archival transcripts of interviews of six eyewitnesses including this study's pioneering air personalities: Taylor, Winslow, and McKinley. Other valuable memories came from transcripts of accounts of one of Winslow's protégés, Art Neville; locally acclaimed singer Irma Thomas; and broadcast and recording studio owner Cosimo Matassa. I analyzed other archival materials as well from the Amistad Research Center, which houses Taylor's and Winslow's collections, each containing various manuscripts; the Library of Congress, which has letters concerning the programming and involvement of the NAACP and the Urban League in New Orleans radio; the Louisiana Division of the New Orleans Public Library, which has a full archive of the *Louisiana Weekly*; and the online archives of the complete contents of a white New Orleans daily, the *Times-Picayune*.

◆ ◆ ◆

Finally, the popularly and functionality of terrestrial broadcast radio may diminish in the years to come considering the rise of audio programming expanded by the use of satellite radio, podcasts, social media, Internet streaming, and the inclination of the listeners to get audio content from new digital mobile communications devices. Such change would occur if and when advertisers increasingly discover that they can track the buying patterns of their consumers and better target ads to existing and prospective customers. Researchers suggest terrestrial radio will decline in popularity similarly as newspapers and magazines. Indicators include younger audio media consumers discovering new music increasingly by relying on Spotify, Pandora, SiriusXM, and YouTube, among other streaming platforms; automobile manufacturers increasingly installing satellite radio capability in new cars; rating services being better able to track digital content compared to broadcast audio; and music listeners tailoring playlists to their individual tastes.[14] Others argue for the viability of radio despite digitization. For example, broadcast radio is free; radio receivers can be purchased cheaply; new technology sometimes does not replace older technology, instead they tend to coexist.[15]

Future studies should explore how the radio and audio industries could change their operations to stall off a retrenchment in operations such as what has happened to the newspaper and magazine industries, which have reduced their publication of print copies and moved content to their websites. In terms of radio programming geared to black youth, scholars could investigate the likely effectiveness of communicating anti–drug use and stop-the-violence messages. Popular radio personalities might contribute to a reduction in occurrences of the illicit behaviors if they aired relevant public service announcements and commentaries. One research question is what factors contribute to effective communications and discussions via radio regarding progressive ideologies and other needed community-based activities.

EPILOGUE

Pioneering black broadcaster O. C. W. Taylor's "Religious Forum of the Air" in 1946 transformed radio in New Orleans into a vehicle that specifically informed black communities about relevant occurrences, issues, and individuals. Such was not the case previously. The medium was perfect for the times. It was especially useful to people who were functionally illiterate. Taylor knew that and provided content that uplifted African Americans and gave them a window through which to look at accomplishments of local blacks. Such knowledge and witnessing contributed to a linked fate, as Michael C. Dawson theorized, wherein African Americans believed that the success of their brethren meant they and their children could travel the long and torturous road toward the American dream.

Local blacks recognized Taylor as a pioneer at each anniversary of the "Forum," which aired on WNOE for twenty-two years until 1968. Leaders of organizations and business owners set up programs to honor him and draw attention to his contributions to African Americans. They sent floods of letters and telegrams recognizing his works. Upon learning that Taylor's alma mater, Wiley College, was considering awarding him an honorary degree in 1972, Daniel E. Byrd, a former executive director of the local NAACP wrote to Dr. Robert E. Hayes Sr., president of Wiley, that Taylor's "journalism, community service record, and his daring opened up new avenues of employment for negroes in the radio and television industries. The impact he has made in this community serves as a reminder to all that 'it can be done.'"[1]

Taylor continued working at WNOE until retiring from the station in 1968 at age seventy-seven. Years earlier, in 1957, after forty-two years, he retired from the Orleans Parish school system after working as a teacher and principal. While employed with the school system, he also organized and directed physical education programs and initiated a nature study and gardening program. He organized infantile paralysis and cancer drives, and during World War II he headed a branch of the Civilian Defense in New Orleans. As deputy state administrator in charge of the sale of war bonds only to blacks, he was responsible for collecting approximately $12 million.

While Taylor was in broadcasting for more than two decades, he never veered far away from his print journalism roots, which included co-founding the *Louisiana Weekly* in 1925 and assuming its first editorship. Throughout his years in broadcasting, he wrote a column for the *Weekly* and was a correspondent for the Associated Negro Press and *Jet* and *Ebony* magazines. He was the state representative for the *Pittsburgh Courier* and the *Chicago Defender*. The Prince Hall Masonic Grand Lodge in 1966 honored him at a civic testimonial dinner at Hayes Restaurant. Taylor continued working as grand director of public relations for the Prince Hall Masons of Louisiana, the Grand Masters Conference, and the United Supreme Council, Ancient Acceptance Scottish Rite of Freemasonry, Southern Jurisdiction. He was a 33rd degree Mason and a member of the Plata Temple No. 15, Ancient Egyptian Arabic Order, Nobles of the Mystic Shrine, P.H.A.[2]

After leaving radio, he became the first black television announcer, producer, and host of regularly scheduled commercial programs. WWOM-TV, channel 26, a UHF outlet whose call letters stood for Wonderful World of Movies, employed him for two-and-a-half years beginning August 1, 1966. He was manager/producer of five hours of live programming at the station in the International Trade Mart building on the edge of the winding Mississippi River. His shows aired from 7 a.m. to noon Saturdays and presented news and commentary from a black perspective, religious discussions, full-length movies, musical presentations, a talent hour, and a teenage dance show. More than a hundred individuals were in the audience to witness the various shows. Blacks again found joy and reasons to celebrate Taylor's accomplishments that said so much about their resiliency. A 1966 letter on *Cleveland Call Post* stationery and signed "Your boy LOEB," a friend of Taylor, said the television shows were viewed as simply the latest accomplishments of "things that others thought beyond the reach of a citizen of color."[3]

Taylor was a visionary. He saw the slings and arrows and used printed words, oral pronouncements, and moving pictures to draw attention to how to overcome ills plaguing blacks. He elevated perceptions of what high black achievement meant. Such was evidence to his organizational leadership. O. C. W.'s broadcasts helped blacks see themselves differently, as educated, successful, and professional. He also indicated to white voyagers who tuned to WNOE that blacks were about the business of self-improvement of their communities and conditions. In 1975 the station's general manager, Eric Anderson, mentioned that it was instructive to hear Taylor talk about issues in the community: "Quite frankly, we need to have listened to only you to learn about New Orleans's problems."[4] He heaped praise on Taylor: "Your wit and charm captivated us, and your grasp of the problems of the community gives me hope that my golden years might be a tenth as productive as yours." Taylor was married to Thelma Ruffin Taylor. They had a daughter, Doris Taylor Goins. On September 29, 1979, following a lengthy illness, Taylor died at St. Charles General Hospital. He was age eighty-seven.

◆ ◆ ◆

Vernon L. Winslow Sr., aka Dr. Daddy-O, became the first black disc jockey in the city spinning records at WWEZ beginning in 1949. That same year, he was a financially struggling faculty member in the art department at Dillard University. He clandestinely took a part-time job at the *Louisiana Weekly* writing a nightlife column and selling ads as the assistant advertising director. After joining the Fitzgerald Advertising Agency, which brokered the radio deal at WWEZ, Winslow spent approximately twelve years disc jockeying at WWEZ, WMRY, and WYLD. He helped popularize New Orleans rhythm and blues musicians. He also contributed to making gospel music more respectable among the masses. In 1961 Winslow left radio and returned to Dillard as an assistant professor. The following year the institution appointed him director of the university news service. By 1968 he had returned to radio as an air personality and continued teaching at Dillard. Daddy-O was also on air at WNNR, after its format changed to black contemporary in 1975. In 1987, at age seventy-five, he revived his classic New Orleans rhythm and blues show, this time calling it "Wavelength," which broadcast over WYLD-AM from 2 p.m. to 4 p.m. weekdays. He played artists he helped popularize between the late 1940s and 1960s, such as Lloyd Price, Little Red Tyler, Charles Brown, Fats Domino, Snooks Eaglin, Allen Toussaint, Earl King, Irma Thomas, and Ernie K-Doe.[5] Daddy-O also hosted his gospel music show at 6 a.m. on WYLD-FM in the late 1980s. By then, during drive time the radio station simulcast programming on WYLD-FM and WYLD-AM. WYLD-FM 98.5 debuted in 1975.

One of Daddy-O's theme songs for his gospel show was "I Don't Care What the World May Do," recorded by Alex Bradford, with lyrics such as "Everyday while I'm walking along, I know I'm in his care / Jesus is walking with me, while my friends and enemies stare / How can I be angry, which my God abides within / I, I, I don't care. I'm going to praise his name." Another one of his favorites was "God is Good" by Deitrick Haddon, who sang: "Oh he's my doctor in a sick room / He's a lawyer in a courtroom / He's a friend when you're friendless . . ." One of Winslow's friends, Walter Ross, mentioned that Daddy-O was his model. Ross was a WYLD announcer who hosted a morning gospel show: "I find myself mimicking him. He was extraordinarily articulate. Had super-smooth delivery. Never stuttered. This was a man who had confidence. When he opened the mike, he knew what he wanted to talk about."[6] Other gospel artists Winslow played included songs by Alex Bradford, the Staple Singers, Dorothy Love Coates, Sister Edna McGriff, and other nationally known musicians. In 1981, he retired from Dillard as an associate professor but continued as a disc jockey at WYLD.

After the first of a two-part interview with a *Times-Picayune* reporter, after Daddy-O's show on a rainy Sunday in December of 1986, he put on his cream-colored coat and carefully packed his gospel albums that were in the broadcast studio at WYLD. The dapper deejay placed the albums in the trunk of his car and drove a half hour to his home on Mirabeau Avenue. Sitting on his sofa in the living room, dressed in a pullover sweater and flannel pants, with his original paintings hanging from the walls, Winslow lamented that painting remains his first love: "These paintings on the wall, they're mine. Had things worked out for me in a way that my talent could support me, I would have been a painter." He was married, but his wife died in 1986. They had two children: a son, Vernon Winslow Jr.; and a daughter, Leslye Higgins. Winslow died from complications due to pneumonia in 2013 at the Lafon Nursing Home of the Holy Family. He was age eighty-two.

❖ ❖ ❖

Cosimo Matassa, a white man who owned the J&M Record Store at Rampart and Dumaine, played a formative role in Taylor and Winslow's early broadcasts. He let Taylor use the studio from which to broadcast installments of the "Religious Forum," as he did for Winslow, who first broadcast "Jivin' with Jax" at J&M. Personnel at the hotels housing the radio stations either refused to allow black professionals into the building or required them to enter through the rear of the building and ride the freight elevator to the broadcast studio. Matassa allowed them to broadcast from his studio because he said he was outraged at such acts compounding white supremacy.

In 1946, with his training from technical school, Matassa bought equipment enabling him to record directly onto a disc. He opened the small J&M Recording Studio in a backroom of his store, where he recorded and distributed the artistry of black musicians. Matassa began recording black musicians as Dr. Daddy-O's popularity grew. Winslow brought into the studio increasing numbers of black musicians whom he interviewed and let perform live. Matassa would go on to record Little Richard singing "Good Golly Miss Molly," Big Joe Turner's "Shake Rattle and Roll," Professor Longhair's "Mardi Gras in New Orleans," and Smiley's Lewis's "I Hear You Knocking," among others.

Matassa's father was an Italian immigrant and entrepreneur. The young Matassa followed in his footsteps but went further, linking black music recording, record distribution, and broadcasting. Matassa was eighteen when he launched J&M, which sold records, radios, and phonographs. He also installed jukeboxes and pinball machines at bars, restaurants, and other places. Before opening J&M, he and his father were partners in a jukebox business.[7] Some whites in the city referred to his business as a "nigger studio" because he treated blacks atypically. Too many whites focused on race. In the early days, his studio was one of only a few places where a black musician could meet up with his white girlfriend and not worry about being arrested. Such rendezvouses were not discussed; they just happened.[8]

Matassa's father also owned a neighborhood grocery store and bars which on the surface were racially segregated. His father rather uniquely arranged two of his bars in a building with a wall separating the establishments. One side was for blacks and the other side for whites, but he cut an opening in the wall between the two bars and placed a phone booth there with a door on each side. Blacks and whites were able to walk through the phone booth, visit the opposite bar, and interact without drawing too much attention. Each bar had its own jukebox, one playing black music and the other stocked with white-oriented tunes. When Matassa visited his father's business, on the white side he heard the popular tunes of the day, some hillbilly, and some Dixieland jazz. On the opposite side, he heard the same genres that local black broadcasters played, boogie-woogie, blues, and New Orleans music, among others. His father also operated a business installing and maintaining jukeboxes and coin-operated pinball machines. Matassa joined his father in the business. While servicing the jukeboxes, the younger Matassa discovered a demand for the used records, which he sold at his store. Soon customers began asking for new releases, so he started selling records fulltime.

According to Matassa, radio programs targeting blacks had an enormous effect on promoting African American music. But the top stations would not play the authentic music because whites sometimes stigmatized blacks and their cultural productions. Managers at mainstream stations said they would lose their white audience if they played black music. Some white people said they were unwilling or afraid to mingle with African Americans, but they would go to concerts and dance to black music. Some said they were more comfortable in segregated places because everybody around them was white. "I've talked to people who have said that even though in their general lives they didn't have much to do with black people period, they'd go out and buy these records and play them. And they loved them, and their kids would hear them and love them," Matassa said. Black music built bridges across the racial divide.[9]

Matassa more and more recognized that music recording and distribution connected perfectly. In 1947 he met David and Julian Braun, who visited New Orleans looking to record musicians who played and sang rhythm and blues (then called race music). The Braun brothers owned DeLuxe Records, based in New Jersey. Matassa recorded musicians for DeLuxe in his studio and situated himself as an informer to representatives of other record labels. Although it was illegal, Matassa took the scouts to segregated nightclubs where blacks performed. When a prospect was found, Matassa was awarded the contract to record the musicians. The arrangement was lucrative. He devoted full attention to his small recording studio and eventually acquired a total of four.[10]

Dr. Daddy-O's significance, Matassa said, was that he presented aspects of black culture including great music to whites who never noticed it or were not aware of it and certainly were not thinking about it. Matassa believed racism in New Orleans was institutionalized during the late 1940s and early 1950s. Blacks and whites, many of whom lived in proximity, were amenable in their mixed neighborhood. Black and white kids played together unaware they were integrating. They were separate, however, in places of public accommodations. Racial problems heightened when blacks began protesting, calling for integration. "I think the whole integration was a mistake because what they should have done was outlaw segregation without promoting integration because that's what ticked off a lot of people . . . feeling that they had something jammed down their throats even when they were being forced to do the right thing."[11]

Matassa went on to produce a majority of the R&B singers recorded in New Orleans between the 1940s and 1970s. He recorded more than 250 nationally charting singles, which were picked up by independent labels such as Chess, Aladdin, DeLuxe, and Atlantic, and twenty-one of the records reached gold. His groundbreaking involvement with black music would earn him a lifetime achievement award at the 2007 Grammys and induction into the Rock and Roll Hall of Fame in 2012. He died on September 11, 2014, after complications from a stroke.

◆ ◆ ◆

Larry McKinley worked as a disc jockey, announcer, and program director at radio stations in New Orleans. He broadcast considerable information concerning the Civil Rights Movement, telling the public where meetings were and what happened at various demonstrations. McKinley let foot soldiers, those engaging in sit-ins and other direct action, tell their stories on air. White broadcasters ignored the progressive activities or reported that demonstrators were lawless.[12] McKinley, from Chicago, was fueled with exuberance concerning the racial conflict. He wanted to join the struggle, but CORE representatives rebuffed his request for membership. He would not turn the other check after being walloped by a white guy in a staged confrontation. Nevertheless, McKinley contributed to the Movement by relaying information that CORE fed him, such as the locations of actions. Several of his on-air colleagues did not have formal knowledge of reporting news. His broadcast contemporaries were not as politically conscious. Most had full-time jobs away from the station and did not have enough free time to cover events. Some simply wanted to spin popular records, comment on athletic games, or play spirituals.

McKinley was not entirely serious on air. He also presented antics. McKinley hosted a show in 1958 from 4 p.m. to 7 p.m. called "Runnin' WYLD," which the station promoted as featuring him and Frank F. Frank, an obnoxious but funny character. The show featured McKinley personifying Frank. People thought Frank was a real person. One day, a guy told him that he suspected Frank and McKinley were the same person. He asked McKinley why does he not hear Frank and Larry talk at the same time. "Well, when I talk, Frank listens. And when Frank talks, I listen. It's as simple as that." The guy wasn't convinced, so McKinley thought of a way to further fool his listeners. The next day, he tape-recorded his alter ego Frank talking. On the air he pretended to speak to Frank repeating the guy's skepticism. McKinley pushed the play button and spoke at the same time the voice recording played. "That blew their mind."[13] The audience did not have much interaction with tape recordings.

McKinley was also an audio entrepreneur. In 1960, while on air at WYLD, McKinley entered the recording industry. He matched record distributor Joe Banashak's approximately $500, and they co-founded the locally based label Minit Records. They employed piano player and songwriter Allen Toussaint as the in-house producer, arranger, and songwriter. They released "Mother-in-Law" by Ernie K-Doe, which was a number 1 hit on the national charts in 1961. Among other New Orleans musicians Minit recorded were Irma Thomas, "Ruler of My Heart," and "It's Raining"; Bennie Spellman, "Lipstick Traces" and "Fortune Teller"; Jessie Hill, "Ooh Poo Pah Doo"; and Chris Kenner, "I Like It Like That." He also promoted local concerts of major acts such as James Brown, Aretha Franklin, the Four Tops, Sam Cooke, and Jackie Wilson.[14]

On air, among his repertoire, McKinley also played music with a message. For example, he played the rhythm and blues duo Sam and Dave's 1967 hit "Soul Man," with lyrics like: "Got what I got the hard way / And I'll make better each and every day / So honey don't you fret / 'Cause you ain't seen nothing yet." McKinley not only played records but he accepted telephone calls from the public. Callers talked about how many young people graduated from high schools such as Booker T. Washington, Walter L. Cohen, St. Augustine, or Xavier Prep. He also allowed students to call in and talk about what was on their minds.

While on a hiatus from radio, McKinley was one of the founding members of the board of directors of the New Orleans Jazz and Heritage Foundation, which has operated the Jazz Festival beginning in 1970. In October of the same year, he was master of ceremonies of the Soul Bowl '70, a concert with nationally known musicians who performed at the Tulane University stadium. Proceeds provided scholarships for blacks to enroll at Tulane. He also went on the road promoting his then-wife Margie Joseph, who recorded on Atlantic as well as Stax Records. During the time McKinley was out of radio, he also worked in public relations and city government for mayor Moon Landrieu. One of his involvements was the Alcohol Safety Action Project. At the time, he was an air personality at WYLD. With the rise of FM radio and the Top 40 charts, music became compartmentalized. Each station appropriated a different style of music, often playing the same thirty songs over and over again. "We were told 'Don't say Crescent City' and 'Don't say black' and 'Don't say right on.' I needed freedom." McKinley left WYLD in 1971.[15]

In 1975 McKinley joined the staff of WNNR, the same year WYLD introduced FM broadcasting at 98.5. WNNR, which stood for Winner Radio, changed formats from "music" in 1964, when it launched, to nostalgic hit music in 1972, and finally to black contemporary music in 1975. In the early 1960s, Supreme Broadcasting Corp. submitted an application to the FCC to transfer its license to operate WJMR, which broadcast at 990 on the dial. The FCC approved the request and the corporation changed the call letters to WNNR. It broadcast 250 watts at the 990 frequency during daytime hours, but changed to 91.7. In August 1964 the *Times-Picayune* began publishing WNNR programming.[16] Originally the station was white-oriented broadcasting from 6 a.m. until 5:30 p.m. weekdays. The station played Latin-American music from 4:35 p.m. to 5 p.m. weekdays and religious music on Saturdays from 7 a.m. to 7:30 a.m. and on Sundays from 8 a.m. to 12:25 p.m. and again from 1 p.m. to 1:30 p.m. In 1966 Roy A. Nelson was president of Supreme Broadcasting. The production and broadcast studios were located at 1544 Canal Street. WNNR was affiliated with the Mutual Broadcasting System (MBS) and the American Broadcasting Company (ABC). Richard Wright, the white managing editor from Channel 12 TV, announced news 7 a.m. to 8 a.m. and 5 p.m. to 5:55 p.m. Mondays through Fridays. On Saturdays WNNR programmed music from 6:05 a.m. to 5:30 p.m. with news bulletins interspersed. On Sundays, the station was on the air from 7 a.m. until 5:30 p.m.[17]

At WNNR McKinley served as the program director. He also hosted "Morning in New Orleans" with Gus Lewis during which he played cuts from albums, 45s, and mixed in social, political, and music commentary.[18] WNNR promoted him to operations manager of the station in 1977, but he continued his 6:15 a.m. to 10 a.m. wake-up show. McKinley added smooth soul music to the lineup. McKinley also produced and loaned his melodious voice to commercials for local public officials including US Rep. William Jefferson, District Attorney Eddie Jordon, and Ernest "Dutch" Morial, who in 1978 become the first black mayor of New Orleans.[19] McKinley was married and had four daughters. He died of chronic obstructive pulmonary disease in 2013 at age 85.[20]

NOTES

Foreword

1. Jack Gibson, interview with Jacquie Gales Webb, January 7, 1996, *Telling It Like It Was: Black Radio Collection*, Archives of African American Music and Culture, Smith Research Center, Indiana University, Bloomington.

2. Martha Jean Steinberg, interview with Jacquie Gales Webb, June 13, 1995, *Telling It Like It Was: Black Radio Collection*, Archives of African American Music and Culture, Smith Research Center, Indiana University, Bloomington.

3. Julian Bond, Interview with Stephen Walsh, August 17, 1995. In author's possession.

4. Fred Ferretti, "The White Captivity of Black Radio," *Columbia Journalism Review* 9, no. 2 (Summer 1970): 35–39.

5. See, Brian Ward, *Radio and the Struggle for Civil Rights in the South* (Gainesville: University Press of Florida, 2004), especially 182–209, 301–9 on black-oriented broadcasting and the freedom struggle in Birmingham.

6. Martin Luther King, "Transforming a Neighborhood into a Brotherhood," *Jack the Rapper* 13, 666 (1989): 1.

Chapter One. Organized Action Colorized White Radio in the Crescent City

1. David Nord, email to Bala Baptiste, April 15, 1998.

2. Daniel J. Czitrom, *Media and the American Mind: From Morse to McLuhan* (Chapel Hill: University of North Carolina Press, 1982); Christopher H. Sterling and John M. Kittross, *Stay Tuned: A Concise History of American Broadcasting*, 2nd. ed. (Belmont, CA: Wadsworth, 1990).

3. William Barlow, *Voice Over: The Making of Black Radio* (Philadelphia: Temple University Press, 1999).

4. Oscar H. Gandy Jr., *Communication and Race: A Structural Perspective* (London: Arnold, 1998), 21.

5. David Paul Nord, Communities of Journalism: A History of American Newspapers and Their Readers (Urbana: University of Illinois Press, 2001), 2.

6. Jurgen Habermas, "The Public Sphere: An Encyclopedia Article," *New German Critique* 1, no. 3 (Fall 1974): 49–55.

7. Jannette L. Dates and William Barlow, eds., *Split Image: African Americans in the Mass Media*, 2nd. ed. (Washington, DC: Howard University Press, 1993).

8. Clifford Geertz, *The Interpretation of Cultures* (New York: Basic Books, 1973), 14; Michael Schudson, "How Culture Works," *Theory and Society* 18 (1989): 155.

9. Schudson, 155.

10. William Barlow, "Commercial and Noncommercial Radio," in *Split Image: African Americans in the Mass Media*, 189; J. Fred MacDonald, *Don't Touch That Dial! Radio Programming in American Life, 1920–1960* (Chicago: Nelson-Hall, 1979), 328.

11. Hal Jackson, with James Haskins, *The House That Jack Built: My Life as a Trailblazer in Broadcasting and Entertainment* (New York: HarperCollins, 2001); Mark Newman, *Entrepreneurs of Profit and Pride: From Black-Appeal to Radio Soul* (New York: Praeger, 1988).

12. Joseph Straubhaar and Robert LaRose, *Media Now: Understanding Media, Culture, and Technology*, 4th. ed. (Australia: Thomson, Wadsworth, 2004), 39; Louis Cantor, *Wheelin' on Beale* (New York: Pharos Books, 1992); MacDonald, 338–39; Barlow, "Cashing in: 1900–1939," 27, 29; Reebee Garofalo, "Crossing Over: 1939–1992" in *Split Image*, 59; Dates, 469.

13. Barlow, "Commercial and Noncommercial Radio," 189; MacDonald, *Don't Touch That Dial!*; Estelle Edmerson, "A Descriptive Study of the American Negro in U.S. Professional Radio, 1922–1953" (M.A. thesis, University of California, Los Angeles, 1954), 21; Barlow, *Voice Over*, 17, 24.

14. MacDonald, 368–69.

15. Erik Barnouw, *The Golden Web: A History of Broadcasting in the United States, Vol. II, 1933 to 1953* (New York: Oxford University Press, 1968), 3–4, 217.

16. MacDonald, 368–69; Barlow, "Commercial and Noncommercial Radio" (1993), 229–30, mentions the sixteen black deejays and cites "Disc Jockeys: Sixteen Sepia Spielers Ride Kilocycle Range in Twenty on Stations," *Ebony*, November 1947, 44–48. Also see Barlow, *Voice Over* (1999), 96.

17. Barlow, *Voice Over*, 25; Barnouw, 3–4.

18. Barlow, "Commercial and Noncommercial Radio," 229–30; Barlow, *Voice Over*, 96.

19. Barlow, *Voice Over*, 27–28; MacDonald, *Don't Touch That Dial!*, 344–45; Joseph Boskin, *Sambo: The Rise and Demise of an American Jester* (New York: Oxford University Press, 1984), 139–40.

20. Alvin J. Aubry, "Know Your Educators," *Pittsburgh Courier*, Louisiana edition, November 2, 1946, in Taylor Collection, no. 360, box no. 3, Amistad Research Center, Tulane University, New Orleans.

21. Kim Lacy Rogers, *Righteous Lives: Narratives of the New Orleans Civil Rights Movement* (New York: New York University Press, 1993), 150.

22. MacDonald, *Don't Touch That Dial!*, 333. C. Joseph Pusateri, *Enterprise in Radio: WWL and the Business of Broadcasting in America* (Washington, DC: University Press of America, 1980), 115.

23. Pusateri, 115.

24. MacDonald, 333. Pusateri discusses the LSU survey, 208, and "Deep South," 189.

25. WWL display advertisement, *Louisiana Weekly*, December 29, 1945, 2; "Radio," June 2, 1946, *Times-Picayune*, in Taylor Collection, no. 360, box no. 3, Amistad Research Center, Tulane University, New Orleans.

26. *Federal Communications Commission Reports,* vol. 13 (Washington, DC: US Government Printing Office, July 1, 1948 to June 30, 1949), 450–52, 456.

27. *Federal Communications Commission Reports,* vol. 13, 448–49.

28. *Federal Communications Commission Reports,* vol. 13, 452–54.

29. Clint C. Wilson II and Felix Gutierrez, *Race Multiculturalism, and the Media: From Mass to Class Communication,* 2nd. ed. (Thousand Oaks, CA: Sage, 1995) 152–53.

30. Barlow, *Voice Over,* 19–20; Donald E. DeVore, "The Rise From the Nadir: Black New Orleans Between the Wars, 1920–1940," M.A. thesis, University of New Orleans, 1983, 60. DeVore cites US Department of Commerce, Bureau of the Census, *Sixteenth Census of the United States, 1940: Housing vol. III Characteristics by Monthly Rent or Value, Part 2.*

31. *Sixteenth Census of the United States: 1940, Population,* vol. II (Washington, DC: US Government Printing Office, 1943), 434; *A Report of the Seventeenth Decennial Census of the United States, Census of Population: 1950,* vol. II (Washington, DC: US Government Printing Office, 1952), 7, 48.

32. WWL transmitted 50,000 watts via 870 kilocycles, was New Orleans's oldest broadcast station, and radiated the strongest signal strength in the city. WSMB and WDSU each transmitted 5,000 watts, the former via 1350 kilocycles and the latter via 1280 kilocycles. WNOE transmitted 250 watts via 1450 kilocycles and radiated the weakest signal strength of the network affiliates. Three local daily newspapers published in the city in 1946: the *New Orleans States,* the *New Orleans Item,* and the *Times-Picayune.* The printed watts and kilocycle data as well as program titles and broadcast times; see "Highlights of Radio," *States,* May 27, 1946, 12, and proximate dates. The *Item* published program titles and times as well but listed shows broadcasted beginning at 7 a.m. and omitted listing the shows that began between 6 a.m. and 6:45 a.m. Both were afternoon newspapers. The *States* and *Item* identified radio programs by slightly different names on occasion. For example, the *States* referred to WDSU's first weekday program as "Yr Mrng Call," an abbreviation of "Your Morning Call." The *Item* listed the same program as "Morning Call." The respective editor likely shortened program titles in order to conserve space. Also see "Radio Programs," *Item,* May 29, 1946, 28, and proximate dates.

33. WJBW transmitted programming via 250 watts and with the use of the frequency 1230 kilocycles. New Orleans dailies omitted publication of WJBW's program schedule in 1946. For WJBW technical data see *Federal Communications Commission Reports,* vol. 12 (Washington, DC: US Government Printing Office, 1950), 902 and passim.

34. Pusateri, *Enterprise in Radio,* 230.

35. Vincent Terrace, *Radio's Golden Years: The Encyclopedia of Radio Programs, 1930–1960* (San Diego: A.S. Barnes & Company, 1981), 138.

36. "Highlights of Radio," *New Orleans States,* May 27–31, 1946; "Radio Programs," *New Orleans Item,* May 29 and 31, June 1, 1946.

37. WWL display advertisement, *Louisiana Weekly,* December 29, 1945, 2; "Radio," *Times-Picayune,* June 2, 1946, see Taylor Collection, no. 360, box no. 3.

38. William Robson, author of "An Open Letter on Race Hatred," in Barlow, "Commercial and Noncommercial Radio, *Split Image,* 208–9.

39. Terrace, *Radio's Golden Years*, 15–16; Melvin Ely, *The Adventurers of Amos 'n' Andy: A Social History of an American Phenomenon* (New York: Free Press, 1991).

40. Pusateri, 89.

41. Paul A. Kunkel, "Modifications in Louisiana Negro Legal Status Under Louisiana Constitutions: 1812–1957," *Journal of Negro History* 44 (1959); 4; Alice Dunbar-Nelson, "People of Color in Louisiana, Part 2," *Journal of Negro History* 2, no. 1 (January 1917): 63.

42. Kunkel, 4.

43. Lerone Bennett Jr., *Before the Mayflower: A History of Black America*, 6th ed. (New York: Penguin, 1993), 475; Joan B. Garvey and Mary Lou Widmer, *Beautiful Crescent: A History of New Orleans* (New Orleans: Garmer Press, 1984), 59; Peirce F. Lewis, *New Orleans: The Making of an Urban Landscape* (Cambridge, MA: Ballinger, 1976), 9, 37; John Hope Franklin and Alfred A. Moss Jr., *From Slavery to Freedom: A History of African Americans*, 7th. ed. (New York: McGraw-Hill, 1994), 114–15, 225.

44. Kunkel, 17.

45. Liva Baker, *Second Battle of New Orleans: The Hundred-Year Struggle to Integrate the Schools* (New York: Harper-Collins, 1996), 34, 46; Donald E. DeVore and Joseph Logsdon, *Crescent City Schools: Public Education in New Orleans, 1841–1991* (Lafayette: University of Southwestern Louisiana, 1991), 114. Adam Fairclough, *Race & Democracy: The Civil Rights Struggle in Louisiana, 1915–1972* (Athens: University of Georgia Press, 1999), 465.

46. Baker, 14, 46; James Gill, *Lords of Misrule: Mardi Gras and the Politics of Race in New Orleans* (Jackson: University Press of Mississippi, 1997), 55; Fairclough, 465, 553.

47. Fairclough, 6.

48. Charles Flint Kellogg, *NAACP: A History of the National Association for the Advancement of Colored People, Volume 1, 1909–1920* (Baltimore: Johns Hopkins Press, 1967), 32–33; Arnold R. Hirsch, "Simply a Matter of Black and White: The Transformation of Race and Politics in Twentieth-Century New Orleans," in Hirsch and Joseph Logsdon, eds., *Creole New Orleans: Race and Americanization* (Baton Rouge: Louisiana State University Press, 1992), 267.

49. *Sixteenth Census of the United States: 1940, Population*, 434.

50. *State of Louisiana Report of Secretary of State to His Excellency*, 1940, 1942, 1946, 1948, 1950, in Special Collections, Joseph Merrick Jones Hall, Tulane University Library, New Orleans (SCTU); Pamela Tyler, *Silk Stockings and Ballot Boxes: Women and Politics in New Orleans, 1920–1965* (Athens: University of Georgia Press, 1996), 28, 247.

51. Jerry Purvis Samson, "Sam Jones, Jimmie Noe, and the Reform Alliance 1940–1942," *Louisiana History* 27, no. 3 (Summer 1986): 267–68; Franklin and Moss, *From Slavery to Freedom*, 356; Fairclough, 104–5.

52. *Louisiana Report of Secretary of State*, SCTU; John L. Androit, ed., *Population Abstract of the United States*, vol. 1 (McLean, VA: Androit Associates, 1983) 321; *Census of Population: 1950*, vol. II, part 18, Louisiana (Washington, DC: US Government Printing Office, 1952), 7.

53. Abraham H. Maslow, *Motivation and Personality* (New York: Harper & Row, 1970) and *Toward a Psychology of Being* (Princeton, NJ: Van Nostrand, 1968).

54. Cantor, *Wheelin' on Beale*, 47.

55. "Meet Jack L. Cooper," *Chicago Defender*, March 5, 1949, cited in Newman, *Entrepreneurs of Profit and Pride*, 55, 76; Barlow, *Voice Over*, 51; Norman W. Spaulding, "History of

Black Oriented Radio in Chicago, 1929–1963," diss., University of Illinois at Urbana-Champaign, 1981; Richard S. Kahlenberg, "Negro Radio," *Negro History Bulletin*, March 29, 1966, 128; Cantor, *Wheelin' on Beale*, 156; MacDonald, *Don't Touch That Dial!*, 338–39.

56. Barlow, *Voice Over*, 25.
57. Jackson, *The House That Jack Built*, 25.
58. Jackson, *The House That Jack Built*, 25–26.
59. Jackson, *The House That Jack Built*, 26–29.
60. Barlow, "Commercial and Noncommercial Radio," 189–264.
61. Barlow, "Commercial and Noncommercial Radio," 189–235.
62. Newman, *Entrepreneurs of Profit and Pride*, x–xi; MacDonald, 338–39.

Chapter Two. Race and Supremacy Contaminated Media

1. Cantor, *Wheelin' on Beale*.
2. Barlow, *Voice Over* 108–9; Newman, *Entrepreneurs of Profit and Pride*, 112; Cantor, *Wheelin' on Beale*, vii.
3. Cantor, *Wheelin' or Beale*.
4. Barlow, *Voice Over*.
5. Stephen Roy James Walsh, "Black-Oriented Radio and the Campaign for Civil Rights in the United States, 1945–1975," doctoral thesis, University of Newcastle, May 1997.
6. Brian Ward, *Radio and the Struggle for Civil Rights in the South* (Gainesville: University Press of Florida, 2004).
7. Barbara Dianne Savage, *Broadcasting Freedom: Radio, War, and the Politics of Race, 1938–1948* (Chapel Hill: University of North Carolina Press, 1999).
8. Robert M. Entman and Andrew Rojecki, *The Black Image in the White Mind: Media and Race in America* (Chicago: University of Chicago Press, 2002).
9. Dates and Barlow, "Introduction: A War of Images," in *Split Image*.
10. Dates and Barlow, "Conclusion: Split Images and Double Binds," in *Split Image*, 523.
11. Antonio Gramsci, *Selections from the Prison Notebooks* (New York: International Publishers, 1971); Dates and Barlow.
12. Stuart Hall, "Signification, Representation, Ideology: Althusser and the Post-Structuralist Debates," *Critical Studies in Mass Communication* 2 (June 1985).
13. Catherine L. Covert, "We May Hear Too Much," in *Media Voices*, 300–301 and passim. Also see David Paul Nord, "The Ironies of Communication Technology: Why Predictions of the Future So Often Go Wrong," *Cresset* 49 (March 1986).
14. Daniel J. Czitrom, "The Ethereal Hearth: American Radio from Wireless Through Broadcasting, 1892–1940," in *Media and the American Mind*; Thomas Streeter, *Selling the Air: A Critique of the Policy of Commercial Broadcasting in the United States* (Chicago: University of Chicago Press, 1996).
15. Michael C. Dawson, *Behind the Mule: Race and Class in African American Politics* (Princeton, NJ: Princeton University Press, 1994).
16. Newman, *Entrepreneurs of Profit and Pride*, 97–98, includes text of an interview of J. C. Danley in 1976. Also see Barlow, *Voice Over*, 96–97.

17. Walter Lippmann, "The World Outside and the Pictures in Our Heads," in *Public Opinion* (1922); published in *Mass Communications* (Urbana: University of Illinois Press, 1960).

18. For discussions of Lippmann's contributions to the concepts of stereotypes and public opinion, see Michael Emery and Edwin Emery, *The Press and America: An Interpretive History of the Mass Media*, 7th. ed. (Englewood Cliffs, NJ: Prentice Hall, 1992), 229. Also see Dates and Barlow.

19. Susan Herbst, *Politics at the Margin: Historical Studies of Public Expression Outside the Mainstream* (Cambridge: Cambridge University Press, 1994).

20. Roland E. Wolseley, *The Black Press, U.S.A.*, 2nd. ed. (Ames: Iowa State University Press, 1990). Also in Bala Baptiste, "(New Orleans) *Louisiana Weekly*: Among America's Oldest Black Newspapers," unpublished M.A. thesis, University of Mississippi, August 1994.

21. Michael H. Burchett, "Notes on the twentieth Century: The History of Black Radio Broadcasting," no. 12, February 2001, mburchet.hypermart.net, accessed May 31, 2018; Statista, "Number of Commercial Radio Stations in the United States from 1952 to 2016," n.d., statista.com, accessed May 31, 2018.

22. J. Fred MacDonald, *Richard Durham's Destination Freedom* (New York: Praeger, 1989).

23. Daniel E. Byrd, letter to Thurgood Marshall, June 15, 1945, in *NAACP 1940–55, Legal File*, microfilm frame 471.

24. Untitled typewritten manuscript, accompanied Byrd letter to Marshall, June 15, 1945, in *NAACP 1940–55, Legal File*, microfilm frames 473–75.

25. Daniel E. Byrd, letter to Thurgood Marshall, June 25, 1945, in *NAACP 1940–55, Legal File*, frame 479.

26. Byrd to Marshall, June 25, 1945, frame 479.

27. Byrd to Marshall, June 25, 1945, frames 473–75.

28. Byrd to Marshall, June 25, 1945, frames 473–75.

29. Gerald Early, ed., *"Ain't But a Place": An Anthology of African American Writings about St. Louis* (St. Louis: Missouri Historical Society Press, 1998).

30. Byrd to Marshall, June 25, 1945.

31. Thurgood Marshall, letter to William H. Hastie, June 27, 1945, in *NAACP 1940–55, Legal File*, frame 472.

32. "Citizens $100,000 Ballot Campaign (?) Starts With Kickoff Meeting (?)," *Louisiana Weekly*, September 8, 1945, 1.

33. Thurgood Marshall, "Memorandum to the Office," September 11, 1945, in *NAACP 1940–55, Legal File*, frame 482.

34. "Radio and the Negro," *Louisiana Weekly*, December 28, 1946, 10.

35. "Radio and the Negro."

36. "Religious Radio Program Becomes Sunday Morning Feature on WNOE," *Louisiana Weekly*, June 1, 1946, 9.

37. "Announces All Negro Radio Program of La.," *Louisiana Weekly*, March 23, 1946, 1.

38. "Announces All Negro Radio Program of La.," *Louisiana Weekly*.

39. "Negro Radio Forum Marks Anniversary," *New Orleans Sentinel*, May 29, 1948, in Taylor Collection, no. 360, box no. 3, Amistad Research Center, Tulane University, New Orleans.

40. Rev. Handy, pastor, First Street Methodist Church; Rev. Davis, pastor, New Zion Baptist Church; and Father Temple, principal, Gaudet Episcopal School; see WNOE program guide typewritten with autograph inserts, 1946, Taylor Collection, no. 360, box no. 4; *Louisiana Weekly*, June 1, 1946, 9; "Negro Radio Forum Second Anniversary Sun.," May 29, 1948, 1.

41. Taylor Collection; "New Orleans Gets Radio Announcer," Houston *Informer*, June 15, 1946; "Negro Leaders Appear on Radio Forum," *New Orleans Informer-Sentinel*, July 6, 1946; John Rousseau, tape-recorded and transcribed interview, New Orleans, July 23, 1971, Oral History Collection of Columbia University; and Fairclough, 61.

42. "Religious Radio Program Becomes Sunday Morning Feature on WNOE," *Louisiana Weekly*, June 1, 1946, 9.

43. John W. Blassingame, *Black New Orleans 1860–1880* (Chicago: University of Chicago Press, 1973), 148.

44. Taylor interview, Columbia University; Alvin J. Aubry, "Know Your Educators," *Pittsburgh Courier*, Louisiana edition, November 2, 1946.

45. Aubry, "Know Your Educators."

46. "Celebrities on Forum," *New Orleans Informer-Sentinel*, July 13, 1946; "Revs. Holmes, Taylor, Harris, on Radio Forum Sunday," *Louisiana Weekly*, June 8, 1946; "Ministers Featured in Radio Forum," *Pittsburgh Courier*, June 6, 1946; "Negro Announcers Over Crescent City Radio," *Chicago Defender*, June 22, 1946.

47. "Conducts All-Negro Radio Forum," *Louisiana Weekly*, July 6, 1946, 3; "Celebrities on Radio Forum on [sic] the Air Sunday," *Louisiana Weekly*, July 13, 1946, 5; "Negro Leaders Appear on Radio Forum," *New Orleans Informer-Sentinel*, July 6, 1946; "Celebrities on Forum," *New Orleans Informer-Sentinel*, July 13, 1946.

48. "Celebrities on Radio Forum on the Air Sunday," *Louisiana Weekly*, July 13, 1946, 5; *Courier* photograph and caption in Taylor Collection; "120 Anniversary of Negro Press Observed with Impressive Radio Broadcast by Local Newspapermen," *Louisiana Weekly*, March 8, 1947, 1; Fairclough, 72–73.

49. Don Juan, "Crescent Mo[portion of headline missing] Seam," *New Orleans Informer-Sentinel*, July 13, 1946.

50. "Religious Forum of the Air" display advertisements in the *Louisiana Weekly* in 1946.

51. "Rev. H. Thomas Primm to Speak Over WNOE," *New Orleans Informer-Sentinel*, October [n.d.] 1946 in Taylor Collection; "Religious Forum" ad, *Louisiana Weekly*, October 12, 1946, 12.

52. M. T. Stringer and E. J. Badgett, letter to Taylor, October 31, 1946, in Taylor Collection.

53. Wright to Taylor, November 4, 1946, in Taylor Collection; ad in *Louisiana Weekly*, October 26, 1946, 12; *New Orleans Informer Sentinel*, October [n.d.] 1946; "Religious Forum of the Air" ad, *Louisiana Weekly*, October 26, 1946, 12.

54. "Home for Incurables to be Dedicated Sun," *Louisiana Weekly*, November 16, 1946; WNOE display advertisements, *Louisiana Weekly*, November 16, 1946, 13, and November 24, 1946, 11; Taylor Collection.

55. "'Y' Membership Drive Gets Off; Holtry and Geddis Heads Campaign," *Louisiana Weekly*, June 22, 1946, 1; "New 'Y' Building to be Dedicated Here Nov. 17," *Louisiana Weekly*, November 9, 1946, 1; "Dedicate New 'Y' Building Here Sunday," *Louisiana Weekly*, November

16, 1946, 1; "Hundreds Attend Dedication of New YMCA Building Here," *Louisiana Weekly*, November 23, 1946, 1.

Chapter Three. Radio Forum Evolved from Religion to Negro

1. "New Orleans Gets Radio Announcer," Houston *Informer*, June 15, 1946, in Taylor Collection; Pusateri, *Enterprise in Radio*, 229.

2. Glenn R. Conrad, general ed., *Dictionary of Louisiana Biography* (New Orleans: Louisiana Historical Association, 1988), 607.

3. Pusateri, *Enterprise in Radio*, 158; Conrad, *Dictionary of Louisiana Biography*, 607.

4. Samson, 246.

5. Hermann B. Deutsch, "New Orleans Politics—The Greatest Free Show on Earth," in *The Past as Prelude: New Orleans 1718–1968*, Hodding Carter, chief ed. (New Orleans: Tulane University, 1968), 234–35.

6. F. Edward Herbert with John McMillan, *"Last of the Titans": Life and Times of Congressman F. Edward Herbert of Louisiana* (Lafayette: Center for Louisiana Studies, University of Southwestern Louisiana, 1976), 105.

7. Herbert with John McMillan, *"Last of the Titans,"* 106.

8. Pusateri, 276.

9. O. C. W. Taylor, transcription of tape-recorded interview, New Orleans, July 24, 1971, Oral History Collection of Columbia University.

10. *State of Louisiana Report of Secretary of State*; "Monogram," typewritten manuscript, March 20, 1972, Taylor Collection, no. 360, box no. 1, Amistad Research Center.

11. O. C. W. Taylor, interview; "Monogram" in Taylor Collection; "Father Temple is Radio Forum Guest," circa November 1946, in Taylor Collection; Alvin J. Aubry, "Know Your Educators," *Pittsburgh Courier*, Louisiana edition, November 2, 1946, in Taylor Collection.

12. Taylor interview, 1971; Baptiste, "(New Orleans) *Louisiana Weekly*: Among America's Oldest Black Newspapers," 76.

13. Taylor interview.

14. Taylor interview.

15. Taylor interview.

16. "Negro Radio Forum Second Anniversary Sun.," *Louisiana Weekly*, May 29, 1948; "Beauticians on Religious Program Here," *New Orleans Sentinel*, November 16, 1946, Taylor Collection; "Radio Forum to Stage Birthday Broadcast Sun.," *Louisiana Weekly*, May 24, 1947, 8.

17. Wolseley, *The Black Press, U.S.A.*, 55, 324–26.

18. Thomas J. Davis, "Louisiana," in Henry Lewis Suggs, ed., *The Black Press in the South, 1865–1979* (Westport, CT: Greenwood Press, 1983), 151–52.

19. "Press Week to be Highlighted via Broadcasts," *Louisiana Weekly*, March 1, 1947, 3; "120 Anniversary of Negro Press Observed with Impressive Radio Broadcast by Local Newspapermen," *Louisiana Weekly*, March 8, 1947, 1–2.

20. "Radio Forum to Stage Birthday Broadcast Sun.," *Louisiana Weekly*, May 24, 1947, 8; "Radio Moderator Given Ovation by Orleanians," May 31, 1947, 4.

21. "National Essay Contest Winners Receive Awards," *Louisiana Weekly*, June 7, 1947, 1.
22. "Dr. Fredericks Speaker on TB Radio Forum Sun.," *Louisiana Weekly*, July 19, 1947, 1; Fairclough, 48.
23. Photograph and caption, *Atlanta Daily World*, July 26, 1947, 1.
24. John W. Blassingame, *Black New Orleans 1860–1880* (Chicago: University of Chicago Press, 1973), 152, 167–68.
25. Photograph and caption, *Louisiana Weekly*, August 23, 1947, 4.
26. Taylor collection, *Louisiana Weekly*, August 23, 1947.
27. Photograph and caption, *Louisiana Weekly*, October 11, 1947, 7.
28. "Radio Broadcasts Focus Attention on Handicapped Week," *Louisiana Weekly*, October 11, 1947, 8.
29. "News and Radio Men in Huddle," *Louisiana Weekly*, August 16, 1947; Oklahoma City *Black Dispatch*, August 23, 1947, in Taylor Collection.
30. *Federal Communications Commission Reports: Decisions and Reports of the FCC of the United States*, vol. 12 (Washington, DC: US Government Printing Office, 1950), 737; "La. Negroes Support a Move to Get Wattage Increase For WNOE," *Louisiana Weekly*, September 6, 1947, 11.
31. *Federal Communications Commission Reports: Decisions and Reports of the FCC of the United States*, vol. 13 (Washington DC: US Government Printing Office, 1954), 450; Alvin H. Jones, letter to FCC, May 29, 1948 in Taylor Collection.
32. O. C. W. Taylor, letter to Beverly Brown, February 28, 1948, in Taylor Collection at Amistad Research Center. Also see Taylor interview, Columbia University.
33. Taylor, letter to Brown.
34. Taylor, letter to Brown.
35. W. Talbot Handy, letter to Taylor, February 29, 1948, in Taylor Collection.
36. Paul A. Landix, letter to Taylor, March 1, 1948; Jas. E. Gayle, letter to Taylor, March 1, 1948, both in Taylor Collection.
37. "Negro Forum to Remain on Air," *Louisiana Weekly*, March 6, 1948, 1.
38. "Taylor Praised as Community Builder," *Pittsburgh Courier*, June 12, 1948, in Taylor Collection.
39. Alvin H. Jones, letter to Taylor, May 20, 1948, in Taylor Collection.
40. Marion P. Barker, letter to Taylor, May 25, 1948; J. O. Richards Jr., letter to Taylor, May 26, 1948; Rev. A. Prince Fortner, letter to Taylor, May 26, 1948; Leon J. Bickham, letter to Taylor, May 27, 1948; W. Talbot Handy, letter to Taylor, May 28, 1948; all in Taylor Collection.
41. E. Lyons Baker, telegram to Taylor, May 30, 1948; Saul's Costume Shop, telegram to Taylor, May 30, 1948; both in Taylor Collection.
42. James E. Gordon, letter to Taylor, June 11, 1948, in Taylor Collection.
43. *Federal Communications Commission Reports: Decisions and Reports of the FCC of the United States*, vol. 15 (Washington, DC: US Government Printing Office, 1965), 935. *Louisiana Weekly*, June 17, 1950, 15.
44. *Federal Communications Commission Reports*, vol. 16, 12, 19.
45. "Greeting to O. C. W. Taylor," typewritten and signed manuscript, n.d. (ca. 1948), in Taylor Collection.

46. *New Orleans Informer-Sentinel*, 1948.

47. "Radio Forum to Salute," 1948.

48. Kopfler, 1948; "Kenner Officials," 1948.

49. Kopfler, 1948; "Kenner Officials," 1948.

50. Baker, 1996; Gill, 1997; Fairclough, 1995.

51. Devore and Logsdon, 1991.

52. "Slidell Mayor," 1948.

53. "Slidell Mayor," 1948.

54. Bennett, 1988.

55. Clancy, 1948.

56. Department of Communications at the University of Maryland, "Voices of Democracy." 2006, retrieved 2013.

57. Arnold, 1948.

58. Theo. O. Hotard, letter to O. C. W. Taylor, 1948, in Taylor Collection at Amistad Research Center.

59. Theo. O. Hotard (1948).

60. *Times-Picayune*, "Radio," June 2, 1946, in Taylor Collection.

61. *Times-Picayune*, "Radio," June 9, 1946, in Taylor Collection.

62. "Religious Radio Program Becomes Sunday Morning Feature On WNOE," *Louisiana Weekly*, June 1, 1946, 9; display ad, *Louisiana Weekly*, October 5, 1946, 7; "'Scoop' Jones' Pot Pourri: The Rhymes that Chime," *Louisiana Weekly*, August 30, 1947, 7.

63. Dawson, *Behind the Mule*, 10, 76.

64. Jerry Wexler, "Rhythm and Blues in 1950," *Saturday Review of Literature*, June 24, 1950, 49; Jerry Wexler and David Ritz, *Rhythm and the Blues: A Life in American Music* (New York: Alfred A. Knopf, 1993).

65. "In Radio Interviews," *Louisiana Weekly*, photograph and caption, July 31, 1948, 9.

66. "NCNW's Impressive Banquet," *Louisiana Weekly*, May 7, 1949, 3; John Hope Franklin, *From Slavery to Freedom: A History of Negro Americans*, 4th ed. (New York: Alfred A. Knopf, 1974), 398, 402, and passim; Dr. Daddy-O, "Boogie-beat Jive," *Louisiana Weekly*, April 1, 1950, 15.

67. Mental Floss, February 9, 2010, accessed November 11, 2017, mentalfloss.com.

68. Rousseau to Taylor, October 2, 1950, Library of Congress.

69. Dorothy W. Wiltz, letter to Taylor, October 4, 1950, Box II: A507, folder 7, Library of Congress.

70. "Archbishop Hails Bunche as 'American,'" *Pittsburgh Courier*, December 24, 1949, in Taylor Collection; "Dr. Ralph Bunche Warmly Received," *Louisiana Weekly*, December 24, 1949, 9; Jessie Dent, interview by Bala Baptiste, tape recording, New Orleans, December 18, 1985.

Chapter Four. Black Culture, Music, and "Hep Phrasing" Permeated Radio

1. George Stephens Jr., aka Tex, interview in author's possession, Bala Baptiste, in New Orleans, January 5, 1998; in "Black Radio," tape-recording, Archives of African American Music and Culture, Indiana University, Bloomington (AAAMC); WJBW display advertisement, *Louisiana Weekly*, May 14, 1949.

Notes

2. Pusateri, *Enterprise in Radio*, 59, 121, 189, 223.

3. Pusateri, *Enterprise in Radio*, 208–9.

4. Cosimo Matassa, "Black Radio," transcription of tape recorded interview, n.d., Archives of African American Music and Culture, Indiana University, Bloomington.

5. Pusateri, 59, 223, 226.

6. Jason Berry, Jonathan Foose, and Tad Jones, *Up From the Cradle of Jazz: New Orleans Music Since World War II* (Athens: University of Georgia Press, 1986, 54.

7. "'Scoop' Jones' Pot Pourri," *Louisiana Weekly*, October 11, 1947, 9; "E-Boping Tina Dixon Remains at Dew Drop," *Louisiana Weekly*, October 11, 1947, 12.

8. *Louisiana Weekly* photograph and caption regarding WJBW, November 1, 1947, 2.

9. "'Scoop' Jones' Pot Pourri: The Rhymes that Chime," *Louisiana Weekly*, August 30, 1947, 7.

10. Stephens, AAAMC collection; Interview by author.

11. "'Scoop' Jones' Pot Pourri: The Rhymes that Chime," *Louisiana Weekly*, August 30, 1947, 7.

12. "'Scoop' Jones' Pot Pourri: The Rhymes that Chime," *Louisiana Weekly*, May 21, 1949.

13. Stephens interview with author.

14. Stephens interview with author.

15. Scoop Jones, "Pot Pourri," *Louisiana Weekly*, May 21, 1949, 9; Browneyes, "Boogie-beat Jive," *Louisiana Weekly*, May 28, 1949, 12; "Gladstone Hotel Radio Show is Groovey Affair," *Louisiana Weekly*, May 28, 1949, 13; Scoop Jones, "Pot Pourri," *Louisiana Weekly*, May 28, 1949, 9; Dr. Daddy-O, "Boogie-beat Jive," *Louisiana Weekly*, July 2, 1949, 12.

16. "Local Talent to be Given Chance on Station WWL," *Louisiana Weekly*, September 27, 1947, 7.

17. Vernon Winslow, interview, n.d., tape recording Bromo 235 and 236, AAAMC, Bloomington, IN.

18. Winslow, interview; Bill Grady, "Dr. Daddy-O in Tune with the Rhythm and Blues of Life," *Times-Picayune*, December 23, 1986; Mark Lorando, "Doctor Daddy-O is Back On," *Times-Picayune*, June 25, 1987; "Radio Star Vernon Winslow, 'Dr. Daddy-O,' Dies at 82," *Times-Picayune*, December 16, 1993; Photograph and caption: "Painter and Designer," *Louisiana Weekly*, February 16, 1946, 3; Bala Baptiste, "How Disc Jockey Vernon Winslow, aka Dr. Daddy-O, Racially Intergraded Radio in New Orleans and Changed the Culture of the Medium," *Louisiana History* 54, no. 2 (Spring 2013): 2002–14.

19. Winslow, "Boogie-beat Jive," *Louisiana Weekly*, January 15, 1949.

20. Winslow, interview; Berry, Foose, and Jones, 65–66.

21. Broven, *Rhythm & Blues in New Orleans*, 233, 234.

22. "'Scoop' Jones' Pot Pourri," *Louisiana Weekly*, December 27, 1947, 5.

23. Winslow, interview.

24. Winslow, interview.

25. Bill Grady, *Times-Picayune*, December 23, 1986.

26. Winslow, interview; Barlow, *Voice Over*, 165; Berry, Foose, and Jones, 65.

27. Berry, Foose, and Jones, 69.

28. Nelson George, *The Death of Rhythm and Blues* (New York: Penguin, 2003); Winslow, interview.

29. Winslow, interview.

30. Winslow, interview; Barlow, *Voice Over*, 165.

31. Barlow, *Voice Over*, 1, 2, 9, and passim; "Radio's Original Poppa Stoppa Now With the Louisiana Weekly," *Louisiana Weekly*, April 9, 1949, 1; Winslow, interview; *Louisiana Weekly*, March 6, 1948, 4.

32. Jones, "Pot Pourri: "Get Hep, Radio Orleans," *Louisiana Weekly*, February 28, 1948, 8.

33. *Louisiana Weekly*, April 9, 1949, 1.

34. Winslow, interview; Berry, Foose, and Jones, 69.

35. Winslow, interview; Rick Coleman, *Blue Monday: Fats Domino and the Lost Dawn of Rock 'n' Roll* (Cambridge: Da Capo Press, 2006), 46.

36. Winslow, interview.

37. Winslow, interview.

38. "Louisiana Weekly Scribe Becomes Crescent City's First Negro Disc Jockey," *Louisiana Weekly*, May 28, 1949, 1.

39. Winslow, interview; Coleman, 46.

40. Winslow, interview; Coleman, 43, 54.

41. *Louisiana Weekly* articles: "Chubby, Roy to be Dr. Daddy-O Guests," June 18, 1949, 13; "'Lil Ella' to be Guest of Dr. Daddy-O Friday," July 9, 1949, 12; "Larry, Lollypop and Ethel on Dr. Daddy-O Radio Show," July 23, 1949, 12; "Roy, Camille Guests of Dr. Daddy-O," photograph, August 20, 1949, 13.

42. Dr. Daddy-O, "Boogie-beat Jive," *Louisiana Weekly*, July 2, 1949, 12; Barlow, *Voice Over*, 2, 11, and passim.

43. "JAX" display advertisement, *Louisiana Weekly*, October 29, 1949, 7.

44. "Regal's New Radio Show: 'Music of New Orleans' Scores Hit in Debut," *Louisiana Weekly*, July 30, 1949, 13; also see "Regal" display advertisements, *Louisiana Weekly*, August 6, 1949, 6, and August 20, 1949, 6.

45. Regarding Bob Parker, see Dr. Daddy-O, "Boogie-beat Jive," *Louisiana Weekly*, September 3, 1949, 12.

46. Scoop Jones, "Pot Pourri," *Louisiana Weekly*, October 29, 1949, 9, and December 24, 9.

47. Dr. Daddy-O, "Boogie-beat Jive," *Louisiana Weekly*, December 3, 1949, 12, and December 17, 12.

48. Winslow, interview.

49. Dr. Daddy-O, "Boogie-beat Jive," *Louisiana Weekly*, October 15, 1949, 12.

50. Winslow, interview; "Dr. Daddy-O Surprises Fans," photograph, *Louisiana Weekly*, January 7, 1950, 13; Dr. Daddy-O, "Boogie-beat Jive," *Louisiana Weekly*, April 1, 1950, 15.

51. Dr. Daddy-O, "Boogie-beat Jive," *Louisiana Weekly*, January 7, 1950, 12; "Warning to Tavern Owners," *Louisiana Weekly*, March 4, 1950, 3; "Here's That Man Again!" Robinson photograph, *Louisiana Weekly*, January 1, 1950, 2.

52. *Louisiana Weekly* columns: Browneyes, "Boogie-beat Jive," April 2, 1949, 12; April 16, 1949, 12; July 2, 1949, 12. Also see *Weekly* advertisements: April 2, 1949, 12, and April 16, 1949, 13. "Papa Celestin Signed for Once A Week Disc Jockey Program on Station WDSU," *Louisiana Weekly*, November 12, 1949, 12.

53. "Hayes Adds Air Conditioning to its Many Features," *Louisiana Weekly*, 23 July 1949, 13; John Lee Neely, *Louisiana Weekly*, June 11, 1949; "Talent Hour Clicks With Radio Fans," *Louisiana Weekly*, July 23, 1949, 13.

54. C. C. Dejoie, *Louisiana Weekly*, June 11, 1949; "Blind Lad," *Louisiana Weekly*, July 16, 1949.

Notes 147

Chapter Five. The Pioneer Mixed a "Batch of 'Congrats'"

1. Dr. Daddy-O, "Boogie-beat Jive," *Louisiana Weekly*, December 3, 1949, 12, and December 17, 12.
2. Barnouw, *The Golden Web*, 289.
3. "Station WMRY Leases Floor at Louisiana Life for Broadcasting Studio with Integrated Staff," *Louisiana Weekly*, May 6, 1950, 1
4. "Plans Nearing Completion for Station WMRY's Grand Opening in La. Life Bldg.," *Louisiana Weekly*, May 13, 1950, 2.
5. "'Tex' Stephens Joins Ranks of Crescent City Disc Jockeys," *Louisiana Weekly*, March 11, 1950, 3.
6. "Plans Nearing," *Louisiana Weekly*, May 13, 1950, 2.
7. Brian Ward, *Just My Soul Responding: Rhythm and Blues, Black Consciousness, and Race Relations* (Oakland: University of California Press, 1998).
8. "WMRY's Grand Opening Slated Sunday; Stars Set to 'Shine,'" *Louisiana Weekly*, May 27, 1950, 1; "Station WMRY Leases Floor at Louisiana Life for Broadcasting Studio with Integrated Staff," *Louisiana Weekly*, May 6, 1950, 1; "WMRY Leases Studio in La. Insurance Bldg.," *Pittsburgh Courier*, Louisiana edition, May 6, 1950; New Orleans *Item*, May 2, 1950.
9. Dr. Daddy-O, "Boogie-beat Jive," *Louisiana Weekly*, March 4, 1950, 11; February 18, 1950, 12; "Promoted," *Louisiana Weekly*, December 2, 1950, 14.
10. Tex interview with Bala Baptiste, New Orleans, January 5, 1998; "Promoted," *Louisiana Weekly*, December 2, 1950, 14.
11. Dr. Daddy-O, "Boogie-beat Jive," *Louisiana Weekly*, March 18, 1950, 15.
12. *Louisiana Weekly*, May 13, 1950, 2; "Gala Celebration Planned for WMRY Opening May 28," *Louisiana Weekly*, May 20, 1950, 8; "WMRY's Grand Opening Slated Sunday; Stars Set to 'Shine,'" *Louisiana Weekly*, May 27, 1950, 1; *Item*, May 28, 1950.
13. "Puts Blatz on the Air," photograph and caption, *Louisiana Weekly*, June 3, 1950, 2.
14. Dr. Daddy-O, "Boogie-beat Jive," *Louisiana Weekly*, June 10, 1950, 14, and December 2, 1950, 14; *Broadcasting & Cable Yearbook 1999* (New Providence, NJ: R.R. Bowker, 1999), D-194.
15. Dr. Daddy-O, "Boogie-beat Jive," *Louisiana Weekly*, May 20, 1950, 14.
16. Dr. Daddy-O, "Boogie-beat Jive," *Louisiana Weekly*, May 27, 1950, 14.
17. Dr. Daddy-O, "Boogie-beat Jive," *Louisiana Weekly*, June 10, 1950, 14.
18. Dr. Daddy-O, "Boogie-beat Jive," *Louisiana Weekly*, July 15, 1950, 14.
19. Dr. Daddy-O, "Boogie-beat Jive," *Louisiana Weekly*, September 2, 1950, 14.
20. Dr. Daddy-O, "Boogie-beat Jive," *Louisiana Weekly*, September 16, 1950, 27–28.
21. Dr. Daddy-O, "Boogie-beat Jive," *Louisiana Weekly*, February 3, 1951, 14.
22. "Disc Jockey Promoted to Sales Director," *Louisiana Weekly*, January 20, 1951, 2.
23. Winslow, interview.
24. Winslow, interview.
25. "WSMB to Air Dr. Daddy-O Show Nightly," *Louisiana Weekly*, June 16, 1951.
26. Keith Frederic, "'Doctor Daddy-O' Born in 1949," *Times-Picayune*, June 20, 1978.
27. Winslow, interview.
28. Winslow, interview; Jason Berry, Foose, and Jones.

29. "Rock 'n' Roll radio in Houston, 1950," April 18, 2010, Wired-for-sound.blogspot.com, accessed July 21, 2017.

30. Winslow, interview.

31. Winslow, interview.

32. Winslow, interview.

33. *Times-Picayune*, January 7, 1962.

34. Dr. Mable John, "Black Radio," transcription of tape recorded interview, April 11, 1995, AAAMC, Indiana University.

35. Frederic, "'Doctor Daddy-O' Born in 1949."

36. Frederic, "'Doctor Daddy-O' Born in 1949."

37. McKinley, interview.

38. Winslow, interview.

39. Winslow, interview.

40. "WBOK, Newest and 1st Integrated Radio Station, Opens Here Jan. 1," *Louisiana Weekly*, December 9, 1950, 1; "WBOK Makes Debut on Airlanes With Mixed Staff of Disc Jockeys," *Louisiana Weekly*, February 3, 1951.

41. Edward F. Haas, *Mayor Victor H. Schiro: New Orleans in Transition, 1961–1970* (Jackson: University Press of Mississippi, 2014), 289.

42. Rollye Bornstein, *Mediatrix Monthly* 1, no. 7 (1986).

43. Dr. Daddy-O, "Boogie-beat Jive," *Louisiana Weekly*, February 24, 1951, 14.

44. "Atlantan Buys Station WMRY," *Times-Picayune*, August 21, 1957; Maud Bryan, "Up and Down the Street," *Times-Picayune*, November 25, 1958, 11.

45. Newspaper accounts referred to Malcolm LaPlace interchangeably as Mal or Mike. See Dr. Daddy-O, "Boogie-beat Jive," *Louisiana Weekly*, June 17, 1950, 14; Jim Hall, "Time Out," *Louisiana Weekly*, July 22, 1950, 6, and July 29, 1950, 6; "First Negro Baseball Broadcasts," display advertisement, *Louisiana Weekly*, July 22, 1950, 7.

46. "To Broadcast Xavier, Dillard Football Games," *Louisiana Weekly*, September 23, 1950, 7.

47. Advertisement, *Times-Picayune*, May 26, 1959.

48. Bob Roesler, "Behind the Scenes," *Times-Picayune*, July 24, 1962, 5.

Chapter Six. Some Black Broadcasters Spoke Concerning the Civil Rights Movement

1. Ward, *Radio and the Struggle for Civil Rights in the South*.

2. Taylor, interview.

3. Christian Allman, "Larry McKinley the Man Behind the Voice," *New Orleans Tribune* (April/May 2004): 8–9.

4. Ed Brooks, "Broadway hit Can Make TV Stars of Bit Players," *Times-Picayune*, January 19, 1954, 18.

5. *Times-Picayune*, March 1965.

6. "Bus Segregation Discussion Topic," *Times-Picayune*, January 20, 1957, 5.

7. Art Neville, "Black Radio," transcription of tape recorded interview, AAAMC, March 16, 1995.

8. Howard McSween, "Earl Long, 1895–1960: Voting Rights Advocate of Political Correctness," *Virginia Quarterly Review: A National Journal of Literature and Discussion* 53, no. 3 (Summer 1995), accessed July 21, 2017.

9. "United Clubs Incorporated Present Reverend Martin Luther King," program sheet, February 1, 1957.

10. "King Predicts Victory for Integration by 1963," *Times-Picayune*, February 2, 1957, 18.

11. McKinley, interview.

12. "'Carry on in Christian Way for Rights' Urges Rev. King," *Louisiana Weekly*, February 9, 1957, 1.

13. Katy Reckdahl, "Prominent Civil Rights Organization was founded in New Orleans 60 Years Ago This Week," *The Advocate*, February 11, 2017; Edwin Lombard, interview by author, September 28, 2017, in author's possession; Tex Stephens, interview transcription.

14. McKinley, interview.

15. McKinley, interview.

16. Dominic Massa, *New Orleans Radio: Images of America* (Charleston, SC: Arcadia, 2014), 117.

17. McKinley, interview.

18. Liva Baker, *The Second Battle of New Orleans: The Hundred-year Struggle to Integrate the Schools* (New York: Harper Collins, 1996).

19. Baker, *The Second Battle of New Orleans*.

20. McKinley, interview.

21. Don Hubbard, interview by telephone, New Orleans, October 23, 2017, in author's possession.

22. Joseph Logsdon and Caryn Cosse Bell, *Creole New Orleans: Race and Americanization*, ed. Arnold R. Hirsch and Joseph Logsdon (Baton Rouge: Louisiana State University, 1992).

23. Paul F. Lachance, letter to O. C. W. Taylor, in Taylor Collection at Amistad Research Center.

24. Hubbard, interview.

25. Hubbard, interview.

26. Irma Thomas, "Black Radio," transcription of interview, n.d., Archives of African American Music and Culture, Indiana University, Bloomington.

27. McKinley, interview.

28. McKinley, interview.

29. McKinley, interview.

30. Elizabeth Mullener, "Civil Rights Movement: Leaders on Both Sides Smoothed way to Integration," *Times-Picayune*, NOLA.com, June 6, 1993.

31. McKinley, transcript; Stephens, transcript.

32. Rogers, *Righteous Lives*; McKinley, transcript; Stephens, transcript.

Chapter Seven. Entertainment Content Required on Black-Focused Radio

1. "New Orleans Places Hit by Fire Bombers," *Times-Picayune*, April 5, 1968.

2. Hubbard, interview.

3. Bill Rouselle, interview with author, in New Orleans, April 1, 2016, in author's possession.

4. Ward, *Radio*, 341.

5. Lombard, interview.

6. Bornstein, *Mediatrix Monthly*.

7. Robert R. N. Ross and Deanne E. B. Ross, *Walking to New Orleans: Ethics and the Concept of Participatory Design in Post-Disaster Reconstruction* (Eugene, OR: Wipf & Stock, 2008).

8. Richard Campanella, *Journal of American History* 94, no. 3, accessed September. 6, 2017, www.historycooperative.org/journals/jah/94.3/campanella.html.

9. Ward, *Radio*; *Encyclopedia of Alabama* (Auburn, AL: Auburn University Press, 2009).

10. Ward, 185.

11. Ward, 188.

12. Ward, 186.

13. Ward, 196.

14. Dates and Barlow, "Commercial and Noncommercial Radio," in *Split Image*, 241.

15. "Build Support," *Times-Picayune*, August 10, 1973.

16. "Build Support," *Times-Picayune*.

17. Barlow, "Commercial Radio," 1993.

18. Jason Chambers, *Madison Avenue and the Color Line: African Americans in the Advertising Industry* (Philadelphia: University of Pennsylvania Press, 2008).

19. Winslow, "What happened to 'Poppa Stoppa'?" *Louisiana Weekly*, December 4, 1948.

20. Chambers, *Madison Avenue*.

21. Hubbard, interview.

22. *Times-Picayune*, June 10, 1962.

23. The Newberry, https:llmms.newberry.org, accessed November 27, 2017.

24. Mallardi to Parris, letter, September 27, 1965; Parris to Mallardi, letter, October 1, 1965, II-V-17 NUL, Library of Congress.

25. Dates and Barlow, 242.

26. Keith Woods, "Promotion Blitz: Waging Air War Over City," *Times-Picayune*, March 13, 1988; Robert Redding Jr., "Black Voices, White Power: Members of the Black Press Make Meaning of Media Hegemony," master's thesis, Marshall University, 2015.

27. Bob Davis, "Tuning Out: Black Radio Stations Face Balky Advertisers as Competition Rises," *Wall Street Journal*, September 23, 1987.

28. Wendy Wilson, "Whites Only: How Advertisers Ignore African American Consumers," *Diversity or Division? Race, Class and America at the Millennium*, nyu.edu, accessed December 22, 2017.

29. Woods, *Times-Picayune*.

30. David Stout, "Robert F. Williams, 71, Civil Rights Leader and Revolutionary," *New York Times*, October 19, 1966, NYT.com, accessed December 5, 2017.

31. Ward, *Radio*, 338.

Conclusion

1. Hope Green, "Scholars Revisit Fiery '57 Critique of Black Middle Class," *B.U. Bridge* vol. 6, no. 1 (August 30, 2002), bu.edu/bridge, accessed December 21, 2017.
2. *Louisiana Weekly*, 1947.
3. Dawson, *Behind the Mule*, 1994.
4. Treva B. Lindsey, "Black No More: Skin Beaching and the Emergence of New Negro Womanhood Beauty Culture," *Journal of Pan African Studies* 4, no 4 (June 2011).
5. Advertisement, *Louisiana Weekly*, September 30, 1950.
6. Advertisement, *Louisiana Weekly*, August 6, 1949.
7. Advertisement, *Louisiana Weekly*, August 20, 1949.
8. *Louisiana Weekly*, May 6, 1950.
9. *Louisiana Weekly*, June 3, 1950.
10. *Louisiana Weekly*, June 3, 1950.
11. Lombard, interview.
12. Neville, interview.
13. Dates and Barlow, *Split Image*, 240.
14. Daniel Sanchez, "Radio is Dead. This Study Proves it," Digital Music News, August 31, 2017; Chris Morgan, "How Much Longer Will Terrestrial (AM/FM) Radio Stations Exist?" *Quora*, quora.com, accessed December 21, 2017.
15. Matt Senne, "Is Radio Dead in 2017," Leighton Broadcasting, May 10, 2017, leightonbroadcasting.com, accessed December 21, 2017; John McDuling, "Streaming Hasn't Killed the Radio Star," Quartz, January 13, 2015, qz.com, accessed December 21, 2017.

Epilogue

1. Robert Hayes, letter to Daniel Byrd, 1972, Taylor Collection.
2. *Times-Picayune*, May 24, 1966.
3. LOBE, letter to Taylor, June 1, 1966, in Taylor Collection.
4. Eric Anderson, letter to Taylor, 1975, Taylor Collection.
5. Mark Lorando, *Times-Picayune*, June 25, 1987.
6. Gwendolyn Thompkins, "Playboys of the Airwaves," *Times-Picayune*, October 13, 1991.
7. Newman, *Entrepreneurs of Profit and Pride*; Berry, Foose, and Jones, 33; Broven, *Rhythm & Blues in New Orleans*, 13–14, 17, 20.
8. Cosimo Matassa, interview, AAAMC; Todd Mouton, "BackTalk with Cosimo Matassa (excerpts from August *OffBeat* feature)," 1997, online at www.offbeat.com/text/cosimo.
9. Matassa, interview.
10. Mouton, "BackTalk."
11. Matassa, interview.
12. Arthur Morrell, interview by author, May 18, 2018, in author's possession.
13. Larry McKinley, "Black Radio," transcription of tape recorded interview, AAAMC, March 13, 1995.

14. Keith Spera, "Larry McKinley, Minit Records Co-Founder and Voice of the New Orleans Jazz Fest, has Died," *Times-Picayune*, NOLA.com, December 9, 2013.

15. Benjamin Morrison, "Man Who Makes WNNR Gumbo," *Times-Picayune*, January 25, 1976.

16. *Times-Picayune*, August 2, 1964.

17. Bornstein, *Mediatrix Monthly*.

18. David Cuthbert, "The First Survivors," *Times-Picayune*, March 22, 1975, 16.

19. Christian Allman, "Larry McKinley: The Man Behind the Voice," *New Orleans Tribune*, April/May 2004; *Louisiana Weekly*, n.d.

20. Tompkins, *Times-Picayune*.

INDEX

ABC. *See* American Broadcasting Companies (ABC)
Abernathy, Ralph, 99
Adams, William R., 95
advertising: aimed at blacks, 8; aimed at whites, 7; for beer, 118; for black entrepreneurs, 79; on black radio stations, 109, 111–12; for Blatz beer, 81, 119–20; for cigarettes, 118; for Delta airlines, 112; for Falstaff beer, 85; for funeral homes, 117, 118; for Hadacol, 53–54, 119; for insurance companies, 76, 91, 117, 118; for Jax beer, 43, 58, 70, 71–75, 84–87, 109, 118–19, 128; for local public officials, 133; for Regal Beer, 73, 119, 120; for skin lighteners, 118; by WNOE, 10
advertising agencies, 6, 7, 19, 43, 44, 58, 80. *See also* Fitzgerald Advertising Agency
African Americans: access to radio programming, 11, 26, 115; and the American Dream, 5, 76, 115, 125; and black institutions, 42–43; disabled, 44; as disc jockeys, 7, 18, 22, 57, 69, 74, 75, 76, 79, 80–81, 85, 88–89, 90, 94, 109–10, 121, 130; legal status of, 14–15; marginalization of, 27, 51–52; in the military, 93; negative stereotypes of, 12, 23–25, 31; as radio broadcasters, 4–5, 8, 57–58, 61, 64, 69; and radio programming, 19; and religion, 32–34, 44, 49, 89; self-actualization of, 16–17; and sports, 43–44, 91–92; voting rights for, 15–16
Afro American, 19
Alabama Christian Movement for Human Rights, 107

Alexander, Avery, 102, 103
Allen, Oscar K., 38
American Brewing Company, 73, 119, 120
American Broadcasting Companies (ABC), 7, 11, 59, 60, 132
Amistad Research Center, 123
Amos 'n' Andy, 12–13
Anderson, Eric, 126
Armstrong, Louis, 8
Arnoult, Henry, 50
Associated Negro Press, 31, 33, 40, 126
Atlanta Daily World, 33
Ayers, Cesta, 85

Baham, Herminie, 81, 83
Baker, E. Lyons, 47
Baker, Marion P., 42, 46
Banashak, Joe, 131
Barlow, William, 19, 22, 24, 69
bebop blues, 72. *See also* blues music
Bel Geddes, Norman, 64
Bell, Caryn Cosse, 100
Bell, Warren, 123
Bethune, Mary McLeod, 53
Bickham, Leon J., 47
Black Dispatch (Oklahoma newspaper), 33
black language. *See* hep phrasing
black magazines, 29, 30, 44, 108, 116, 126
black music, 6–7, 129–30; blues, 21, 72, 79, 129; boogie woogie, 6, 72, 129; contemporary, 132; funk, 5; gospel, 5, 6, 21, 79, 87–89, 90, 107, 118, 127–28; in New Orleans, 5; "race music," 52, 59, 60, 62, 130; rap, 112; religious, 9 (*see also*

153

gospel); rhythm and blues, 5, 6, 21, 52, 59, 64, 79, 90, 113, 117–18, 127, 130, 131–32; soul, 113, 133; white listeners' reactions to, 59; on WWEZ, 66. *See also* jazz music
black musicians, 75; acceptable to white audiences, 59, 66; interviews with, 72; in Jax commercials, 84; jazz, 81; local talent, 65–66; nationally known, 66, 70, 87; recorded by Matassa, 128–30; recorded by McKinley, 131; rhythm and blues, 127; visiting, 61
black newspapers, 15, 18, 27–30, 32–33, 41, 44, 60, 93, 99, 122, 123, 126. See also *Louisiana Weekly*; other black newspapers by name
Blassingame, John, 33
"Blatz Radio Show," 81
Blayton, Jesse B., Sr., 115
blues music, 21, 79, 129; bebop, 72. *See also* rhythm and blues
boogie-woogie music, 6, 72, 129
"Boogie-beat Jive" (Winslow), 69, 79, 80, 89, 119
Borikins, Naomi, 43, 70
Boyton v Virginia, 102
Braun, David, 130
Braun, Julian, 130
Bringier, Ernest "Ernie the Whip," 80–81, 83, 120
"Bronze Review," 19
Brown, Beverly, 44
Browneyes, 65, 68, 74
Bunche, Ralph J., 54–55
Burns, Leonard, 106
Byrd, Daniel E., 28, 30, 61, 125

Caire Associates, 80
Cantor, Louis, 21
Carlson, Charles C., 58
Carlson, Louise Elsie, 58
Cassimere, Raphael, Jr., 123
Castle, Doris Jean, 103
Castleberry, Eddie, 108
CBS. *See* Columbia Broadcasting System (CBS)

Celestin, Oscar "Papa," 75, 119
Champion, Jesse, 108
Chicago Defender, 32, 33, 41, 126
Christophe, H. J., 42
Civil Rights Movement, 28, 94–103; in Birmingham, 107; and black radio broadcasters, 94–95, 97–98, 101, 103; bus boycotts, 95; and Congress of Racial Equality, 97, 99, 101–2; coverage by black newspapers, 93; dichotomy between light- and dark-skinned African Americans, 100–101; Freedom Riders, 102; march through Central City, 102; and Martin Luther King Jr., 96–97; in New Orleans, 93–97; role of black radio, 120–22; school desegregation, 98–99; and Southern Christian Leadership Conference, 96–97
"Civil Rights Roundup," 110
Clancy, Frank J., 49
Clark, Peter W., 34
Clay, Joyce Lena, 42
Coley, C. C., 19
Columbia Broadcasting System (CBS), 7, 8, 11, 51, 59, 60
comedy shows, 7, 11, 12–13, 18, 51
commercials. *See* advertising
communism, 49–50
community building, 4, 5–6, 57
Compromise of 1877, 14
Congress of Racial Equality (CORE), 97, 99, 101–2, 103, 105, 107–8, 131
Connell, Pat, 110
Consumers League, 99
Cooper, Jack L., 18, 108, 115, 116
Cornish, Samuel E., 27, 41
Covert, Catherine L., 26
Creoles, 13, 15; and Civil Rights Movement, 100–101
Crisis (NAACP magazine), 30
cultural duality, 100
cultural production, 6, 24, 51, 52, 129
Curry, Ernest, 34

Darnley, J. C., 26
Dates, Janette, 24
Davis, Abraham Lincoln, Jr., 32, 95, 96, 102, 106, 116
Dawson, Michael C., 26, 52, 125
Deep South Broadcasting Corporation, 10–11
Dejoie, Constance C., Sr., 40, 44, 65
DeLuxe Records, 130
Dent, Albert W., 8–9, 54, 106
Dent, Ernestine Jessie Covington, 54
"Destination Freedom," 22
Dew Drop Inn, 59–61, 65, 71, 79, 89, 117
disc jockeys: black, 7, 18, 22, 57, 69, 74, 75, 76, 79, 80–81, 85, 88–89, 90, 94, 109–10, 121, 130; white, 7, 58, 72, 79, 109
Dixieland jazz, 75, 129. *See also* jazz
Dooky Chase restaurant, 99–100
double consciousness, 24
Double V Campaign, 93
Dr. Daddy-O, 4, 71, 74–75, 79, 84, 85–86, 87, 101, 108, 116, 117, 119, 127, 128, 130; on Civil Rights Movement, 23–24. *See also* Winslow, Vernon L., Sr.
dramas, 7, 9, 11, 31, 51, 60; blacks excluded from, 22–23
Dryades YMCA, 35, 41, 43, 57, 58, 76, 80
Du Bois, W. E. B., 24, 25, 30
Dunlap, Norman, 84
Dupree, Henry, 63
Durand, Eldon, 54
Durham, Richard, 22

Elie, Lolis, 102
Enquirer, 27
Ernie "The Whip." *See* Bringier, Ernest "Ernie the Whip"
Evans, Leon, 108

Faush, Erskine, 108
Federal Communications Commission (FCC), 3, 8; broadcast policies, 10
Fifteenth Amendment, 16

Fitzgerald Advertising Agency, 43, 70, 72, 85, 109, 117, 127
Fortner, A. Prince, 46
Frank, Frank R., 131
Franklin, G. B., 51
Frazier, E. Franklyn, 116
Frederick, Rivers, 42, 76, 80, 116
Freedom Riders, 102
Freedom's Journal, 27, 41
Fritchie, H. G., 49
funk music, 5

game shows, 7, 60
Garroway, David "Dave," 64, 85
Gay, Connie B., 90–91
Gayle, James E., 32, 33, 35, 46
Gibson, Joseph Deighton, Jr., 121–22
"Glory Road," 86
Goins, Doris Taylor, 127
Good Samaritans, 43
"Goodnight Mother," 86, 87
Gordon, James E., 11, 47
gospel music, 5, 6, 21, 79, 86–89, 90, 107, 118, 127–28
Graham, William B., 109
Gramsci, Antonio, 25
Gray, Paul A., Sr., 81, 120
Green, Eddie, 119–20
Gretna and Lower Coast Radio and Broadcasting Company, 47

"Hadacol Talent Hour and Jamboree," 54, 119
Haley, Oretha Castle, 99, 102
Hall, Jim, 91
Hall, Juanita, 94
Hall, Stuart, 25
Handy, W. Talbot, 32, 45, 47
Hardy, John "Honeyboy," 90
Hastie, William H., 30
Haydell, C. C., 42
Hayes, Robert E., Sr., 125
hep phrasing, 61, 64, 66, 84; and sexual euphemisms, 68

Herbert, F. Edward, 38
Herbst, Susan, 27
hierarchy of needs, 16, 17
Higgins, Leslye, 128
hillbilly music, 90, 129
hipster dialect. *See* hep phrasing
Holtry, J. A., 35
Holtry, Maxine, 53
Hoover, J. Edgar, 50
Hotard, Theo. O., 51
House Committee on Un-American Activities, 50
Howard, Clara Mae, 42
Hubbard, Don, 99, 101, 123
Human Rights Law (New York 1945), 6
Hutchinson, James, 111
Hychew, Elgin, 52

ideological hegemony, 24–25
independent stations, 7
Informer (Houston newspaper), 32, 86
Informer-Sentinel (New Orleans newspaper), 32, 33, 44
integration, 130; of public library, 8–9; in public sector, 93; of radio broadcasting, 4, 5–6, 9, 12, 19, 23–24, 30–32, 37, 108; of schools, 97–99. *See also* segregation
Inter Urban Broadcasting, 111
Interdenominational Ministerial Alliance, 95

Jack the Rapper, 121
Jackson, Hal, 18–19, 115
Jackson Brewing Co., 43, 70, 84, 116. *See also* Jax beer
"Jam, Jive & Gumbo," 68–69, 71, 79
Jax beer, 43, 58, 70, 71–75, 84–87, 118–19, 128. *See also* "Jivin' with Jax"
Jazz Age, 6
Jazz Festival, 132
jazz funerals, 5
jazz music, 5, 6, 22, 26, 62, 73, 79, 81, 113; Dixieland, 75, 129; swing, 72

Jefferson, Denton, 84
"Jim Hall's Louisiana Weekly Sportscast," 91
"Jivin' with Jax," 71–73, 79, 87, 118, 119, 128; in Houston, 85–86; interviews with musicians, 72
John, Mable (Dr. Mable John), 87
Johnson, Lyndon, 110
Jones, Alvin H., 46
Jones, Clarence, 6
Jones, Gladys, 34
Jones, Joseph "Scoop," 52, 61, 66, 69, 74
Jones, Lucius L., 41, 44, 84, 91
Jordan, Louis, 70–71
Jordon, Eddie, 133
Joseph, Margie, 132

Kabacoff, Lester, 87
Kaman, Lester, 90
KFFA radio (Helena, Arkansas), 26
King, Martin Luther, Jr., 5, 95–97, 99–100, 105, 110, 116, 122
Kopfler, Joseph S., 48
Kruttschnitt, E. B., 14
KTHT radio (Houston, Texas), 85–86
Ku Klux Klan, 102, 113
KYW radio (Westinghouse station), 6

Labat, Emile, Jr., 42
Landix, Paul A., 45
LaPlace, Malcolm, 81, 83, 84, 91
Laws, Clarence A., 41, 42
Leche, Richard W., 38
Lewis, Guy, 133
Lewis, Leon, 44
"Life of Anna Lewis," 108
Lindsay, Treva B., 118
Lippmann, Walter, 26–27
"Listeners' Choice," 94
Logsdon, Joseph, 100
Lombard, Edwin, 106, 121, 123
Long, Earl K., 95
Long, Huey P., 37–38
"Louisiana Gospel Train," 75

Louisiana Industrial Life Insurance Company, 80
Louisiana Undertaking Company, 75, 118
Louisiana Weekly: advertisements in, 32, 34, 60, 71, 119–20; and black press, 44; and Civil Rights Movement, 93, 97, 101; Jax beer advertisement, 72–73; Jones's column, 52–53, 61, 66, 69; news reporting, 46, 61, 71, 92, 96, 116, 122; reporting on radio shows, 31, 32, 44, 46, 117; started by Taylor and Dejoie, 40; Stephens's column, 97; Taylor's involvement with, 39–42, 55, 126; Winslow's column, 65, 69, 74, 79, 80–81, 83–84

MacWilliams, Clement, 53, 63
Mallardi, Vince, 110–11
Mardi Gras Indians, 5
marginalization, 27, 51–52
Marshall, Thurgood, 30, 99
Maslow, Abraham, 16
Matassa, Cosimo, 40, 66, 71, 118, 123, 128–30
Mayoral, George, 67
MBN radio, 7
MBS. *See* Mutual Broadcasting System (MBS)
McKinley, Larry, 4, 88, 94–95, 116, 130–33; and Civil Rights Movement, 98–103, 107–8, 123, 130–31; at WMRY, 4; at WNNR, 132–33
McNamara, Ray, 63
Miller, Rice, 26
Minit Records, 131
Montgomery bus boycott, 95
Montgomery Improvement Association, 95
Morial, Ernest "Dutch," 99, 133
"Morning in New Orleans," 133
Morrell, Arthur, 123
Mr. Cool, 80. *See also* Stephens, George Joseph Emery "Tex," Jr.
music: Dixieland jazz, 75, 129; European art, 75; hillbilly, 90, 129; New Orleans, 72, 73, 81, 129; nostalgic hit, 132; rock and roll, 21. *See also* black music; jazz music
"Music of New Orleans," 73, 119
Mutual Black Network, 108
Mutual Broadcasting Network, 8
Mutual Broadcasting System (MBS), 11–12, 28, 44, 51, 60, 132

National Association for the Advancement of Colored People (NAACP), 11, 15, 99, 105, 110, 123; campaign for radio integration, 31–32; Citizens Committee objectives, 28–29; enlisting help from black journalists, 29–30
National Association of Radio Announcers, 121–22
National Black Network, 108
National Broadcasting Company (NBC), 7, 11, 51, 59, 60, 119
National Council of Negro Women (NCNW), 53
National Negro Network, 94, 108
National Urban League, 110
Native Americans, 40
NBC. *See* National Broadcasting Company (NBC)
"NBN Shorts," 108
"NBN Stage Door," 108
Negro American Labor Council, 110
Negro Citizens Committee, 8, 30–33, 35
"Negro Forum of the Air," 31–35, 37, 42, 49, 55, 116, 117; popular support for, 44–47; promoting black achievement, 52–53; schedule reported by the press, 51–52; Taylor's efforts to expand, 48; white concern regarding, 49–51
"Negro News," 55
Negro Newspaper Publishers Association (NNPA), 41
Negro Newspaper Week, 41–42
Negro South Magazine, 44
"Negro Sports Roundup," 91
"Negro Talent Hour," 53–55, 76

"Negro Talent Show," 118
Nelson, Roy A., 132
Neville, Art, 88, 95, 121, 123
Neville Brothers, 88, 95
New Orleans: black music in, 5; Committee on Race Relations, 54; legal status of blacks in, 14–15; NAACP in, 15; nonviolence in following King assassination, 105–6; political history of, 13; radio frequencies (1950), 55; radio stations (1947), 57; radio stations with black-oriented programs (1940), 63; relationship between whites and blacks in, 13–15; segregation in, 14–15; unique history of, 5; voting rights for blacks, 15–16
New Orleans Improvement League, 95
New Orleans Informer, 41, 52
New Orleans Item, 51
New Orleans Jazz and Heritage Foundation, 132
New Orleans music, 81, 129. *See also* black music; jazz music; music
New Orleans States-Item, 38
New York Enquirer, 41
Newman, Mark, 26
news broadcasts, 10, 86, 94
"Night Talk," 108
Nixon, Sondra, 103
Noe, Anna Gray Sweeney, 37
Noe, James Albert, 8, 9, 115; involvement with radio broadcasting, 39; political experience, 37–38
nonviolent resistance, 6, 105, 112–13

Ofori, Kofi, 111
"Old Ship of Zion," 86
"One Black Man's Opinion," 108–9
Ortique, Revius, 99

Paglin, Jules J., 90
Painia, Frank, 59–61
Parker, Bob, 61, 62, 74, 83, 84, 91
Parks, Rosa, 95

Parris, Guichard, 111
Payne, Sonny, 26
Percy, Leslie, 31
Perry, Robert N., Jr., 34
Picayune (New Orleans newspaper), 51–52
Pinkney, Addison, 31
Pittsburgh Courier, 32, 33, 34, 41, 44, 46, 91, 93, 116, 122, 126
Pleasure, Moses, 42
Poppa Stoppa, 67–69, 70, 71, 72, 87
Priestley, Alfred C., 34
Primm, H. Thomas, 34
public affairs radio program, 8, 9, 22, 51
public health, 46
public service programming, 10, 31, 90
public sphere, 6

quiz shows, 12

"race music," 52, 59, 60, 62, 130. *See also* black music
racism, 3, 5, 11, 23–24, 64, 93; NAACP action against, 28–29
radio broadcasting: changes in, 5; integration of, 4, 5–6, 12, 19, 21, 23–24, 30–32, 37, 108; New Orleans radio frequencies (1950), 55; New Orleans radio stations (1947), 57. *See also* radio programming
Radio Education Project, 22
Radio Free Dixie, 113
radio programming, 11–12; and African Americans, 8, 19, 21–22, 48, 63, 79, 94, 107, 110, 117; by black broadcasters, 31; and black imagination, 26; block programming, 9; current effectiveness of, 124; decline in popularity of, 123; integration of, 31–32; portrayals of blacks, 12, 125; public affairs, 22; sports, 18–19; by Urban League, 110–11; on WBOK, 110; and white imagination, 26; at WNNR, 132–33; at WNOE, 55; on WYLD, 110. *See also* radio broadcasting

radio stations: black-owned, 28, 111; independent, 7, 60, 77, 79; network-affiliated, 60; survey of popularity, 59. *See also specific radio stations by name*
Ray, Stanley W., Jr., 67, 90
Reconstruction, 14, 15, 43
religion, and the black church, 32–34, 44, 49, 89
"Religious Forum of the Air" (WNOE), 8, 10, 31–35, 37, 42, 116, 118–19, 125, 128. *See also* "Negro Forum of the Air"
rhythm and blues, 5, 6, 21, 52, 59, 64, 79, 90, 113, 117, 127, 130, 131–32
Rich, Ray, 75
Richards, J. O., Jr., 46
Richardson, Alvin, 72
Riesling, Richard, 62
Robinson, Cleveland, 110
Robinson, Jackie, 85, 120
rock and roll, 21
Roesler, Bob, 92
Roosevelt, Franklin D., 50
Ross, Bennett B., 28
Ross, Sherwood, 110
Ross, Walter, 127–28
Rounsaville, Robert W., 90
Rouselle, Bill, 123
Rousseau, John E., Jr., 41, 44, 54, 116
Rousseve, Ferdinand, 35
Rousseve, Numa, 53
Royal Broadcasting Corporation, 47
"Runnin' WYLD," 131
Russwurm, John B., 27, 41
Rustin, Bayard, 110

Salaam, Kalamu ya, 123
Savage, Barbara Dianne, 22
Seals, London Thomas, Jr., 34
segregation, 49; in mass media, 6; in New Orleans, 14–15; outlawed by US Supreme Court, 105; in public spaces, 40–41, 96, 105; in public transportation, 95, 102, 105; in schools, 23–24, 97, 98–99; in state laws, 107. *See also* integration
self-actualization, 16–17
self-determination, 17
Sengstacke, John H., 41
"Sepia Homemaker," 81
Settles, Glenn T., 34
Shuttlesworth, Fred, 107
Silverman, Mort, 79, 81, 83, 98
Simpson, Percy "Windbag," Jr., 81, 83
slavery, 5, 100; abolition of, 14
Smith, Elwood, 73
Smith, James "Okey Dokey," 97, 110
Smith, Jerome, 101–2
Smith v. Allwright, 16
"Smoky Joe and Tee Tain," 13
soap operas, 9, 23, 60, 94, 108
Soproco Singers (gospel group), 32, 34, 55
Soul Bowl, 132
soul music, 113, 133
Southern Christian Leadership Conference, 5, 96–97, 105, 116
"Southern Melodies," 81
Southland Broadcasting Company, 80, 90
sports broadcasting, 18, 23, 43–44, 91–92, 117
St. Charles, John L., 42
States (New Orleans newspaper), 51
Stephens, George Joseph Emery "Tex," Jr., 80, 81, 83, 84, 91, 97, 108, 116–17; and Civil Rights Movement, 103
stereotypes: of African Americans, 23–25, 31; media construction of, 27
"Story of Ruth Valentine," 94, 108
Student Nonviolent Coordinating Committee, 105
Sullivan, David, 109
Supreme Broadcasting Company, 60, 132
"Sweet Talkin' Time," 81
swing jazz, 72. *See also* jazz

talk shows, 4, 5, 6, 7, 21, 58, 79
"Tan Timers Club," 80
"Tan Town Homemakers," 81

Taylor, Orlando Capitola Ward ("O. C. W."), 3, 8, 29, 31–32, 33, 37; background, 38; and black print media, 39–42, 55, 126; and Civil Rights Movement, 123; as community organizer, 125; and Negro Forum, 31–33, 40–41, 43, 44–52, 115–16, 125; and "Negro Talent Hour," 76; promoting black achievement, 52–55; as radio broadcaster, 57; teaching experience, 39–40, 125; as television announcer, 126

Taylor, Thelma Ruffin, 127

television, 12, 13, 23, 24, 25, 39, 51, 63, 79, 112, 125, 126

Temple, James, 32

Thiele, Duke, 68–69

Thirteenth Amendment, 14

Thomas, Irma, 101, 123

Thornhill, Eloise, 34–35

Times-Picayune, 60, 73, 86, 87, 92, 123, 132

"Tippin' with Tex," 80

Tuesday (radio trade magazine), 108

Tureaud, Alexander Pierre, Sr., 100, 106

Turner, Joe, 61

Union Benevolent Association, 43

United Clubs, 95

United Federal Savings and Loan Association, 87

Urban League, 8, 105, 110–11, 123

Urban League of Greater New Orleans, 8, 99

variety shows, 7, 11, 12, 18, 62, 74, 108

Voter Education project, 106

voter registration, 15–16, 28, 29, 61, 95, 99

Walker, Joe, 91–92

Walsh, Stephen Roy James, 22

Ward, Brian, 22

Warren, Jim, 79, 81, 83, 91

Waters, Ethel, 8

"Wavelength," 127

WBNO radio, 9. *See also* WNOE radio

WBOK radio, 90, 97, 110; and King assassination, 106

WCAP radio (Washington, DC), 18, 115

WCBS radio (New York), 110

WDIA radio (Memphis), 17, 21

WDSU radio, 11–12, 51, 59, 60, 118, 120; black programming, 75

Weiss, Carl, 38

WENN radio (Birmingham), 107

Wexler, Jerry, 52

White, Paul "Tall Paul," 108

White, Walter, 41

white broadcasters, 7, 58, 72, 79, 109

white newspapers, 27, 41, 51, 60, 109, 123

white supremacy, 6, 7, 11, 12, 14, 15, 23–24, 29, 52, 71, 93

Wilkins, Roy, 30

Williams, A. Victor "Vic," 42, 53, 74

Williams, Nat D., 17

Williams, Robert, 112–13

Williamson, Sonny Boy, 26

Willis, Jimmy, 84

Willis, Louise, 44

Wilson, Larry, 54

Wiltz, Dorothy W., 54

Winslow, Vernon L., Jr., 128

Winslow, Vernon L., Sr., 3–4, 43, 64, 116, 117; as advertising consultant, 87, 109, 117–18; and Civil Rights Movement, 108, 123; as columnist, 65, 69, 71, 79, 80, 81, 83–84, 89; as disc jockey, 4, 43, 64, 71, 72, 83, 84, 97, 101, 102, 116, 117, 127–28; as emcee, 87; with Jackson Brewing Co., 70; at Jax block parties, 74–75, 85; as news announcer, 86; proposal to WJMR, 66–67; proposal to WWL, 66; as radio broadcaster, 57; at WJMR, 57–58, 67–69; at WMRY, 84, 86, 127; writing radio scripts, 68–69; at WWEZ, 4, 58, 71–73, 75, 86–87, 117–18, 119, 127; at WYLD, 86, 87–88, 127–28. *See also* Dr. Daddy-O

WINX radio (Washington, DC), 18–19, 115

WJBW radio, 11, 58, 59, 63, 79, 117, 120; Dew Drop Inn broadcasts, 60–61; Gladstone broadcasts, 62
WJLD radio (Birmingham), 107
WJMR radio, 57, 58, 60, 63, 65, 79; "Jam, Jive & Gumbo" show, 68–69, 70; Winslow's proposal to, 66–67
WMAQ radio (Chicago), 22
WMRY radio, 4, 74, 79, 80–81, 88, 90, 98, 117, 120, 127; black programming, 94; May 1950 program schedule, 82; news broadcasting, 86; sports broadcasting, 91–92
WNNR radio, 88, 132
WNOE radio, 3, 8, 9, 11–12, 28, 31, 32, 33, 37, 40, 51–52, 57, 58, 59, 60, 63, 115; black programming, 75–76; change in programming and operating assignment, 10–11, 47; music broadcasting, 66; request for more broadcast power, 10–11, 44; talent show, 62. *See also* "Negro Forum of the Air"
Wolfe, Roger, 75
Wonder Orchestra, 6
Wood, Roy, 109
WQUE-FM radio, 112
Wright, James Skelly, 98
Wright, Richard, 132
WSMB radio, 11–12, 51, 59, 60, 119
WTPS radio, 60, 86, 91, 119
WWEZ Radio Inc., 4, 60, 66, 79, 86, 117, 127. *See also* "Jivin' with Jax"
WWL radio, 9, 11–12, 51, 59, 60, 65; lack of black programming, 63; Winslow's proposal to, 66
WYFE radio, 91
WYLD radio, 86, 88, 90, 91, 111, 117, 123, 127, 131, 132; and Civil Rights Movement, 103, 110; and King assassination, 106

Young, Andrew, 99
Young, Ethel, 42
Young, Whitney M., Jr., 110

CPSIA information can be obtained
at www.ICGtesting.com
Printed in the USA
BVHW040859270619
552087BV00002B/2/P